THE NATIONAL QUESTION
AND ELECTORAL POLITICS IN QUEBEC AND SCOTLAND

DEMOCRACY, DIVERSITY, AND CITIZEN ENGAGEMENT SERIES

Series editor: Alain-G. Gagnon

With the twenty-first-century world struggling to address various forms of conflict and new types of political and cultural claims, the Democracy, Diversity, and Citizen Engagement Series revitalizes research in the fields of nationalism, federalism, and cosmopolitanism, and examines the interactions between ethnicity, identity, and politics. Works published in this series are concerned with the theme of representation – of citizens and of interests – and how these ideas are defended at local and global levels that are increasingly converging. Further, the series advances and advocates new public policies and social projects with a view to creating change and accommodating diversity in its many expressions. In doing so, the series instills democratic practices in meaningful new ways by studying key subjects such as the mobilization of citizens, groups, communities, and nations, and the advancement of social justice and political stability.

Under the leadership of the Interdisciplinary Research Centre on Diversity and Democracy, this series creates a forum where current research on democracy, diversity, and citizen engagement can be examined within the context of the study of nations as well as of nations divided by state frontiers.

The National Question
and Electoral Politics
in Quebec and Scotland

ÉRIC BÉLANGER
RICHARD NADEAU
AILSA HENDERSON
EVE HEPBURN

McGill-Queen's University Press
Montreal & Kingston · London · Chicago

ISBN 978-0-7735-5326-2 (cloth)
ISBN 978-0-7735-5327-9 (paper)
ISBN 978-0-7735-5413-9 (ePDF)
ISBN 978-0-7735-5414-6 (ePUB)

Legal deposit second quarter 2018
Bibliothèque nationale du Québec

Printed in Canada on acid-free paper that is 100% ancient forest free
(100% post-consumer recycled), processed chlorine free

We acknowledge the support of the Canada Council for the Arts, which
last year invested $153 million to bring the arts to Canadians through-
out the country.

Nous remercions le Conseil des arts du Canada de son soutien. L'an
dernier, le Conseil a investi 153 millions de dollars pour mettre de l'art
dans la vie des Canadiennes et des Canadiens de tout le pays.

Library and Archives Canada Cataloguing in Publication

Bélanger, Éric, author
   The national question and electoral politics in Quebec
and Scotland / Éric Bélanger, Richard Nadeau, Ailsa Henderson,
Eve Hepburn.

(Democracy, diversity, and citizen engagement series ; 3)
Includes bibliographical references and index.
Issued in print and electronic formats.
ISBN 978-0-7735-5326-2 (cloth). – ISBN 978-0-7735-5327-9 (paper). –
ISBN 978-0-7735-5413-9 (ePDF). – ISBN 978-0-7735-5414-6 (ePUB)

   1. Nationalism – Political aspects – Québec (Province).
2. Nationalism – Political aspects – Scotland. 3. Elections – Québec
(Province). 4. Elections – Scotland. 5. Political parties – Québec
(Province). 6. Political parties – Scotland. 7. Voting – Québec
(Province). 8. Voting – Scotland. I. Nadeau, Richard, 1956–, author
II. Henderson, Ailsa, author III. Hepburn, Eve, author IV. Title.
V. Series: Democracy, diversity, and citizen engagement series ; 3

JC311.B45 2018   320.5409411   C2017-908010-5

This book was set by True to Type in 10.5/13 Sabon

Contents

Tables and Figures

FIGURES

Acknowledgments

Producing this book has been a research endeavour that we would never have been able to complete without the crucial help of many individuals and organizations. We must first thank the Social Sciences and Humanities Research Council of Canada for its financial contribution (grant number SSHRC 410-2011-1439). This aid was of course instrumental in enabling us to travel back and forth "across the pond" several times over the past few years, particularly during the planning stages of data collection and writing. But it also allowed us to hire a number of fantastic research assistants whose work was essential in seeing us through the significant amount of data collected for this project. We thus thank El Hadj Touré at the Université de Montréal and Robert Liñeira at the University of Edinburgh. At McGill University, we benefited from the work of Gaby González-Sirois, Eva Falk Pedersen, and Catherine Collerette. Still at McGill, Chris Chhim deserves special mention. Not only did he perform most of the party manifesto coding and analysis on top of myriad other tasks, but he also stepped in for one of us (who had been ill) to present the preliminary draft of one of the chapters at a conference. Chris's level of commitment and enthusiasm for the project from day one was very much appreciated by all of us.

Several colleagues have read the manuscript, in parts or in whole, during the writing stage. We first thank Michael Keating, James Mitchell, and Maurice Pinard for their very useful feedback. The anonymous reviewers selected by McGill-Queen's University Press made extremely helpful comments that contributed to significantly improve the manuscript. Also, preliminary versions of the chapters were presented at two conferences: the 2014 Elections, Public Opinion and Parties (EPOP) conference held in Edinburgh, and the 2015 European Consortium for Political Research (ECPR) general conference held in

Montreal. We thank Chris Carman, Harold Clarke, Patrick Dunleavy, and the other attendees for the useful remarks and suggestions they offered us at these occasions. We also wish to acknowledge the invaluable help of Élodie Fabre in developing with us the manifesto coding scheme used in this book, as well as the hospitality of the European University Institute where Bélanger and Hepburn spent a week in the spring of 2014 working on parts of the manuscript.

The book has found a welcoming home at McGill-Queen's University Press and we thank our editor, Kathleen Kearns, for her tremendous care and efficiency in handling the manuscript throughout the publishing process there. We are also very appreciative of the strong support of Alain-G. Gagnon, who has included our book in his Democracy, Diversity, and Citizen Engagement Series at this press. Our managing editor Ryan Van Huijstee and our copyeditor Ellie Barton also deserve special thanks for their remarkable work in the final stages of production.

Finally, we thank our families for the patience and understanding that they have displayed, and the deep support that they have provided, in the face of the many sacrifices that the completion of this book has entailed. Our very last word of appreciation goes out to all the parliament members and citizens of Quebec and Scotland that we interviewed for this research project. It is their answers to our many questions that form most of the empirical core of this study, and we would not have had much to say in this book without their collaboration.

THE NATIONAL QUESTION
AND ELECTORAL POLITICS IN QUEBEC AND SCOTLAND

I

The "National Question" as an Electoral Issue in Quebec and Scotland

Quebec and Scotland are both substate nations within multinational, multilevel states. In this they are similar to other "usual suspect" nations such as Catalonia, the Basque Country, and Flanders. The two are often compared, not least because they are legislative polities with social democratic nationalist parties, and both have held referendums on additional sovereignty. They share historical connections to the British Empire and in both cases the relationship with their respective English-dominated central state has been complex. A comparison of these two specific cases makes even more sense since the devolution settlement of the 1990s that provided Scotland with a substate government of its own, albeit with fewer powers than those enjoyed by the Quebec provincial state (Henderson and Coates 2005). Calls for constitutional change not only structure political debate within Quebec and Scotland but also ensure that the accommodation of national demands features in statewide political debate.

This book explores the impact of the "national question" on the behaviour of political parties and voters in these two substate nations. With respect to parties, we explore how they position themselves on the national question. For voters, we are interested in analyzing what role attitudes towards the "national question" play in their electoral decisions. Within the broad label of the "national question," we include attitudes towards constitutional change, a sense of national identity, and a perception of national grievance. The national question thus provides a lens through which to view all of these issues, and it can therefore be characterized as a "multiple-ordering" issue in substate party systems that have a strong nationalist basis of party competition (Hepburn 2009a).

The analysis presented in this book offers two key innovations on the various works that have compared Quebec and Scotland (e.g., Keating 1996; Paquin 2001; Tierney 2004; Henderson and Coates 2005; McEwen 2006; Henderson 2007; Béland and Lecours 2008; Kennedy 2013). First, it not only compares Quebec and Scotland but examines dynamics both within the nation and at the level of the multinational state. That is, it examines electoral competition at the provincial/devolved level as well as in Canadian and UK general elections. Second, we are interested in both the supply and the demand sides of electoral competition. While previous works have examined parties in Quebec and Scotland (Chhibber and Kollman 2004; Lynch 2005; Hepburn 2010a; Kennedy 2013) or voting behaviour in the two nations (Henderson and McEwen 2010, 2015; Barker 2015), comparatively few have explicitly examined both voter and party behaviour together. We can think of two exceptions (Keating 1996; Henderson 2007), but as path-breaking as these studies are, they do not address directly the strategic behaviour of political parties nor do they make use of identical survey questionnaires for modelling voting behaviour in these nations. Our main objective is to understand the electoral calculus underlying the stances of parties and voters in Quebec and Scotland. Here we argue for a reciprocal relationship, with voters taking cues from parties, but with parties devising strategies likely to win them votes by taking into account both the state of public opinion on the national question and their competitors' own positionings on this issue.

While Quebec and Scotland are both substate nations, this does not automatically make them instructive comparators. On the face of it the socially democratic nationalist political parties, each seeking to achieve independence through a referendum, would seem to suggest that the two are quite similar. The value of the comparison, however, is in the variation in institutional setting, the extent to which the nation is tied to particular demographic groups, and the level of autonomy wielded by their legislatures. These sources of variation do not always point in the same direction. On the one hand, we might expect to find that the national question plays a greater role in Quebec given its higher levels of self-rule and shared rule within the Canadian state, as well as the relationship between the nationalist project and the majority francophone community in Quebec. On the other hand, the electoral fortunes of Scottish nationalist parties in the past ten years would suggest that the national question plays a greater role in influencing party and voter behaviour in Scotland. Compared with other substate nations, we might well be more likely to see evidence of the national question at work in Quebec and Scotland, but the differences between the two cases raise the possibility that the two should not be seen as cut from the same cloth. Nonetheless, the two are similar enough so as to allow meaningful generalizations regarding electoral politics in substate nations.

Our empirical analysis in this book covers the 2010–14 period of Quebec and Scottish electoral politics. Before we can compare the impact of the national question in Quebec and Scotland during that period, we must of course compare the political context in which the two nationalist movements operate. The two regions possess different demographic profiles with respect to the larger state; furthermore, they exist within different institutional architectures, and their nationalist movements have different trajectories. The following historical section outlines these differences of context. The rest of the chapter will then present our theoretical and empirical approach to the study of Quebec and Scottish electoral politics. It will offer (a) an operational definition of the "national question" that highlights its multidimensional nature, (b) theoretical expectations about the behaviour of political parties and voters vis-à-vis the national question in substate nations, and (c) a brief presentation of the empirical data to be used to test these expectations.

OVERVIEW OF QUEBEC AND SCOTTISH ELECTORAL POLITICS

Quebec

Quebec is a province within a federation. It has possessed its own legislature – the Quebec National Assembly – since Canadian Confederation in 1867. Following Confederation, two parties – the Liberal Party (the *rouges*) and the Conservative Party (the *bleus*) – contested seats at both federal and provincial levels. The parties contesting seats today, however, have a more recent history. The current deviation between parties contesting Quebec seats in Canadian elections and those contesting seats for the Quebec National Assembly has its roots in the middle of the twentieth century (Rayside 1978).[1] The period of intense socioeconomic development in Quebec (otherwise known as the Quiet Revolution) saw an important transformation in the predominant national identity held by Quebecers, gradually moving from a "French-Canadian" identity to a "Québécois" one (see Bélanger and Chhim 2016). This

Table 1.1
Results in Quebec for provincial elections since the 1970s

Election year	Parti Libéral %	Parti Québécois %	ADQ/ CAQ %	Québec Solidaire %	Option Nationale %	Union Nationale %
1970	**45**	23	-	-	-	20
1973	**55**	30	-	-	-	5
1976	34	**41**	-	-	-	18
1981	46	**49**	-	-	-	4
1985	**56**	39	-	-	-	-
1989	**50**	40	-	-	-	-
1994	44	**45**	7	-	-	-
1998	44	**43**	12	-	-	-
2003	**46**	33	18	-	-	-
2007	**33**	28	31	4	-	-
2008	**42**	35	16	4	-	-
2012	31	**32**	27	6	2	-
2014	**42**	25	23	8	1	-

Notes: ADQ = Action Démocratique du Québec. CAQ = Coalition Avenir Québec. Figures are percentages of valid votes. Figures in bold indicate the party forming the government.

transformation was accompanied by the creation in 1968 of a new nationalist, pro-independence party, the Parti Québécois (PQ), founded by former Parti Libéral du Québec (PLQ) member René Lévesque. The realignment of the provincial party system (Lemieux, Gilbert, and Blais 1970) effectively ended in 1976 with a PQ victory (see table 1.1) and a new two-party system based on different constitutional preferences: a sovereignist PQ and a federalist PLQ.[2] The PQ government introduced legislation for a referendum on "sovereignty-association." The referendum, which took place on 20 May 1980, asked Quebecers whether they agreed to let their government negotiate a new political and economic partnership with the rest of Canada. The question raised the prospect of a second referendum on any eventual agreement and therefore sought a mandate for change. The pro-independence Yes side earned 40 per cent of the vote, with 86 per cent of registered voters having cast a ballot.

Despite the referendum defeat, the constitutional question was still very much at the forefront of political debates at both the federal and the provincial levels. The post-referendum patriation of the Canadian Constitution from the United Kingdom, without the consent of the Quebec government, fuelled existing grievances. Offering to solve them

Table 1.2
Results in Quebec for Canadian federal elections since the 1970s

Election year	Liberal %	Conservative %	NDP %	Bloc Québécois %	Social Credit %
1972	**49**	17	6	–	24
1974	**54**	21	7	–	17
1979	62	**14**	5	–	16
1980	**68**	13	9	–	6
1984	35	**50**	9	–	–
1988	30	**53**	14	–	–
1993	33	**14**	2	49	–
1997	37	22	2	38	–
2000	**44**	6	2	40	–
2004	34	9	5	49	–
2006	21	**25**	8	42	–
2008	24	22	12	38	–
2011	14	**17**	43	23	–
2015	**36**	17	25	19	–

Notes: NDP = New Democratic Party. Figures are percentages of valid votes. Figures in bold indicate the party forming the government.

brought the Progressive-Conservative Party to power in the 1984 federal election, helped in part by substantial support from Quebec voters. Indeed, one Quebec voter in two supported Brian Mulroney's party in that election (see table 1.2). It was Liberal Quebec premier Robert Bourassa who negotiated a new constitutional agreement with the other provinces and federal government that would hopefully satisfy Quebec's core demand to be formally recognized as a "distinct society" within Canada, a new official status that had the potential to grant the province additional powers. Signed in 1987, the Meech Lake Accord required ratification by each of the ten provincial legislatures within three years.[3]

By the deadline of June 1990 the Meech Lake Accord was still missing ratification by two of the ten provincial legislatures, and so did not come into effect. The failure of the Accord sparked a rise in support for independence among Quebecers, with public opinion polls reporting clear majority support for this constitutional option between 1990 and 1992 (Pinard, Bernier, and Lemieux 1997; Yale and Durand 2011). A second constitutional agreement, the Charlottetown Accord, was rejected in a pan-Canadian referendum in October 1992.[4] More than a decade of constitutional negotiations therefore preceded the return of the Parti Québécois to office in Quebec. Upon election it proposed legislation to hold a second referendum on independence. The 30 October 1995 referendum on "sovereignty-partnership" saw a similar result as in 1980, but a significantly smaller margin for the victors (50.6%). The PQ was re-elected in the 1998 provincial election but started to experience a slow decline in its electoral support in the years that followed. It briefly returned to power in 2012 with 32 per cent of the vote and a minority of seats, only to be voted out of office in the 2014 election, receiving its lowest support since 1970 (25 per cent; see table 1.1).

Meanwhile, notwithstanding the surge in support for independence following the failure of the Meech Lake Accord, the Parti Libéral du Québec under Robert Bourassa did not press for special constitutional status for Quebec, a decision that left the more nationalist members of the PLQ deeply dissatisfied. In 1994 a splinter group composed of disaffected PLQ members decided to create a new party, the Action Démocratique du Québec (ADQ), dedicated to pursuing greater political autonomy for Quebec within Canada. Over the years the ADQ also came to take a number of controversial stances on the questions of immigrant integration (arguing for a more restrictive, assimilationist model – see Hepburn 2011) and governance (pushing for cutbacks in Quebec's welfare state and questioning the interventionist model of economic development). After several years of varying electoral fortunes (see Bélanger and Nadeau 2009; Tanguay 2013), the ADQ finally decided in 2012 to merge with the Coalition Avenir Québec, which was newly created by former PQ member François Legault and campaigned under this name.

A fourth party, Québec Solidaire, currently holds three out of the 125 seats in the Quebec National Assembly. This party was created in 2006 as a reaction to what its members perceived as a drift towards the socioeconomic right within the Quebec party system, including within the traditionally progressive Parti Québécois. Although Québec Solidaire is in favour of Quebec's independence, its main priority and thus axis of competition remains the left-right dimension (Nadeau and Bélanger 2013). Another current secessionist party is Option Nationale, a splinter party created in 2011 by former PQ member of the National Assembly Jean-Martin Aussant, who felt that the Parti Québécois was not pushing hard enough for independence. This new party received 1.9 and 0.8 per cent of the vote in the 2012 and 2014 provincial elections (see table 1.1) and has no representation in the National Assembly, hence we do not consider Option Nationale further in this book.

While constitutional politics has played a larger role for parties contesting Quebec elections, it has also occupied parties contesting federal seats. During the 1980s the Progressive-Conservative Party (renamed Conservative Party of Canada in 2004) sought to respond positively to the province of Quebec's constitutional demands, although attention to constitutional challenges waned under Stephen Harper's government (2006–15). For its part, the New Democratic Party (NDP), a social democratic formation, has shown some openness to Quebec's demands for more autonomy. Although the NDP has never formed a federal government and so has yet to be in a position to act on this issue, this more accommodative stance has nonetheless informed the party's discourse in recent years, thus overcoming its long-standing – if perhaps unwarranted – reputation in Quebec as being a political party in favour of more centralization.

For a good portion of the twentieth century – in effect, since the time of Wilfrid Laurier, Canada's first prime minister of French-Canadian origins (1896–1911) – the Liberal Party of Canada (LPC) has claimed to be the best defender of French-Canadians' interests in Ottawa (Dion 1975; Bickerton, Gagnon, and Smith 1999). And indeed, Quebecers regularly voted en masse for the federal Liberals before the adoption of the 1982 Constitution Act. The party averaged 58 per cent of support in Quebec between 1972 and 1980, for example (see table 1.2). This level of support fell after the 1982 constitutional patriation. Since then, the Liberals' stance on the Quebec question has mostly been a nonaccommodative one, with the party presenting itself as the champion of Canadian unity in the face of the separatist "threat" on the Quebec provincial scene.

The fourth main party contesting seats in Canadian elections is the Bloc Québécois. Ever since its creation in 1991 as a direct reaction to the Meech Lake Accord collapse, the BQ has promoted independence as well as sought to defend Quebec's regional interests in the Canadian Parliament. The BQ has enjoyed considerable success, garnering 49 per cent of the Quebec vote on two occasions (1993 and 2004; see table 1.2) – although its success has been more impressive in terms of parliamentary representation than actual votes because the regional concentration of its support has been rewarded by the single-member plurality (SMP) electoral system (Bélanger and Nadeau 2016). Support for the BQ fell in the 2011 election to 23 per cent, which translated into four of the seventy-five Quebec seats. The NDP was the main beneficiary of the BQ's collapse in that election, in a vote that seemed more driven by left-right considerations than by constitutional preferences (Fournier et al. 2013). The BQ's decline continued further in the 2015 election, where it regained a few seats (for a total of ten MPs elected) but with an even lower share of the popular vote (19 per cent).

Scotland

Scotland is a devolved region within a unitary state. From 1707 – at the time of its Union with England and Wales – until 1999 Scottish voters could vote in local/regional elections and could elect Scottish MPs to the UK House of Commons. Voting opportunities expanded in 1999 with the first elections to the Scottish Parliament.

In the early twentieth century the Liberal and Conservative parties dominated UK elections, and the same was true in Scottish constituencies. The Scottish Conservative and Unionist Party (SCUP) has separate origins in Scotland and was an independent party until 1965. It was the first party to make a commitment to a (weak) form of devolution (Mitchell 1998; Chaney 2013). Upon its integration into the UK party, it abandoned any commitment to devolution (Hepburn 2010b). The Scottish Liberal Democrats have always supported home rule as part of a wider federalist agenda, a view which translates into a federal party structure that has allowed the Scottish branch to exercise greater autonomy over policy than its competitors. It was not until 1922 that Labour replaced the Liberal Party as the chief rival to the Conservatives, although Liberal support remained strong in Scotland to a greater extent than in England, particularly in the Highlands and islands. The three main parties occupy different positions on the left-right spectrum, with Labour and the Conservatives at the left and right poles and the Liberal (Democrats) in between. There has been some movement over time. The creation of the Liberal Democrats following the short-lived Labour-breakaway Social Democratic Party leaves them in the centre group, and Labour moved decidedly to the centre under Tony Blair's leadership.

The three main parties adopted different positions with regard to constitutional politics. In the early part of the twentieth century the focus was less on Scotland than on Ireland and home rule, with the Liberals championing home rule, a position that, to some degree, the Liberal Democrats retain. Labour attitudes to home rule for Ireland and, later, some form of self-government for Scotland have been less consistent (Keating and Bleiman 1979; Hepburn 2010b), with internal jurisdictional divi-

Table 1.3
Results in Scotland for UK general elections since the 1970s

Election year	Labour %	Conservative %	Lib/Dem %	SNP %
1974	**36**	25	8	30
1979	42	**31**	9	17
1983	35	**28**	25	12
1987	42	**24**	19	14
1992	39	**26**	13	22
1997	**46**	18	13	22
2001	**44**	16	16	20
2005	**40**	16	23	18
2010	42	**17**	19	20
2015	24	**15**	8	50
2017	27	**29**	7	37

Notes: SNP = Scottish National Party. Figures are percentages of valid votes. Figures in bold indicate the party forming the government.

sions seen as an obstacle to international socialism by some within the party (Keating and Bleiman 1979; Geekie and Levy 1989).

The Scottish National Party (SNP) was formed in 1934 as an amalgam of previous nationalist parties and social movements supportive of nationalism. Much like the Parti Québécois, it is currently a social democratic pro-independence party. At various points it has been a broad church on one spectrum while more unified on the other, and the dominant position within the party, whether on left-right placement or the Constitution, has shifted over time. In the 1970s it was a centrist party, nicknamed the "Tartan Tories,"[5] and it contains within its ranks supporters of independence as well as devolution max or enhanced devolution.

The electoral fortunes of these parties have varied over time (see table 1.3). Throughout most of the postwar period Scots have demonstrated greater support for the Labour Party than have voters in England, although this is likely due to a mix of greater sympathy for its social and economic policy in a region with higher levels of employment, and the party's perceived national values of communitarianism and egalitarianism (McCrone 1992; Brown, McCrone, and Paterson 1996; Henderson 2007), as well as its support for devolution. The Conservatives have seen a steady erosion in support since 1951, although levels plummeted under Margaret Thatcher due to her perceived indifference to Scottish distinctiveness and devolution (Seawright 1996, 2004).

During the twentieth century, Scots have been to the polls twice in referendums related to constitutional politics. The first was in 1979 over plans to create a Scottish Assembly. Originally proposed by the Labour government at Westminster under the Scotland and Wales bill, internal Labour divisions – and fear that the proposals would fail due to lower levels of support in Wales – led to separate legislation for Scotland and Wales and the promise of a referendum subject to a 40 per cent electorate threshold. The Conservative Party opposed the proposals while the SNP supported them. Labour was divided (Newell 1998). The referendum results – 52 per cent in favour but with only 64 per cent turnout – failed to meet the necessary threshold for success.

Under a succession of Conservative governments (1979–97), proposals for devolution to Scotland received extensive backing from particular civil society organizations. At this time Labour and the Liberal Democrats were strong advocates of devolution. The election of a Labour government in 1997 led to another referendum, this time on proposals that had received the benefit of twenty years of thinking about the specifics of what the legislature would control and how it would be structured. The two-question referendum – one question on the existence of a Parliament, the other on tax-raising powers – passed in September 1997, and the first elections for the 129-seat Scottish Parliament were held in May 1999 (see Trench 2007; Mitchell 2009; Jeffery and Mitchell 2010; and Keating 2010 for more on this period).

The first two Scottish administrations, elected under a mixed member proportional system in 1999 and 2003, were Labour-LibDem coalitions (see table 1.4). Having facilitated the arrival of devolution, both parties became advocates of the constitutional status quo. Where once three parties (Labour, LibDems, and SNP) had advocated change, now only one campaigned for further devolution (SNP). The immediate aftermath of devolution also coincided with the UK Labour party moving to the centre. The relative lack of policy deviation between the UK and Scottish parties ensured that Scottish Labour also moved to the centre, although arguably to a lesser degree than the UK party as a whole (Bradbury 2006).

A minority SNP government was elected in 2007, followed by a majority administration in 2011. This marked the beginning of partisan variation across Westminster and Holyrood elections, with continued support for Labour in UK elections and greater support for the SNP in Scottish elections. The expectation has been that the left-right axis, as

Table 1.4
Results in Scotland for devolved elections, constituency vote (regional list vote in parentheses)

Election year	Labour %	Conservative %	Liberal Democrat %	SNP %	Green %	Socialist %
1999	**39 (34)**	16 (15)	**14 (12)**	29 (27)	– (4)	1 (2)
2003	**35 (29)**	17 (16)	**15 (12)**	24 (21)	– (7)	6 (7)
2007	32 (29)	17 (14)	16 (11)	**33 (31)**	0 (4)	0 (1)
2011	32 (26)	14 (12)	8 (5)	**45 (44)**	– (4)	– (0)
2016	23 (19)	22 (23)	8 (5)	**46 (42)**	1 (7)	– (0)

Notes: SNP = Scottish National Party. Figures are percentages of valid votes. Figures in bold indicate the parties forming the government.

well as the capacity to form a government, would play a greater role in vote choice in Westminster elections than in devolved elections. As a government, the SNP administration continued with the centre-left socioeconomic agenda of the previous Labour-LibDem coalition governments such as free care for the elderly and free university tuition for Scottish (and therefore EU) students. Constitutional issues played a relatively small role in the first SNP administration, and voters rewarded their good record with a majority in the 2011 election (Johns, Carman, and Mitchell 2013), paving the way to a referendum on the issue of Scottish independence.

Although the right to hold a referendum was initially contested by the UK government, the 2012 Edinburgh Agreement signed by both levels of government marked the start of a two-year-long referendum campaign. The agreement precluded a multioption referendum, and so voters debated the relative merits of independence and a (somewhat shifting) status quo. The 2012 Scotland Act, which was to give the Parliament enhanced powers, was not to come fully into effect until 2015, and "No" campaigners, including leaders of the main UK parties, proposed – in a move oddly reminiscent of the 1980 Quebec referendum – some form of constitutional change in the event the "Yes" side lost. The 18 September 2014 referendum's eventual result, 55 per cent against independence with 85 per cent turnout, was followed by plans to transfer additional powers to Scotland through the Smith Commission. Despite losing the referendum, the SNP saw its membership soar, and in the May 2015 UK general election the party won fifty-six of the fifty-nine Scottish seats, with 50 per cent of the Scottish vote (see table

1.3). The SNP's gains came at the expense of Labour in particular, who performed significantly worse in Scotland than normal and, for the first time in decades, worse in Scotland than in England. The popularity of the SNP, and the decline of Labour in Scotland, were seemingly confirmed in the May 2016 devolved elections (see table 1.4). The SNP remained the first party in Scotland after the snap general election of June 2017 but lost twenty-one seats. Half of them went to the Conservative Party, confirming the latter's rise to second party place in Scotland. Labour's enhanced electoral fortunes occurred despite a modest improvement in vote share.

It should be noted that the SNP is not the only substate party seeking Scottish independence. Two smaller parties – the Scottish Green Party and the Scottish Socialists – have also made independence a policy aim, though for very different reasons. While the Greens believe independence would enable Scotland to improve the welfare system and its environmental record, the Socialists wish to see an independent Scotland implement sweeping redistributive reforms. However, despite supporting independence, the Greens and Socialists have not polled more than 7 per cent of the vote in Scottish parliamentary elections from 1999 to 2016 (see table 1.4).

MAKING SENSE OF QUEBEC AND SCOTTISH ELECTORAL POLITICS

Having provided an overview of the Quebec and Scottish party systems and trends in voter support, the remainder of this book examines more closely the effect of the national question on Quebec and Scottish party and voter behaviour in the period under study (2010–14). This section and the next elaborate our theoretical framework in more detail by, first, defining the national question and, second, proposing some general hypotheses about party and voter behaviour in Quebec and Scotland that will guide the empirical analysis to be presented in the remainder of this book. We believe that these theoretical expectations go a long way towards helping us to make sense of electoral politics in these substate nations.

The National Question: No Longer a Niche Issue

Michael Keating (2005, 266) has noted how the national debate constrains competition between the main political parties in these two territories: "In both Quebec and Scotland, the party cleavage, at least between the biggest and second biggest parties, is structured by the national question." We wish to develop this idea further and to analyze in more depth how the national question structures party competition and voting behaviour in Quebec and Scotland. Our study of political party strategies draws its inspiration from previous works having shown that a political party's positioning on a key issue depends on three main factors: its previous position on the issue, the current position of its competitors, and the general state of public opinion (see, most notably, Meguid 2008).

The overview presented in the previous section has already suggested that Quebec and Scottish political parties have some, but rather limited, flexibility with regard to the national question. The national question is generally an important concern for Quebecers and Scots and is, therefore, central to the political debate in both territories. This situation forces all parties (not just nationalist ones) to adopt a relatively clear and constraining position on this issue. That said, the ebb and flow of public opinion has some influence on party positioning (Klüver and Sagarzazu 2016). The importance given to the national debate by the parties and the specific party positions on this issue also depend on the state of public opinion during electoral campaigns. Parties are generally more likely to respond to voter attitudes and priorities than the reverse (Steenbergen, Edwards, and de Vries 2007; Adams, Ezrow, and Somer-Topcu 2011), and this includes nationalist parties (Young and Bélanger 2008).[6] A party's previous stances certainly constitute a significant inertia factor, but they do not entirely prevent a party from strategically changing its positioning vis-à-vis its competitors on the nationalist dimension.

We believe that there are two core research questions that arise when the national question is studied as an *electoral issue* that matters to party politics and to voter behaviour. The first question is to establish whether the national question in Quebec and Scotland constitutes a niche issue for just one party in particular – the dominant nationalist party – or a mainstream issue that structures the party system as a whole. To answer this question, an essential distinction has to be made concerning the nature of this issue in statewide and substate elections. In the case of state-level elections we might expect this issue to have the characteristics of a "niche" issue that stands outside the main set of economic issues that generally structure party competition in developed democracies (Meguid 2008). Within the arena of Canadian federal politics, one political party, the Bloc Québécois (BQ), has made defending the interests of Quebec and promoting the province's political independence its central goal (Noël 1994; Young and Bélanger 2008). In doing so, the BQ has behaved not only as a regional party (fielding candidates only in a particular region) but also as a regionalist one, campaigning for greater autonomy, if not outright independence, for the region (Brancati 2008). The slogans used by this party are in and of themselves revealing. In 1993, when the BQ first contested state-level elections, it asked Quebec voters to give themselves "true power" (*le vrai pouvoir*). A decade later, thanks to a whimsical play on words in French, this same party ran in an election (2004) dominated by the issue of corruption under the slogan of "un parti propre au Québec" (the double entendre referring to a party that belongs to Quebec and that is a clean/uncorrupt political party).

The political positioning of the other statewide Canadian parties is also revealing. The Conservative Party, the Liberal Party, and the New Democratic Party all present themselves as "national" (i.e., pan-Canadian) parties, as opposed to the Bloc Québécois, which presents itself as a regional (Québécois) party. The statewide parties field candidates in all Canadian provinces including Quebec and also present themselves as parties with a comprehensive political platform on all substantive policy issues. Their platforms include taking a position on relations between the central government and the provinces.

The parallels between Canada and the prevailing situation in the United Kingdom are quite clear. Like the Bloc Québécois, the Scottish National Party has also used the Scottish "national question" as a niche issue during UK-wide elections (see Meguid 2008, 192–246). It has presented candidates only in Scotland, and its role has essentially consisted of making Scotland's concerns known at Westminster. Within UK elections, the SNP has thus typically competed for votes as a niche party, seeking to defend Scotland's interests (in terms of both fiscal and constitutional arrangements), although since the emergence of New Labour it has simultaneously sought to portray itself as a viable social democratic alternative to the other parties. By contrast, all other major parties have fielded candidates across the UK and have devoted less attention to constitutional matters in general.[7] In short, in both the Quebec and Scottish case the national question is exploited, on the state level, as an issue that allows one particular party to occupy a specific niche and seek to win votes by defining itself as the party that best defends the interests of a particular nation or region.

The political dynamics play out differently at the substate level, where questions of regional identity and interests are much more important.

In these regions, the national question, far from being a niche issue, often becomes the fundamental political cleavage around which all substate political parties position themselves (Keating 2005). In moving from the national to the regional level, this issue evolves from being niche to one of the structuring pillars of electoral politics (Deschouwer 2003; Jeffery 2009a). On the regional level, it is an unavoidable question and all parties have an official stance on it (Bélanger and Nadeau 2009; Bechhofer and McCrone 2010; Hepburn 2014a). In that sense, the national question becomes something like a "super issue," that is, a general issue that serves as a summary of policy preferences, like left-right ideology is in many political systems (see Laponce 1970; Inglehart and Klingemann 1976; Inglehart 1984, 1990; Dalton 1988; Fuchs and Klingemann 1989; Gabel and Huber 2000), and can dominate all other cleavages in determining vote choice. In other words, a super issue is a mainstream issue by definition, but not all mainstream issues are "super issues" that dominate electoral politics. At the state level, the conceptual opposition is between niche and mainstream issue, whereas at the substate level we would argue that it is between mainstream and super issue, with the latter being more likely when it comes to characterizing the national question.

This situation is clear in the case of Quebec, where the national question has been the dominant electoral cleavage since the late nineteenth century and even more so at the provincial level since the first coming to power of a sovereignist party in the 1970s. The case of Scotland is interesting because this evolution of the national question, from a niche to a mainstream issue at the substate level, has arguably accelerated following devolution. With the attainment of devolution, the Labour Party in Scotland has struggled to articulate a new territorial position. The SNP has instead set the terms of the debate, facilitated by a devolved Scottish political arena to air its concerns. This means that, now even more than before, all parties in Scotland are claiming to stand up for Scottish interests and to demand greater powers for Scotland.

These dynamics suggest that characterizing nationalist parties as "niche" parties may be inappropriate, at least when it comes to the study of substate party systems (Jeffery 2009b; Elias, Szöcsik, and Zuber 2015). Some of the extant literature tends to include substate nationalist parties in that category together with Green and radical right parties (Gunther and Diamond 2003; Adams, Ezrow, and Somer-Topcu 2006; Meguid 2008; Jensen and Spoon 2010). Scholars of nationalist parties often agree, pitting these actors against "the rest" in the party system, and even arguing that they represent antiestablishment or antisystem actors that seek to destroy, or at least unhinge, the state (Sartori 1971; Esman 1977; Schedler 1996; Keren 2000; Swyngedouw and Ivaldi 2001; Cento Bull and Gilbert 2001). Nationalist parties are considered part of the niche party family because they are seen as competing mostly on a small number of "noneconomic" issues (Wagner 2012) or as emphasizing a narrow range of policy areas neglected by their rivals (Meyer and Miller 2015; Bischof 2017). Yet, at the substate level it may make more sense not to treat these parties as niche ones (Alonso, Cabeza, and Gómez 2015; Chhim 2016), just as it is more appropriate to think of the national question as a mainstream, even a super, issue instead of a niche one in substate politics.

Unpacking the National Question

A second key question is to ask if the national question has the characteristics of a "valence issue," that is, an issue on which political parties and public opinion are in broad agreement (Stokes 1963; Stokes and Dilulio 1993). The economy is often presented as the valence issue par excellence in that all (or almost all) parties and voters can agree on lowering unemployment and maintaining price stability (Bélanger and Nadeau 2014).[8] Can we say in the same vein that the national question in Quebec and Scotland is a valence issue? In the eyes of voters, are all substate political parties expected to defend the region's interests, identity, and language? Are all substate parties judged with regard to whether they are working towards these goals or their ability to do so? Past research has shown that parties that want to differentiate themselves on a valence issue must show that they are the most determined and competent party to reach these goals (Budge and Farlie 1983; Petrocik 1996; Bélanger and Meguid 2008). In order to understand the complex answer to this question, we must first recognize that the issue of the "national question" consists of many dimensions.

As Mitchell (2014, 4) points out, the national question involves a "mix of linked issues." The characteristics of the national question as a political (and electoral) issue are indeed numerous. We take inspiration from the theoretical work of Mitchell (2014, 8–16) and Hepburn (2009a) and argue that the national question – which can also be referred to as the "territorial dimension" of electoral competition – combines issues of self-determination, identity, culture, social policy, economic policy, and supranational engagement. Each of these aspects of the territorial issue is important to the national debate and is used by political parties for mobilizing voter support.

These various aspects can be regrouped into broader conceptual dimensions of the national question. We posit that the political parties' positioning on this issue in Quebec and Scotland rests on an equilibrium between three fundamental dimensions of the national debate itself: (a) the promotion of constitutional options, (b) the affirmation of a regional identity, and (c) the defence of regional interests. The objective of this research is therefore to see how political parties exploit these three central dimensions of the national debate in their attempts to form a winning electoral coalition.

In Scotland and in Quebec, there is no consensus among substate parties when it comes to the promotion of a constitutional option. One could instead say that this question has the characteristics of a "positional" issue. The case of Quebec is telling in this regard. For the past forty years, Quebecers have been divided between two constitutional options. The first option, political independence, is spearheaded by the Parti Québécois but also endorsed by Québec Solidaire (QS). The second option is keeping Quebec within the Canadian federation, and the Parti Libéral du Québec (PLQ) has been the most outspoken advocate of this option. The fourth most important substate party in Quebec, the Coalition Avenir Québec (CAQ), also supports a federalist position but seeks a stronger settlement for Quebec than the Parti Libéral. The opposition between federalists and sovereignists (or independentists) is the dominant cleavage in Quebec's political life (Bélanger and Nadeau 2009; Pelletier 2012; Tannahill and Kanji 2016). All political parties in the province must have a clear position on this question (that is, federalist or sovereignist); those who decide to take a middle-of-the-road position are often accused, by adversaries and pundits alike, of either eluding the question or being confused about their own stance. This dividing line with regard to constitutional options is often more important than the line between left and right. The centrality of the constitutional debate in Quebec challenges mainstream theories of party competition that the left-right cleavage structures everything (Nadeau, Guérin, and Martin 1995; Godbout and Bélanger 2002; Bélanger and Nadeau 2009; Gidengil et al. 2012).

Likewise, in Scotland the SNP is the only major party that promotes the independence of the region. The other three main parties have adopted broadly unionist perspectives on the Constitution. The views of parties have broadly tracked their party supporters' views, reflecting

Conservative support for the status quo (but with some changes per the 2014 Strathclyde Commission's report), a Liberal Democrat preference for federalism, and Labour support for (enhanced) devolution. Whereas all parties agree that devolution was a positive evolution and that the role of the governing parties in Holyrood should be to defend Scotland's interests and identity, the same parties differ on the future of the region. As in Quebec, this dimension of the national question in Scotland thus presents the basic characteristics of a positional issue.

While the promotion of decentralization (or more regional autonomy) also falls under the constitutional dimension, we believe that decentralization is distinct from the question of independence per se in that it offers a less radical form of change and tends to divide the electorate less. Most voters, and most political parties, desire some powers to be transferred from the central government to the regional government, even though they may not seek (and may not agree with the goal of) political independence. This is an important nuance to keep in mind when we analyze and interpret party positions and voter preferences with regard to the constitutional dimension of the national debate. Another point of nuance regarding decentralization is that it may also be pursued as a means of defending regional interests (our third dimension to be discussed below). But asking for more powers and placing this goal as a central component of a party's positioning on the national question are two different things. For instance, the PQ may ask for more powers in immigration, but it may not believe that this incremental approach is the right one for Quebec – and many sovereignists are likely to think that such an approach is counterproductive since it may create the illusion that Canadian federalism is open to accommodate Quebec's distinctive needs. On the other hand, the PLQ is not against getting more powers for Quebec but does not seem to believe that it is crucial for the nation; the status quo is basically fine. The "more powers" constitutional option is different. Gaining more powers and autonomy is the cornerstone of this option, and this objective is seen as neither counterproductive nor superfluous.

In contrast with the constitutional dimension, the other two dimensions of the national question may be construed as "valence" ones. The second dimension involves the promotion of the specific identity of a particular region. The key question has to do with the way in which parties define national identity and the strategies they adopt in order to be perceived as being most capable of affirming this identity (on this, see Schlesinger 2009; Bechhofer and McCrone 2010; and Leith and

Soule 2011 for the Scottish case, and Bélanger and Nadeau 2009 for Quebec). The identity issue notably encompasses the challenges brought forth by rising cosmopolitanism and diversity, and the tensions that can arise at the substate level when it comes to balancing the goals of integrating immigrants and preserving an existing culture that is distinct within a larger ensemble (Kymlicka 2001; Hepburn 2009a, 2011; Barker 2015). In a general sense, elite emphasis on the values shared by members of the substate national community can contribute to define the collective conception of national identity (Henderson and McEwen 2005), although citizens' perceptions of inclusion and exclusion are in no way shaped entirely by nationalist discourse as the cases of Scotland and Quebec also illustrate (Henderson 2007).

In Quebec, the question of identity is particularly relevant due to the precariousness of the French language on the North American continent (Blais, Martin, and Nadeau 1995; Nadeau and Fleury 1995). That Quebecers believe they have a distinct identity that should be protected and promoted by their regional government is largely undisputed (Blais and Nadeau 1992; Martin and Nadeau 2002; Bélanger and Perrella 2008). Thus, the question of protecting and promoting Quebecer identity is largely consensual, and all parties must subscribe to this objective. That said, while supporting this general goal, parties sometimes disagree on the means necessary to arrive at these ends and differ in the intensity (or zeal) with which they defend this question. These differences were particularly apparent during past debates over language laws in Quebec and more recently during the debate over the adoption of the Charter of Quebec Values, a proposal that would have affirmed the secular nature of Quebec society (see chapter 2).

The defence of regional interests constitutes a third important dimension of the national question, one that nationalist parties are usually, but not always, able to capture. This dimension captures the notion that any government in power in the substate capital, be it Edinburgh or Quebec City, must vigorously defend the interests of this region vis-à-vis the central state. This defence can take several forms. It can consist of defending the prerogatives of the regional parliament against any encroachment by the central government, while also ensuring that the region's integration within a supranational ensemble does not impede its economic and political interests. It can also mean defending the distinct character of the region's social and economic model (even though there may be disagreements over the exact definition of this distinct model). It is along this objective of defending regional interests that the national question truly takes on the characteristics of a valence issue. All substate political parties must have a clear stance on this question and show that they will vehemently and effectively defend the interests of their region (Nadeau et al. 2001; Bélanger and Nadeau 2009), at the risk of being portrayed by their adversaries and perceived by voters as not being "true patriots." Governments from other regions of the state often aim to defend their interests as well, but this defence does not tend to involve the preservation of a distinct, national way of doing things as it does in the case of substate nations.

Taking Scotland as an example, these various goals now appear to be largely shared among political parties. It seems, in accordance with the definition of valence issues, that major parties in Scotland broadly agree with the objectives of promoting Scotland's interests and identity while trying to distinguish themselves through their firmness and commitment in reaching these goals. This consensus is relatively recent. And, as seen earlier in this chapter, the positions of these parties on the constitutional dimension of the national question have changed over time with the effect that partisan competition has become more crowded first on the side supporting significant constitutional change (devolution) and now on the side opposing significant constitutional change (independence) but advocating some form of additional powers. Of course, political parties do not arrive at policy positions in a vacuum: such movements are attributable, to a large extent, to parties seeking to appeal to voter preferences on the national question. In that sense, parties in Scotland and Quebec behave rationally according to expectations set forth by theories of the median voter, which emphasize the proximity between parties' and voters' *issue positions* (Downs 1957; Enelow and Hinich 1984), and by theories of issue ownership, which emphasize the parties' competence at handling *valence (consensual) issues* and voters' perceptions of that competence (Stokes 1963; Budge and Farlie 1983; Petrocik 1996; Egan 2013).[9]

To sum up, we see the national question as comprising three dimensions. We assume that two of these, the affirmation of a regional identity and the defence of regional interests, have the characteristics of a valence issue. The third dimension, the promotion of constitutional options, we believe is more positional in nature because it leads to more disagreement, among parties and voters, about the political goals to be achieved.

EXPLAINING THE BEHAVIOUR OF PARTIES AND VOTERS

Party Behaviour: Issue Salience and Direction

As suggested above, the national question ought to be considered as an electoral issue that substate parties simply cannot avoid. In that sense, the national question may be best conceived as a mainstream issue, even a "super issue," in substate electoral politics. Since all competing parties need to address this issue, the question then becomes, *How* exactly do they address the issue of territory?

The debate surrounding the national question in substate nations often asks whether that nation should become independent from the central state. As explained in the previous section, this is the constitutional dimension of the national question, and it generally leads to disagreement among parties (and voters). Indeed, if there was agreement among parties (and voters) on that dimension, then the debate would end and independence would be either realized or never pursued by anyone. The most extreme nationalist parties will naturally advocate political separation. The most extreme opponents of separation will advocate unionism. Others will take a position in between, arguing for greater decentralization within the existing state structure. In all accounts, the issue of whether constitutional change is needed or not takes on a positional character (Downs 1957; Enelow and Hinich 1984).

That said, as argued in the previous section, the national question includes much more than just the issue of political independence. On other aspects of the question, substate parties take more or less the same position (although they may disagree on the means to implement this position or differ in their levels of commitment towards it). These other dimensions make the national question more of a valence issue at the substate level in that there is more agreement, not only among political actors but also among voters, on the general direction that policies ought to take (Stokes 1963). Meguid (2008, 24–30) calls this phenomenon the "convergence" of mainstream parties to the position of the niche party. When there is such convergence, not only does the issue become a mainstream one – as opposed to a niche one – but specific issue positions do not really matter anymore; the issue has become a valence one because of the overall agreement over the policy goal.

Issue ownership theory has recently been developed to account for party competition behaviour around valence, or consensus, issues (Petrocik 1996; Egan 2013). If there is agreement on policy goals, then what becomes central to the parties' ability to differentiate themselves from each other is voters' perception of which party is most committed and likely to achieve the universally desired goal. This strategic goal serves to reinforce the party's constituency base, but more importantly to expand it. The corollary of this theoretical proposition is that, on a given issue, voters support the party that is viewed as the "owner" of that issue – the party that is seen as the most credible proponent of that issue (Bélanger and Meguid 2008; Green and Jennings 2017).

The roots of the issue ownership concept lie with Robertson's (1976) and Budge and Farlie's (1983) work on issue saliency. According to this body of work, and as would the theory of issue ownership (Petrocik 1996) predict, a party that owns an issue should emphasize it over other issues because it is believed to confer an electoral advantage to the extent that the issue is a priority for a sizable portion of the electorate. A party that does not own the issue should emphasize it only if it has a reasonable hope of "stealing the issue"; otherwise, the party should downplay (even ignore) this issue in its message – in other words, try to decrease its saliency. Thus the question to be examined has to do with the salience of territorial issues in electoral politics, and with how much individual parties address the national question (Pogorelis et al. 2005; Libbrecht et al. 2009). To reiterate, in addition to analyzing the *direction* of positions on the national question, it is necessary to examine the *salience* of the issue as well (Fabre and Martinez-Herrera 2009; Libbrecht, Maddens, and Swenden 2013). Both aspects – direction and salience – are important and complementary in an assessment of party behaviour with regard to a given electoral issue (Meguid 2008).

Based on this view of party and voter behaviour, we hypothesize that substate parties will take a position on the national question and its various dimensions – notably the issue of the substate nation's constitutional future – but also will seek to appear as the best defenders of substate identity and interests. We may expect substate nationalist parties to be the traditional owners of the national question and to have an "edge" on the various dimensions of the issue, but not necessarily, and not necessarily on all dimensions. Other substate parties will also seek to present themselves as the most Scottish/Québécois party representing and defending Scottish/Québécois identity and interests. In addition, depending on the actual distribution of the public's constitutional preferences, voters may favour parties that adopt federalist/unionist stances – unless that pole of party competition is too crowded.

Chapters 2 and 3 will address these questions as they pertain to the strategic behaviour of political parties in Quebec and Scotland, respectively. On the question of the salience of territorial issues, our analysis of party programs and rhetoric will show variation across parties. That said, we can expect that the priming of the national question by the parties that dominate on this issue, as well as the valence nature of some of its dimensions, will exert pressure on all parties to take sides in this debate and to address issues of regional identity and interests. On valence issues there should not be a great deal of difference between parties in terms of salience or direction (excluding the constitutional dimension of course), although we might well expect nationalist parties to emphasize the national question the most. While we expect parties to react to positions of other parties, we anticipate that parties do so only insofar as it will win them votes.

Another important consideration is the multilevel nature of electoral politics in both Quebec and Scotland. As the national question becomes mainstream and, to some extent, a valence issue across the substate party system, it is not only nationalist parties that oppose central-state policies; the policies of all substate parties more or less diverge from central-state policies. In agreeing to defend substate identity, interests, and powers – with varying degrees of zeal and commitment – substate parties may act as a "territorial bloc" against the wishes of central state governments. This can create particular tensions for statewide parties, whose substate regional branches may have diverged from the party line or even broken organizationally from the statewide party. As a result, one could argue that the real disagreement in party positioning on the national question takes place along the centre-periphery cleavage between central-state and substate electoral politics. While the above description ought to be viewed as an extreme case, it nonetheless suggests that in general we are more likely to identify divergence across levels (substate versus statewide) than within the substate party system since the national question is more likely to remain a niche issue at the state level (Alonso 2012).

Cleavage theory can be used to explain this type of divergence, in particular the resilience and refashioning of the centre-periphery cleavage in multilevel states. By taking the multilevel dimension of electoral politics into account, we can link back to classical theories and interpretations of party competition (e.g., Lipset and Rokkan 1967). But these must be nuanced, as devolution reshapes the centre-periphery cleavage in multilevel states. Because the national question is more likely to operate as a valence issue at the substate level than at the state level, this territorial bloc phenomenon should accentuate the centre-periphery cleavage within the state. The national question thus has the potential to pit substate and state party actors at loggerheads in multilevel political systems.

Voter Behaviour: The National Question as a Vote Determinant

In electoral politics, parties are but one side of the coin. They take stances on electoral issues, including the national question in substate politics, so as to appeal to voters' preferences and mobilize their support at the polls. For their part, voters look for parties that will deliver on their policy preferences, including those preferences that pertain to the constitutional status, identity, and interests of their substate nation, and they will take the parties' issue messages into account when making their voting decision. Parties thus react to voters, who in turn cast votes for parties, both sides entering into a reciprocal relationship. In that sense, voters and parties represent two sides of the same coin, and in this book we seek to study both of these sides equally. We set out to examine the extent to which political parties in Quebec and Scotland are successful at maximizing their support on the basis of the national question.

In order to estimate parties' relative success at doing so, we need to assess the extent to which citizens in substate nations take the issue of the national question into account when voting the way they do in statewide and substate elections. A related research question in the literature is whether elections are treated as first- or second-order contests by voters. According to Reif and Schmitt (1980), elections in which there is less at stake, in other words where the level of jurisdictional authority is limited, are more likely to be "second order" elections (see also van der Eijk, Franklin, and Marsh 1996; Norris and Reif 1997; Marsh 1998). In such contests, voter turnout is expected to be lower, and voters cast their ballots not on the basis of preferences related to the second-order venue but according to political issues relative to the first order. In other words, according to this framework, second-order elections mainly serve as referendums on the first-order government. While this view was originally formulated to account for dynamics in supranational elections like those to the European Parliament, it can also be applied to the case of substate elections (e.g., Hough and Jeffery 2006). The question of interest thus becomes, Are substate-level elections considered by voters as first or second order? Hough and Jeffery (2006) found that most substate elections in Western Europe appeared to be second order (see also Dinkel 1978; Jeffery and Hough 2003; Pallarés and Keating 2003). But more recent work has tended to provide a more nuanced view on this question, and substate elections are now increasingly being viewed by scholars as distinct in character from state-level elections – and thus as "first order" contests in their own right (Jeffery 2009a, 2009b; Schakel and Jeffery 2013; Henderson and McEwen 2010, 2015; Golder et al. 2017; Thorlakson and Keating 2017).

This conclusion certainly falls in line with the literature that has highlighted the distinctive nature of voting behaviour in Canadian provincial elections (Blake 1985; Cutler 2008; Cross et al. 2015). It is particularly true in the case of Quebec, which has a relatively long tradition of provincial election studies (Lemieux 1969; Lemieux, Gilbert, and Blais 1970; Latouche, Lord, and Vaillancourt 1976; Pinard and Hamilton 1977, 1978; Bernard and Descôteaux 1981; Crête 1984; Monière and Guay 1995; Pinard 2005; Bélanger and Nadeau 2009; Bastien, Bélanger, and Gélineau 2013). The centrality of the constitutional debate raises the stakes when it comes to Quebec substate elections. This in turn makes Quebecers' voting decisions rest, to a significant degree, on their constitutional preferences rather than on an assessment of the performance of the Canadian government. The same situation is true for Quebecers' voting behaviour in statewide elections (Nadeau, Guérin, and Martin 1995; Bakvis and Macpherson 1995; Gidengil et al. 2012; Nadeau and Bélanger 2012; Gagnon and Boucher 2017). To paraphrase Cutler (2008): from a Quebec voter's point of view, provincial (substate) and federal (statewide) elections appear to constitute "two first-order" elections.[10]

The study of voting behaviour in Scotland is well developed too, but has notably faced two limitations. The first is that despite the assumption of distinctiveness, the expression of Scottish political preferences occurred for almost all of the twentieth century in non-Scottish democratic contests, or rather in contests where the boundaries were either entirely internal (local elections) or external (UK, Europe) to, but never coterminous with, Scottish borders. The challenge is that this polity, which by most measures was considered by its voters and political class to possess a distinct political culture with its own political administrative institutions, lacked the opportunity to express its partisan preferences at the level at which they were most significant. Before devolution, this meant that studies of Scottish voting behaviour focused primarily on Scottish preferences in UK elections (Budge and Urwin 1966; Brand, Mitchell, and Surridge 1993; Brown, McCrone, and Paterson 1996; Brown et al. 1999).

With the arrival of the Scottish Parliament, the Scottish electorate had the first opportunity to express itself at a territorial scale matching its borders, and this had a knock-on effect on studies of Scottish voting (see, for example, Paterson et al. 2001; Curtice et al. 2009). A key focus was determining if voters expressed different preferences at different levels, a task made more complicated by the use of a different electoral system (MMP) for devolved elections.[11] In a Scottish context the implication of Reif and Schmitt's (1980) view is that votes in devolved elections could be cast on the basis of the performance of the UK government. As in Quebec, such a view has been proven not to apply to Scotland (Thorlakson and Keating 2017), and vote choice (Denver and Johns 2010; Carman, Johns, and Mitchell 2014) and turnout (Henderson and McEwen 2010, 2015) are driven by predictors specific to Scotland. In the case of turnout and vote choice, these predictors include a sense of national identity and attitudes towards the Constitution.

The national question ought to contribute to make Quebec and Scottish substate elections first order. If such is the case, we should see the positions of Quebecers and Scots on the constitutional debate and their attitudes about the other two (valence) dimensions of the national question – identity/culture and regional interests – having a significant influence on their vote choice. Chapters 4 and 5 will empirically assess whether these general theoretical expectations are met in the cases of Quebec and Scotland, respectively.

We assess the importance of these issue attitudes to vote choice in two ways. First, we compare the impact of these views with that of other, more usual determinants of voting behaviour like sociodemographic characteristics and socioeconomic orientations. Several studies in Quebec have shown that constitutional preferences and feelings of national identity are important motivations behind referendum voting (e.g., Blais and Nadeau 1992; Blais, Martin, and Nadeau 1995; Nadeau and Fleury 1995; Martin and Nadeau 2002; Bélanger and Perrella 2008), but few have shown their direct effects on electoral choice. The link between these variables and vote choice at election times has received more attention in Scotland (Paterson et al. 2001; Curtice et al. 2009; Carman, Johns, and Mitchell 2014) but has led to some diverging results when it comes to the identity variable (Bond 2000; Johns et al. 2009). The opinion measure generally used to operationalize sense of identity is the "Linz-Moreno" question (Linz et al. 1981; Moreno 1988), which consists of a five-point scale measuring whether a respondent feels more Québécois (or Scottish) than Canadian (or British) or the inverse. Yet other indicators of identity can be looked at as well, notably the respective level of attachment to the state-level and substate-level community (Mendelsohn 2002). Such indicators have the advantage of not imposing a hierarchical approach to multiple identities, contrary to the Linz-Moreno measure (Sinnott 2006; Levy 2014; Guinjoan and Rodon 2016). We include both types of identity measures in our analysis.

The defence of regional interests, and the perceived ability of political parties to deliver on this issue, can also be expected to influence vote choice in territories where the national question is politically salient. This valence aspect of voting behaviour has been studied in some detail on the federal level in Canada (Nadeau and Blais 1990; Nadeau et al. 2001; Clarke, Kornberg, and Scotto 2009) but has received only limited attention on the provincial level (Bélanger and Gélineau 2011). Until now, the competence of political parties has remained an overlooked dimension of Scottish voting behaviour: "Valence concerns, which have been neglected in studies of Scottish voting to date, need to be much more prominent [in future studies]" (Johns et al. 2009, 230). The notion that voters are concerned less with positional issues and more with valence issues is a recent theme in British politics (Clarke, Sanders, et al. 2004, 2009; Green 2007; Clarke, Kornberg, and Scotto 2009; Green and Jennings 2017) as well as Scottish politics (Johns 2011; Johns et al. 2009; Johns, Carman, and Mitchell 2013; Johns and Mitchell 2016). Our comparative analysis of voting behaviour thus seeks to include attitudes towards the social and economic interests of a region in explaining vote choice in Quebec and Scotland, and see which parties appear to own these issues in voters' minds.

A second way to determine the national question's influence on voter behaviour is to test whether the *importance* given by voters to the national question itself actually conditions the influence of their constitutional preferences on their vote choice. How voters' individual positions on political issues influence vote choice is a topic that has attracted the attention of many specialists of electoral behaviour over the years (e.g., Downs 1957; Franklin, Mackie, and Valen 1992; Lewis-Beck et al. 2008). Some of the most recent work on issue voting suggests that the impact of issue assessments is greater when the issue in question is "salient," that is, considered to be very important by an individual (e.g., Fournier et al. 2003; Bélanger and Meguid 2008). Previous studies on this topic, both in Scotland and in Quebec, have looked at the impact of constitutional preferences on vote choice, but none have verified whether this influence was moderated by the importance given by individuals to the national question. Therefore, we intend to examine how an individual's positioning on the constitutional dimension interacts with how important the national question is to his or her vote choice.

This is the general approach that will guide our analysis of voter behaviour. That said, three important nuances must be noted. First, as pointed out in the previous section, while we might expect nationalist parties to claim ownership over the valence dimensions of the national question, and they might be perceived by voters to care most about certain aspects of the national question, positional dimensions might well introduce different electoral dynamics. Indeed, on the constitutional dimension the "owner" of the issue is more likely to be the party whose position is the closest to the majority opinion among the electorate – which of course could well mean that the party is sharing this position with one or more competitors. Thus the issue owner might not be the same political party on all dimensions of the national question. This is likely to be the case in Quebec, where the Parti Québécois may be viewed as the party that best stands up for the nation's identity and interests, but the Parti Libéral du Québec (the only party clearly opposed to independence) may be the one owning the constitutional dimension since the majority of Quebecers do not support the independence option. The Scottish National Party, on the other hand, might well own the constitutional dimension (in addition to the other two dimensions) because, contrary to the Quebec case, voters who are opposed to independence (and who also form a majority) are divided among three major political parties.

Second, it may be one thing for a party to claim ownership of an issue – for example, by emphasizing it in its manifestos and campaign speeches – and another to be perceived as the rightful owner of this issue and to be rewarded as such by voters at the polls. In most instances, the two will coincide because parties tend to emphasize issues (or dimensions of an issue) that they *think* will confer an electoral advantage to them (Budge and Farlie 1983). But we need to keep in mind that claims to issue ownership may not always automatically translate into voting decisions that are based (a) on this issue, and (b) on the claims of commitment and competence made by political parties concerning this issue.

Finally, we expect the national question to have a greater impact on substate vote choice than on state-level voting behaviour. Statewide elections are first-order contests of a different kind than substate elections. More importantly, the priming effect of the national question within the party system is less important at the state level since, as argued above, this issue is more niche than mainstream at that level. Since we expect the national question to act as a super issue in structuring vote decisions at the substate level, it should have more of an influence in determining the outcome of devolved elections than of contests held at the state level. That said, the greater impact of the national question in substate elections certainly does not prevent other policy issues or concerns (like health, education, etc.) from being debated by the parties during campaigns held at that level and from factoring into voters' decisions.

CARRYING OUT THE STUDY

The empirical analysis carried out in this book makes use of multiple data sources. Chapters 2 and 3 focus on party behaviour and provide a study of the strategies of Quebec and Scottish political parties. In the context of this comparative project, it is crucial to closely examine how parties, both nationalist and unionist/federalist, define their positions on the national question and how specific institutional and cultural contexts in Quebec and Scotland may shape party discourse and competition across levels of government.

To study party behaviour, we have access to two important sources of data. We first look at the parties' electoral manifestos, as they reflect how a party explicitly portrays its political position to voters during an election campaign (Budge et al. 2001; Klingemann et al. 2006). In order to assess the positions of the different parties on the national question and its various dimensions, we have carried out a content analysis of the manifestos from recent substate and statewide elections in both regions: the 2011 Canadian and 2014 Quebec elections, and the 2010 UK and 2011 Scottish elections. Since the manifesto coding schemes employed by comparative projects tend to focus on statewide issues, we have developed a manual coding scheme better suited to the study of substate elections and constitutional politics, along the lines of the innovative work of Alonso and colleagues (2013) (see also Pogorelis et al. 2005; Libbrecht et al. 2009; Libbrecht, Maddens, and Swenden 2013; Basile 2015).

The second source of information comes from semistructured interviews with party elites. These allow us to reveal, for example, the underlying strategy behind decisions taken by political parties with regard to their constitutional orientations, something that cannot typically be deduced from the manifest content of political party platforms. Documents produced by parties for public consumption also rarely make direct reference to the arguments of their competitors, at either the state or substate levels. We carried out interviews with elected representatives from the major parties at each level of government, in both regions.

A third source of data is public opinion surveys conducted in both Scotland and Quebec in 2012 and again in Quebec in 2014. These surveys, to be used in chapters 4 and 5, allow us to examine citizen opinions on the dimensions most vital to our study. Since the independent and dependent variables of interest to us are not typically included in the same survey, new opinion research was necessary. In addition, these new surveys allowed us to ask practically identical questions to respondents in both regions, something that greatly strengthens the Quebec-Scotland comparison of voter behaviour. More details on our methodology and data are provided in chapters 4 and 5, which explore the motivations behind vote choice in Quebec and Scotland at both the state and the substate levels, as well as in the appendices.

The book ends with chapter 6, which takes the main findings from the previous four chapters in order to draw a number of conclusions regarding the comparative impact of the national question on party and voter behaviour in Quebec and Scotland. The chapter also reflects more generally on the past, present, and likely future role and influence of the "national question" – in all of its dimensions – on state and substate electoral politics, and on the study of them, in these two territories and beyond.

2

Party Behaviour in Quebec

As underlined in chapter 1, while the national question has been very much on the agenda in Scotland ever since the Scottish National Party formed its first government in 2007, in Quebec the issue has experienced two decades of slowly declining salience following the 1995 referendum defeat. In some ways, the record-low level of electoral support recently received by Quebec's two most prominent separatist parties – the Parti Québécois (PQ) in the substate election of 2014 (25.4 per cent) and the Bloc Québécois (BQ) in the statewide election of 2015 (19.4 per cent within the province, representing only 4.7 per cent of the Canada-wide vote) – can be interpreted as a symptom of a larger mobilization problem that confronts the nationalist movement in Quebec at the beginning of the twenty-first century.

Yet, political parties in Quebec still compete on the issue. They still talk regularly about the national question, even if for some of them it is merely to say that Quebecers need to focus on priorities other than independence for the time being. Seeking or preserving Quebec's autonomy within the Canadian federation remains a fundamental aspect of the parties' discourse in the province. The resilience of the national question as an electoral issue in Quebec is understandable. It has underpinned the substate party system ever since the socioeconomic and political modernization of the province starting in the 1960s, a period known as Quebec's Quiet Revolution (Pelletier 2012; Godbout 2013). With the advent of the PQ, the first serious political party advocating independence, the question has polarized the substate party system, with "sovereignists" gravitating towards the PQ and "federalists" mainly represented by the Parti Libéral du Québec (PLQ). In other words, the national question has structured the party system for so long, it is no wonder why it is difficult for the parties to get rid of the issue or to simply stop addressing it. It is very likely that parties on both sides of the debate believe that they still benefit from the issue, in that it allows them to keep their core supporters mobilized (either in favour of independence or against it at all costs). Even at the state level, the question of the defence of Quebec's interests also continues to structure the competition between federal parties in the province, especially since the arrival of the Bloc Québécois (BQ) in the 1993 election (Hinich, Munger, and De Marchi 1998; Johnston 2000, 2008). Almost all of the statewide parties feel the need to propose one form or another of collaborative approach to Quebecers, while the BQ continually tries to keep the idea of political independence, or at the very least enhanced autonomy for Quebec, on the federal agenda.

This chapter thus seeks to understand the electoral calculus underlying the stance that Quebec parties take with respect to the national question. Following on from our theoretical framework, it employs the concept of issue ownership to understand how, and to what extent, the territorial dimension structures party competition in Quebec. Based on the issue ownership perspective, we presented the general hypothesis in chapter 1 that parties in Quebec need to take a position on the national question and its various dimensions – the constitutional issue, national identity, and regional interests – to win over the electorate. Furthermore, we put forward the hypothesis that whoever "owns" the issue of the national question – and here we believe it is most likely to be the nationalist parties themselves – has the potential to have an influence on the positioning of the other parties. Thus, while the Parti Québécois – as the main nationalist party in Quebec – may be the long-term owner of the national question issue, it also faces competition from other parties in presenting itself as the most pro-Quebec party. Yet we do not believe that there is convergence across all dimensions of the national question. In particular, we believe that the constitutional dimension remains a positional issue for political parties, while other aspects of the national question – identity and regional interests – are valence issues, in the sense that there is general agreement between political parties on the direction of policies, although there may be differences in the parties' level of commitment to defending these aspects and in their proposed means for achieving these goals. A more specific set of hypotheses can be expressed as follows:

1 Given its importance in Quebec, the national question is an issue on which all parties take a position that becomes a central component of their political positioning.

2 The most nationalist parties in Quebec, the Parti Québécois and the Bloc Québécois, "own" the valence dimensions of the national question, and therefore emphasize this issue the most.

3 The most nationalist parties in Québec, the Parti Québécois and the Bloc Québécois, and the least nationalist one, the Parti Libéral du Québec, emphasize the constitutional dimension the most because they each stand to benefit the most from the polarization of the electorate on this dimension.

4 The priming of the national question by the parties dominating this issue, and the valence nature of some of its dimensions, exert pressure on other parties in the substate party system, inciting them to take stronger stances in this debate. This phenomenon is more marked at the substate level, leading substate parties to act as a territorial bloc in opposition to state-level parties and policies.

In order to fully test these hypotheses, this chapter unpacks each of the principal dimensions of the national question in Quebec to gauge the degree to which the parties are priming (a) the constitutional dimension; (b) the identity dimension (including positions on cosmopolitanism and language); and (c) the regional interests dimension (including social policy, economic policy, and supranational policy). Looking at issue salience will allow us to test the first three hypotheses, whereas conclusions about the last hypothesis will mainly come from an examination of issue direction. (The extent to which these priming efforts succeed at making parties be perceived as the "issue owner" in the eyes of citizens will be analyzed in the public opinion chapters – chapter 4 for Quebec and chapter 5 for Scotland.)

To determine and analyze the parties' positions on the national question in Quebec, we use two sources of data. The first comes from a content analysis of recent campaign manifestos published by the political parties at the substate and statewide levels. These manifestos reveal how provincial and federal parties portray their political orientations to Quebec voters during elections. We used a specially adapted coding scheme to measure the issue profile of substate and statewide parties on the national question. The coding scheme (presented in more detail in appendix table A1) captures the main dimensions of the national question as conceptualized in the theoretical framework. We rely on the manifestos from the

April 2014 substate election[1] and the May 2011 federal election, with a total of eight manifestos covering substate and state parties: the 2014 manifestos of the Parti Québécois (PQ), the Parti Libéral du Québec (PLQ), Coalition Avenir Québec (CAQ), and Québec Solidaire (QS); and the 2011 manifestos of the Bloc Québécois (BQ), Liberal Party of Canada (LPC), Conservative Party of Canada (CPC), and New Democratic Party (NDP).

The manual coding procedure involved the division of each manifesto into "quasi sentences," each representing an argument expressed by a sentence or part of it, and assigning individual quasi-sentences to (a) an exclusive "issue salience" category and (b) an exclusive directional category to determine the relative positioning of parties on substate issues along a five-point continuum going from -2 (centralist direction) to +2 (autonomist direction), with 0 representing a position in favour of the status quo (see appendix table A2). This approach enabled us to determine the salience and positioning of parties on each of the dimensions of the national question.

The second source of data comes in the form of semi-structured elite interviews with senior party officials. The interviews posed a series of questions on the three themes of the national question: the constitutional issue, the identity issue, and regional interests. These interviews provided us with a valuable source of "insider information" not captured in official manifestos. We were also able to compare what was said by politicians in a one-on-one setting with what the party officially states in its election manifestos. Interviews were conducted between February and December 2013 with at least one member from the four most important parties on each level of government in Quebec: members of the National Assembly (MNAs) for the PQ, PLQ, CAQ, and QS; and Quebec-elected members of Parliament (MPs) in Ottawa for the BQ, LPC, CPC, and NDP, for a total of nine interviews.[2] (Two MNAs from the CAQ were interviewed, one a former *adéquiste* and the other a former *péquiste*,[3] as a way to ensure that the CAQ's viewpoint presented in this book was not biased one way or the other.)

THE CONSTITUTIONAL DIMENSION

The first dimension of the national question that deserves attention is the position of the various political parties on the current and future constitutional status of Quebec. Is there disagreement (or polarization) among the parties' stances on this aspect? Or does it take on characteristics of a valence (or consensual) issue?

The data from our manifestos analysis indicate that the Coalition Avenir Québec is the substate party that emphasized the constitutional issue the most in the 2014 election campaign in Quebec. As figure 2.1 shows, the Parti Québécois came in second place with eleven references made, about half as many as the CAQ (twenty references). Of particular interest is the absence of any references to the constitutional issue in the PLQ manifesto. However, we posit that this lack of attention in the PLQ manifesto is misleading because the Liberals and their leader, Philippe Couillard, did emphasize the constitutional issue in speeches and press releases during the campaign (Maioni 2014; Bélanger and Falk Pedersen 2015). In particular, the PLQ focused a great deal of attention on the speech made by the PQ's newly recruited star candidate, businessman Pierre Karl Péladeau. To the apparent astonishment of the then PQ leader Pauline Marois, Péladeau declared – with a victory fist in the air – that his deep motivation for wanting to go into politics was to obtain independence for Quebec (Journet 2014). The Quebec Liberals sought to highlight this speech as a reminder of the Parti Québécois's priority – independence – which was unpopular at the time among the public (as shall be seen in chapter 4) and had up to that point been downplayed by the PQ leadership. Instead, the Liberals used Péladeau's independence speech to contrast it with their own policy priority, the economy (see figure 2.9 below). The fact that the PQ did not emphasize the constitutional issue as much as the CAQ reflects Marois's decision to focus on other dimensions of the national question, especially identity, as an emphasis on independence may have been seen to be an electoral liability among an unsympathetic electorate (see figures 2.3 and 2.5). On paper, the PLQ's behaviour does not conform to our expectation, but the lack of emphasis on this dimension in its manifesto can also be interpreted as support for the constitutional status quo.

At the state level, the claim to ownership of the constitutional issue could not be clearer: the Bloc Québécois made 145 references to it in its manifesto, while the three federalist parties barely mentioned it.[4] The BQ emphasized independence because, unlike the PQ in 2014, the party leadership did not seem to consider it a liability during the 2011 election (Fournier et al. 2013). However, the results from that election – whereby the BQ suffered steep electoral decline – indicate that the BQ somewhat overestimated the Quebec public's appetite for sovereignty. Despite this, the BQ elected a new leader in 2014 – Mario Beaulieu – who criticized the PQ (and to a lesser extent the BQ itself) for being too timid on the independence issue, and pledged to make it an even

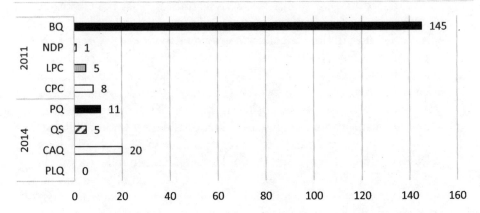

Figure 2.1 Salience of the constitutional issue in Quebec and statewide party manifestos

stronger priority in BQ campaigns. It is telling that only a couple of months before the October 2015 federal election, the party brought back its former leader Gilles Duceppe to replace Beaulieu, seeing as the party seemed to be running into a wall – yet the return of Duceppe failed to reverse the party's continuing decline (Bélanger and Nadeau 2016). In short, it seems that by behaving in accordance with our third hypothesis, the BQ has been severely punished at the polls in the last two federal elections since opinion polarization tended to favour the federalist camp in both contests (see chapter 4).

What about the parties' positions on the constitutional dimension? The directional coding of the manifesto data presented in figure 2.2 indicates that all substate parties took a positive position on the constitutional issue – except, of course, the Parti Libéral du Québec, which made no reference to the issue at all, as stated above. The Parti Québécois, Québec Solidaire, and the Coalition Avenir Québec are all in favour of more constitutional autonomy, with the first two of these parties advocating independence and the CAQ seeking enhanced autonomy for Quebec within the Canadian federation. This similarity in party positions is as one would expect based on our fourth hypothesis, not taking into account the more divisive question of independence itself.

Turning now to the federal election manifesto data, we can see that most of the Conservative Party's references were in a positive direction, while the single reference made to the constitutional issue in the NDP manifesto (addressing regional fiscal autonomy) was also positive. Only

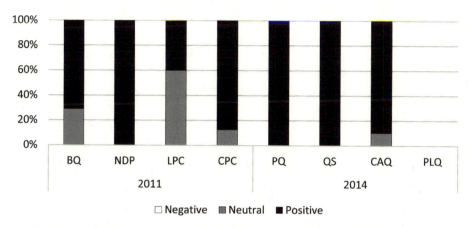

Figure 2.2 Direction on the constitutional issue in Quebec and statewide party manifestos

the Liberal Party appears to resist accommodation on this question, as only two of its five references were positive (in favour of more influence for Quebec in central government decisions) with all others being neutral. A sizable number of the Bloc Québécois's references were neutral in nature, but this ought to be expected given the very large number of references made to the constitutional issue in the party's (extremely lengthy) manifesto.

The interviews tend to confirm these observations while bringing a number of important nuances to the analysis. On the surface, there is no denying the clear polarization among substate parties on the question of whether the province of Quebec should separate from the rest of Canada. As the PQ MNA that we interviewed states, "The goal of the Parti Québécois, the very reason for its existence, is to win Quebec's political independence" (interview, 15 August 2013). The creation of a sovereign Quebec state has been the goal of the PQ since its birth in 1968, although the party – like its Scottish counterpart – has sought to emphasize continuing (monetary and political) linkages with the rest of Canada following any transition to independence. On the other hand, the Liberal MNA interviewed claims that her party "remains a federalist option within the National Assembly, so our preference is always to maintain the link with Canada" (interview, 13 May 2013). She even goes as far as saying that her involvement in politics is primarily motivated by the threat that the PQ poses to the integrity of the Canadian federation.

Between these two poles, the other parties navigate less easily. While Québec Solidaire sides with the PQ's pro-independence option, the QS MNA is quick to add that the party's preference is to maintain a form of association between the two states of Canada and Quebec, with the sharing of a number of core responsibilities (currency and defence) and possibly the creation of some form of supranational representational institution. For its part, the Coalition Avenir Québec refuses (at the time of our interviews) to take a position on the constitutional future of Quebec, with one interviewee stating that this lack of position actually constitutes the "founding axis" of their new party (interview, 22 February 2013). Indeed, during the 2014 provincial election, the CAQ leadership – sensing public disaffection with the constitutional issue – pledged that the party would never hold a referendum on independence in Quebec. The CAQ believes that the national question in Quebec has reached a temporary dead end, and so Quebecers ought to start dedicating their time and energy to other policy priorities. Despite this stern approach, however, if one looks carefully at CAQ manifestos and speeches, the party does support more powers for Quebec – especially over the economy – but not full independence. This emphasis on more autonomy became the CAQ's official position on the constitutional issue at the fall 2015 general meeting of the party membership (Castonguay 2015).

On that note, if we leave aside the issue of whether Quebec ought to separate or not, we find a relatively large consensus among Quebec's substate parties when it comes to the broader thrust of decentralization, with all parties seeking to increase the province's powers. Put differently, while the substate parties take various positions on whether to seek secession per se, they are all in favour of more constitutional autonomy, although they certainly display varying levels of commitment towards that goal.

While in power between 2012 and 2014, the Parti Québécois even adopted a strategy to that effect, which it called *gouvernance souverainiste*. The PQ MNA defined "sovereignist governance" as follows: "If we cannot make independence, then let's use to a maximum the provincial autonomy that we already have ... Quebec is already sovereign in a certain number of policy areas so let's occupy our jurisdiction fields, the sovereignty space that we have already" (interview, 15 August 2013). The PQ's turn in power was too brief for the party to really put this doctrine into practice, but sovereignist governance is the principle that guided the PQ's ideas and strategies under Pauline Marois's tenure.

The Coalition Avenir Québec's position as being a pro-autonomy party also emerged more clearly from the interview data. One of its MNAs underlined the fact that seeking greater autonomy for Quebec had always been the constitutional position of the Action Démocratique du Québec (ADQ), the party that merged in 2012 with the newly formed CAQ. The ADQ sought greater provincial autonomy for Quebec within Canada, and in that sense the CAQ remains truthful to the legacy of its parent party. In the MNA's words, it is a "Quebec-first approach" whereby the CAQ pledges to defend Quebec's interests first and foremost (interview, 22 February 2013). The second CAQ MNA whom we interviewed concurred, adding that autonomy is to be sought within the framework of Canadian federalism in the form of additional powers: "We will try to obtain the most powers that we can within the federal framework so as to improve Quebec's lot ... I think that's our top priority" (interview, 22 March 2013).[5]

The interview data revealed that both the PQ and the CAQ adopted a "more powers" approach partly because a significant minority of Quebecers continue to support outright independence. But while the PQ – to use a well-known idiom – sees the glass as being "half full" in having some public support for independence, the CAQ sees it as being "half empty." On one hand, according to the PQ, the core question facing the party in the current period is: "How to be an independentist in a state that, for the time being, does not have the necessary popular support for making independence? ... How to be an independentist and play the Canadian game?" (interview with PQ MNA, 15 August 2013). Seeking more autonomy thus becomes a fallback strategy for the PQ in this context, mainly due to the constraints of public opinion: "As we have already held two [failed referendums] we cannot afford losing a third. So when the time comes to call a third one, we need to have more than reasonable chances of winning. So we need to have strong support within public opinion. The current level of support is not enough, we must recognize it" (interview, 15 August 2013). On the other hand, for the CAQ the sizable constituency that will always be in favour of independence in Quebec presents a problem: "The fact that there is at least a quarter, if not a third, of Quebecers who are, who remain, and who will always be sovereignists must be taken into account ... This is not a negligible minority, and so we have to deal with it. Hence the approach which in my view is the most open one, which is that of autonomy, where we remain within the Canadian framework but also fully assume our destiny" (interview with CAQ MNA, 22 February 2013).

For its part, Québec Solidaire is also in favour of more constitutional autonomy (as well as independence) for Quebec, although the issue
of power devolution is not as central to QS as for the PQ or the CAQ. According to one of its MNAs, Québec Solidaire "does not ask itself what
powers ought to be sought within the current institutional framework,
that is to say, look at which policy areas fall under the federal government's jurisdiction and see whether we can obtain them or not" (interview, 27 February 2013). The party is much more concerned with establishing what it calls a *souveraineté populaire*, that is, a genuine
grassroots sovereignist movement in which the whole independence
process is controlled by the population through a constituent assembly
that would provide a counterweight to the influence of big businesses
and financial interests over Quebec's national debate.

The Parti Libéral du Québec appears to resist the autonomy drive
most strongly out of all substate parties, but even then, it does not publicly come out against wanting more powers for Quebec. One of its
MNAs indicates that the party wants provincial competencies to be respected by the federal government, and is in favour of more provincial
powers in the domains of health care, education, and culture. This position is in line with the nationalist demands formulated by the PLQ in
2001 in the Pelletier Report,[6] which remains the reference point for
party policies according to this interviewee. More importantly, the party
wishes to rectify an important historical grievance of the Quebec state:
"Whether we want it or not, we have a rendezvous with 1982 one day
or the other because [that year] there was the imposition of the Constitution's repatriation by the nine provinces without Quebec's consent, and it remains a problem ... It remains a wish of our party that
one day this situation can be resolved" (interview with PLQ MNA, 13
May 2013). This wish forms the central objective of the PLQ government's "national affirmation policy" that was made public in the spring
of 2017 (Canadian Press 2017).

Shifting the focus to statewide parties, one finds an opposite portrait
of party behaviour. That is to say, (non-nationalist) statewide parties
tend to agree on the separation issue – being very much against it – but
they disagree on the question of the further enhancement of Quebec's
constitutional autonomy.

At the state level, only the Bloc Québécois is in favour of Quebec's
independence. Canada's three other statewide parties – the Liberals,
Conservatives, and NDP – are staunchly against the idea of Quebec's separation from the rest of Canada. For the Liberal Party, "Quebec's place

within Canada does not constitute a problem; that's where we can grow. It is a state that we created with the other Canadians. Being both a Quebecer and a Canadian is not a contradiction, it is a great complementarity" (interview with LPC MP, 13 March 2013). The Conservative Party MP concurs with this view: "I believe that Quebec takes great profit from being able to develop and grow within the Canadian federation" (interview, 6 December 2013); but she still views the question of whether Quebec should separate or not as a perfectly legitimate one that ought to be debated. As for the NDP, its MP suggests that there will always remain a number of staunch independentists in the province, but that Quebecers in general have priorities that are more important than the national question such as health care, the economy, and environmental protection (interview, 16 August 2013). This position contrasts with that of the left-wing Québec Solidaire at the substate level, which endorses independence as a means to achieve a more socially just society in Quebec. Indeed, one party ancestor of the current QS – the Nouveau Parti Démocratique du Québec (NPDQ) – disaffiliated from the federal NDP in 1989 on this very issue: the federal party had disagreed with the NPDQ's more favourable attitude towards Quebec nationalism.

The statewide parties' views on Quebec's constitutional autonomy are much more varied, however. In one corner, the Bloc Québécois is very much pro-autonomy. In fact, it is exactly because Quebec has not been able to become more autonomous within the Canadian federation that the BQ advocates its independence: "Every time Quebec has wanted to distinguish itself, Canada has always said no. So I think that's where the conflict comes from" (interview with BQ MP, 22 March 2013).

In the opposite corner, the Liberals and Conservatives are opposed to more autonomy for Quebec (unlike the Liberals at the provincial level). As one Liberal MP argues, Canada "is already a very decentralized federation; on several aspects the most decentralized possible. The province of Quebec fully utilizes the room to manoeuvre that the Constitution grants it. There is also some recognition of Quebec's distinctiveness in the Constitution, such as the civil code, language planning, etc." (interview, 13 March 2013). The Conservative Party also believes that the Quebec government already has ample powers. The Conservative MP we interviewed claimed that the more important question in her party's view is that the central government be respectful of Quebec's areas of jurisdiction – a position that, for a time, actually formed the core of the Conservative Party's approach of "open federalism"[7] (interview, 6 December 2013).

In between these two extreme positions, one finds the NDP. While the party considers Quebec to be already quite autonomous, it remains in favour of further decentralization in some policy areas, but not outright secession (unlike the provincial left-leaning QS). This constitutional position was defined in the so-called Sherbrooke declaration adopted at the NDP's 2005 general meeting of its Quebec section.[8] According to the NDP MP that we interviewed, the declaration remains the party's official position regarding the national question. The Sherbrooke declaration "recognizes the importance of having a cooperative and asymmetrical federalism ... It also recognizes, of course, Quebec as a nation; and in fact it was recognized as such by the NDP since its founding ... The vision of two founding nations [of Canada] is something that is really part of the NDP's principles" (interview, 16 August 2013). It is on this basis that the NDP considers the demands for more power devolution as a legitimate prerogative of the Quebec government – demands that a federal NDP government would be open to discuss and negotiate, especially if devolution would allow Quebec more political and financial freedom to create its own institutions and policy programs.

To sum up, with regard to the constitutional dimension of the national question, we can see the clear contours of a centre-periphery cleavage. On one hand, substate parties are all pro-autonomy to varying degrees, and two of them – Parti Québécois and Québec Solidaire – are in favour of Quebec's independence. On the other hand, only two statewide parties – Bloc Québécois and NDP – are open to more constitutional autonomy for the Quebec government, and only one (BQ) advocates independence. As a result of different degrees of support on the question of more autonomy at the two levels, we find that the party system at the substate level pulls more in one direction while the statewide party system pulls more in the other, thus offering initial confirmation of our fourth hypothesis. This state-substate centre-periphery cleavage will materialize again when we examine the multi-level dynamics of the national question later on in this chapter.

IDENTITY

Cosmopolitanism

The second dimension of the national question that we are interested in is national identity. Here, cosmopolitanism – by which we mean the cultural diversity of the nation – is the first aspect of the identity dimension that we analyze in terms of salience and directional position-ing in the party manifestos. Findings regarding the salience of this issue are presented in figure 2.3. At the substate level, it is the Coalition Avenir Québec and the Parti Québécois that have claimed ownership of this issue, by emphasizing questions of immigrant integration (with twenty-eight and twenty-two references, respectively). In contrast, Québec Solidaire made few references to this issue in its manifesto (nine mentions), and the Parti Libéral du Québec barely mentioned it at all.

Cosmopolitanism turned out to be a salient issue in the 2014 provin-cial election because of the PQ government's proposal to create a Char-ter of Quebec Values, which was made public in fall 2013 and de facto abandoned after the PQ's subsequent electoral defeat in 2014.[9] The PQ had proposed that Quebec adopt a charter of secularism, but its most controversial provision – the ban of any "ostentatious" religious symbols for all public sector employees – was met with outright criticism by several parties at the substate and statewide levels. In particular, the char-ter was strongly opposed by the PLQ and QS, both of which restated their commitment to the principles of multiculturalism, while the CAQ endorsed the secularism charter (Tessier and Montigny 2016). Among statewide parties, the BQ emerged as the only supporter of the charter, emphasizing the issue more than any other party (with a substantial 133 references).

The findings about the parties' directional positions (figure 2.4) com-plement those about salience. At the state level we also find the Bloc Québécois to be isolated, this time in terms of the direction of its po-sition: the party is in favour of the Quebec model of immigrant inte-gration called "interculturalism," which unlike the Canadian model of multiculturalism places a strong emphasis on assimilating into Que-bec's culture (see Bouchard 2015). Meanwhile, the other statewide parties are mostly neutral on this issue, with some references unsur-prisingly going in the opposite direction (i.e., support for multicultur-al recognition of minorities – a federal policy that was created by Pierre Trudeau's Liberal government in the 1970s). Among substate parties, as aforementioned, we observe more support for a distinct model of in-tercultural integration on the part of the PQ and CAQ. The PLQ's single manifesto statement that fell under the theme of cosmopolitanism was positive in relation to Quebec's distinct identity, as it put forward the Liberals' willingness to develop closer ties with the Indigenous com-munities of northern Quebec in implementing their economic devel-

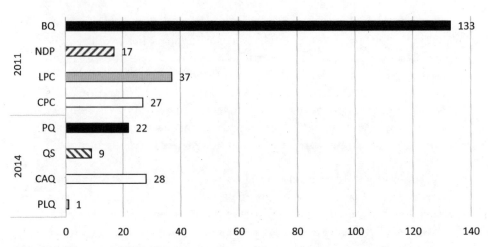

Figure 2.3 Salience of cosmopolitanism in Quebec and statewide party manifestos

opment plan for this area of the province (dubbed Plan Nord). In sum, our second hypothesis that the most nationalist parties own this valence dimension is mostly confirmed, except for the CAQ emphasizing this issue slightly more than the PQ.

Our interviews confirm cosmopolitanism to be one aspect of the national question that is highly contested among parties in Quebec. We find two opposing blocs. The PQ and the CAQ are in favour of a distinct model of integration based on interculturalism, an approach whereby newcomers are encouraged to – at a minimum – adopt the French language since it is the common public language in Quebec. The PLQ and QS meanwhile remain supportive of a multicultural approach to integration, which encourages newcomers to maintain and valorize their cultural values and their language. The clash between these views was at the forefront of political debates during the period under study due to the PQ's proposal to adopt a secularism charter.

As the PQ MNA explains, the idea of adopting a strict secular model like the proposed charter stemmed from the perception that Quebecers' values are very different from those of other Canadians. The Quebec model of integration ought to be distinct from Canada's multiculturalist one so as to better accommodate this difference in values. Quebecers "wish that newcomers integrate with an existing system; therefore the multiculturalist ideology that claims that you can keep your cultural difference in the margin of the majority cul-

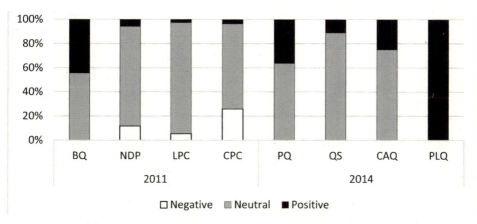

Figure 2.4 Direction on cosmopolitanism in Quebec and statewide party manifestos

ture ... is not shared by Quebecers" (interview with PQ MNA, 15 August 2013). In particular, the idea of various religions requesting some form of accommodation for their specific values is problematic in the eyes of the PQ because it goes against Quebecers' century-long efforts at asserting their own set of values (as a minority in Canada, but constituting a majority within the province of Quebec): "Most of the gains [regarding secularism] started with the Quiet Revolution, and we do not want these gains to be questioned by reintroducing religion into the public sphere and requiring special treatments that challenge [our values]."

For the most part, the CAQ agrees with these views. The party's opposition to multiculturalism is as clear as the PQ's position on the matter: "I don't think that Quebecers have adopted Mr Trudeau's multiculturalism policy. Quebec and all Quebecers have never adhered to it ... We believe more in the idea of two founding nations than in a multicultural nation or in Trudeau's vision of a nation" (interview with CAQ MNA, 22 March 2013). Accordingly, the party expressed support for the proposed secularism charter, although it argued that the prohibition from wearing religious signs should apply only to authority figures such as judges, police officers, prison guards, and (more controversially) education workers.

It is important to note that the CAQ's position regarding the accommodation of religious values is consistent with that developed by its parent party, the ADQ, during the so-called reasonable accommodation crisis in 2006–07 (Hepburn 2011). During that period, several incidents – including the adoption of a highly assimilationist "code of conduct" by the town of Hérouxville to prohibit non-Western cultural practices – fuelled widespread public debates on the extent to which minorities in Quebec should be able to publicly practice and express their religious beliefs. The ADQ's answer to this question was that they should not be accommodated, and its leader Mario Dumont argued for a decrease in immigration and the reinforcement of Quebec values and identity. In many ways, it can also be argued that the ADQ's antimulticulturalism position greatly influenced the discourse adopted by the PQ in the aftermath of its 2007 electoral defeat (Hepburn 2011). Indeed, the PQ's turn towards a less inclusive definition of immigrant integration – arguably crystallized in the charter of secularism project – has been viewed by some in Quebec (e.g., Dupré 2012; Caron 2013) as an abandonment of the civic nationalist discourse that was put forward by that party in the years that followed the 1995 referendum and PQ leader Jacques Parizeau's infamous referendum-night speech in which he partly attributed the Yes defeat to "some ethnic votes."

In contrast to the views expressed by the PQ and the CAQ, one finds more support for multiculturalism among the PLQ and QS parties. The Liberal MNA remains cautious regarding the question of whether Quebec has values that are distinct from those found in the rest of Canada: "I don't see that we have a society that is completely different here; there are differences, but the core values are shared from coast to coast." She goes on to argue that Quebec does not need more powers in the area of immigrant integration ("there's a limit because it's still in Canada that people immigrate"). Nor does it need to adopt more stringent rules on integration (we need to "be as respectful as possible of others") (interview, 13 May 2013). Along similar lines, the QS MNA claims that her party puts forward a view of "openness to the world." She feels that the Quebec model of integration needs no further distinction or revision; instead, the problem lies with the actual means of applying the model: "We don't want to impose an identity, a language, a culture; but we want to repair, reduce the resistance of our institutions" to immigrants in order to allow a better integration (interview, 27 February 2013). Like the PLQ, QS was a staunch opponent of the PQ's proposed Charter of Quebec Values.

At the federal level, there is more agreement regarding the multiculturalism model among statewide parties. Only the Bloc Québécois opposes it, seeing the multicultural model as former Prime Minister Pierre

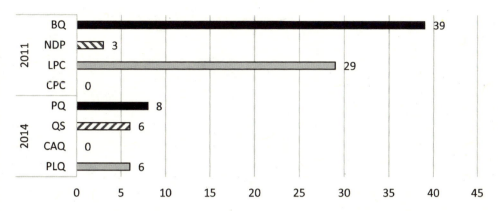

Figure 2.5 Salience of language in Quebec and statewide party manifestos

Trudeau's method of culturally marginalizing Quebec within the greater Canadian ensemble (which has been a similar accusation of the PQ against multiculturalism). The other three parties – the Liberals, Conservatives, and NDP – are clearly in favour of multiculturalism and believe that Quebecers' values are closer to those of other Canadians than what is generally claimed. An interesting nuance, however, is suggested by the NDP MP, who argues that in practice the multicultural and the intercultural models are almost identical, in that they both try to respect individual differences but also to ensure that there is a minimal degree of adherence to the dominant culture (interview, 16 August 2013).

Language

In contrast to the cosmopolitan dimension of identity, the language issue in Quebec proves to be more consensual but more so among substate than statewide parties. The manifestos analysis (figure 2.5) indicates that substate parties all made between six and eight references to language, except the CAQ, which did not address the issue at all. At the state level both the BQ and the Liberals made mention of language (thirty-nine and twenty-nine references, respectively), while the Conservatives and NDP barely mentioned it. As for directional positioning (figure 2.6), the coding reveals that statewide parties tended to differ in their positions on the language issue with the BQ being the most positive, the NDP the most neutral, and the Liberal Party somewhere in-between those positions. At the substate party level, both the PQ

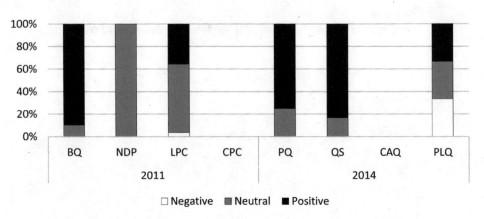

Figure 2.6 Direction on language in Quebec and statewide party manifestos

and QS adopted a largely positive position on protecting the French language, while the Liberals appeared more ambiguous – their references to language were evenly balanced between positive, neutral, and negative statements (particularly focusing on the place of English-language training in schools). Thus, for the language issue, our fourth hypothesis that the valence nature of this dimension incites parties to adopt the same position seems to apply at the substate level, whereas our second hypothesis about issue ownership appears to be confirmed at both levels.

The relative consensus among all parties on the language issue comes across more clearly in the interviews. All of the parties are in favour of defending and preserving the French language in Quebec, with the Parti Québécois and the Bloc Québécois seeking slightly more protection. As one PQ MNA points out, "One of the reasons why Quebecers define themselves first and foremost as Quebecers is because they have the feeling of being different ... For many years, and it's still true to some extent even if it's less so now, language has been the main factor of cultural difference between Quebecers and other Canadians" (interview, 15 August 2013).

While language remains at the heart of the PQ's identity politics, it is interesting to note that this same PQ MNA remained more or less silent during the interview regarding her government's proposed changes to Quebec's language policy.[10] The Marois government's Bill 14 was abandoned in November 2013 due to a lack of support from the opposition parties. It aimed at updating the Charter of the French Language (also

known as Bill 101) with a number of controversial, coercive provisions
such as introducing a mandatory French proficiency test for Quebec
high school pupils and CEGEP graduates, and forbidding businesses
with twenty-five to forty-nine employees to use English in the workplace. The use of additional coercive measures in the area of language
planning in Quebec has been decried by virtually all of our other interviewees. According to one CAQ MNA, the current version of Bill 101
is perfectly fine (interview, 22 March 2013). Meanwhile, the QS MNA
states that "there's a limit to coercion ... Sure, there is the necessity – in
the Canadian, Quebec, North American context – to compete with the
cultural appeal of the United States ... But Quebec has done well. It has
done well, after all, like many other small nations have managed to do"
(interview, 27 February 2013). The MNA for the Liberal Party concedes
that French-language promotion "will always be a critical primary responsibility for any Quebec government," but coercive measures that
are too excessive may actually damage the image of Quebec abroad (interview, 13 May 2013).

Statewide parties also agree with the goal of French-language protection in Quebec. In the words of one Liberal MP, "We must remain
vigilant; the assimilation force of English is enormous. But overall, one
of the successes has been to ensure that the French language is the language of Quebec" (interview, 13 March 2013). That said, all of the federal-level politicians we interviewed underlined an additional reason
for why it is important to keep the French language alive in Quebec. As
one Conservative MP states, "There are many francophones everywhere
across Canada, and these people rely on Quebec to continue to provide
radiance to a francophone linguistic and cultural diversity" (interview,
6 December 2013). The NDP MP adds that all francophones across the
Canadian state share a number of common interests and that "this sharing is part of what defines the Canadian identity" (interview, 16 August 2013).

In short, language is clearly a valence issue in Quebec at both the
substate and the statewide levels, even though there remains some disagreement over the use of coercion, and some parties (in particular the
PLQ) do not appear as deeply committed to this issue as others are. Another minor point of divergence among the substate parties has to do
with the notion of promoting the learning and use of English in Quebec. Both the PLQ and the CAQ are clearly in favour of this policy. As stated by the two CAQ MNAs we spoke to, English "is the language of the
twenty-first century" (interview, 22 February 2013) and "we need to take

into account that French is not the only language in Quebec" (interview, 22 March 2013). In contrast, the question of the importance of English is generally not addressed by the PQ.

REGIONAL INTERESTS

Social Interests

The third dimension of the national question that we are interested in is the question of regional interests. Three aspects of this question are worth exploring. The first one involves social interests. The so-called Quebec model of governance is usually characterized by an interventionist state (Bourque 2000). For example, in contrast with the governing approach that prevails in the rest of Canada, the Quebec state does not shy away from subsidizing a number of domestic economic sectors and industries. In addition, since the mid-twentieth century it has established a series of progressive social policies that now form a far-reaching regional welfare state. In this subsection we focus on the social aspect of the Quebec model.

To what extent are Quebec's social interests emphasized by parties in their electoral manifestos? Figure 2.7 indicates that social interests do not take up much space in the parties' electoral platforms. The only exception to this, among statewide parties, is the Bloc Québécois, which made eighty-five references to Quebec's governance, thus acting as a true owner of this aspect of the national question. The BQ also emphasized Quebec's distinctive brand of social values and preferences, and criticized the other mainstream Canadian parties as all being the same when it came to addressing Quebec's own interests (figure 2.8). In fact, the silence of the other statewide parties on this issue may be viewed as evidence of the BQ's claims in that regard.

For their part, all substate parties – save the PLQ – mentioned social interests at least once. However, it is the PQ that emphasized this issue the most (seven references, all in a positive direction) and insisted on defending Quebec's distinctive voice and model of governance. The single reference made by QS to the governance of Quebec was neutral, while two of the three CAQ references on this theme were coded as positive since they advocated the limitation of the federal spending power and the elimination of costly duplication between levels of government, both of which are consistent with the CAQ's "Quebec-first" approach.

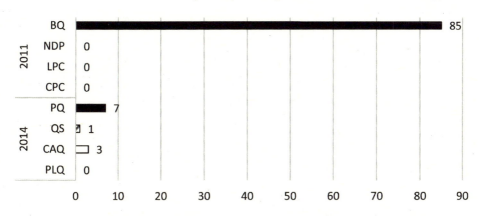

Figure 2.7 Salience of social interests in Quebec and statewide party manifestos

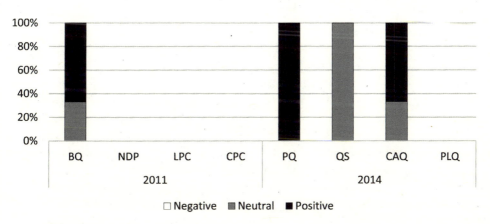

Figure 2.8 Direction on social interests in Quebec and statewide party manifestos

In recent years the Quebec model has come under criticism, as some parties have challenged the notion that Quebec values are naturally in favour of state intervention. Mario Dumont's former Action Démocratique du Québec played an important role in this nascent reform movement, and the Coalition Avenir Québec has taken up this mantle in the current substate party system. As one of its MNAs indicates, the Quebec model in its social dimension is not necessarily as distinct from the rest of Canada as is often claimed. She highlights the existence of a vigorous left in some English-Canadian provinces, and considers that there are as many right-leaning people in the province as there are outside Quebec (interview, 22 February 2013). The other CAQ MNA we interviewed observed that the Conservative Party does have some support base in Quebec, contrary to the popular view (interview, 22 March 2013). In short, the CAQ calls into question the image of Quebec as a more socially progressive province. The party does concede that Quebecers pay for social programs that other provinces do not have, but considers that this situation needs to change if only because the Quebec state does not have the financial means to sustain social protection in its current form over the long term (interview with CAQ MNA, 22 February 2013). To that end, the CAQ believes that Quebec needs to push through with austerity measures. The PLQ MNA broadly shares the CAQ's assessments and tends to reduce the Quebec model to a mere tradition of social policy innovation within the Canadian federation (interview, 13 May 2013).

The other two substate parties – Parti Québécois and Québec Solidaire – appear much more favourable to protecting what they see as Quebec's distinctive positions on social policy. According to the PQ MNA, "Quebec's ideological centre of gravity is closer to the centre-left than the political centre of gravity in the rest of Canada ... The value of solidarity is stronger here than elsewhere" (interview, 15 August 2013). She links this solidarity to Quebec's historical past, when French Canadians – who were in a position of social and economic inferiority – had to stick together and create their own institutions, leading to a conception of civic life that puts more emphasis on sharing than elsewhere in the Canadian state. The QS MNA adds that Quebecers' solidarity trait also derives from their European heritage, especially French republicanism. Again, this solidarity trait contributes to that party's definition of a progressive social model that is distinct from the rest of Canada and that needs to be nourished and preserved (interview, 27 February 2013).

To sum up, on social interests we observe disagreements among substate parties along the left-right ideological spectrum, with a sharp divide between left-of-centre (PQ/QS) and right-of-centre (CAQ/PLQ) parties on a Quebec social model. But these disagreements have more to do with defining the nature of the social model to be promoted than with the more consensual goal of defending it. And the most nationalist parties are the ones emphasizing this issue the most, in line with our second hypothesis.

We find this disagreement on the nature of the Quebec model to be mirrored in the statewide party system. In fact, it is striking how the viewpoints expressed by MPs are practically identical to those held by MNAs. Both the Bloc Québécois and the NDP MPs argue that the Quebec social model is distinct from the rest of Canada because it is adapted to Quebec's society, its history, and its specific interests. The BQ MP also mentions the creation of Quebec's firearms registry and the more positive attitude towards euthanasia among Quebecers as recent examples of this distinctiveness in terms of social policies and interests (interview, 22 March 2013). By way of contrast, both the Conservative and Liberal MPs offer a more nuanced assessment of the Quebec model's distinctiveness. They highlight the existence of even more progressive provincial governments outside Quebec, and they emphasize the contemporary convergence of social preferences between Quebecers and other Canadians in terms of health care, crime, security, and sustainable development. The Liberal MP claims that the Quebec model of governance was actually more distinctive *before* the onset of the Quiet Revolution in the 1960s, when there was no professional state bureaucracy and the health and education systems were under the control of the Catholic church (interview, 13 March 2013).

Economic Interests

The second aspect of the regional interests dimension worth considering is the economy, and specifically the protection and defence of Quebec's economic interests. The manifestos analysis presented in figure 2.9 shows that the Parti Libéral du Québec is clearly the substate party that mentioned Quebec's economic interests the most, with a total of 222 references – nearly half of those being about the need to build a strong regional economy. While this finding goes contrary to our second hypothesis, it comes as no surprise as the PLQ has traditionally enjoyed the reputation of being the best party at dealing with the economy in Quebec (see chapter 4, as well as Lemieux 2006; Bélanger and Gélineau 2011). Indeed, the Liberals centred their 2014 campaign almost exclusively on this issue, as they have tended to do in past elections. To illustrate, their 2014 slogan "We take care of the real business" (*On s'occupe des vraies affaires*) aimed at opposing the "real" issue, the economy, to the PQ's priority issue of independence. However, the PLQ's usual emphasis on the economy cannot really be interpreted as a form of economic nationalism. That would be more the domain of the Parti Québécois, and especially the Coalition Avenir Québec, which in recent years has been adept at, for example, attacking the Quebec gov-

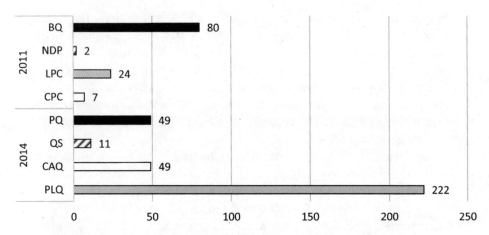

Figure 2.9 Salience of economic interests in Quebec and statewide party manifestos

ernment's inaction in preventing the sale to non-Quebec interests of a number of high-profile Québécois companies.

While the Liberals acted as the owner of the economic issue, the other substate parties also strongly emphasized this issue in their respective manifestos: both the Coalition Avenir Québec and the Parti Québécois had forty-nine references, and Québec Solidaire had eleven. Note, however, that most of these references about the economy were neutral, with QS being moderately more positive overall than the other parties and the CAQ being the only party that made a number of negative, or critical, statements regarding Quebec's current approach towards the economy – one third of their references were negative as shown in figure 2.10.

Understandably, statewide parties did not make as many references to regional economic interests as substate parties. That said, two parties did put some emphasis on this issue in their 2011 manifestos: the Bloc Québécois made eighty references to it (mostly on the need to build a strong Quebec economy) whereas the Liberals made twenty-four. Almost all of the Liberal statements involved natural resources (e.g., helping Quebec to develop renewable energy sources), and their statements were neutral on the whole. The only two NDP references also had to do with natural resources but were coded negatively since these statements involved working with other provinces – not just Quebec – in the federal framework. Overall, in similarity to several other issues examined above, the question of regional economic interests was championed by

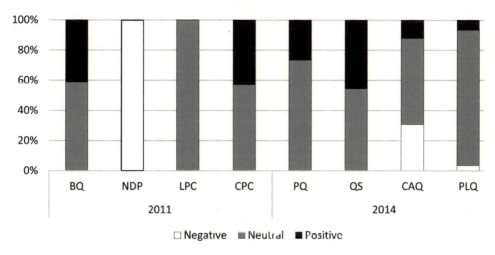

Figure 2.10 Direction on economic interests in Quebec and statewide party manifestos

the nationalist Bloc Québécois at the state level as our second hypothesis would lead one to expect.

The substate parties' different directions in their issue positioning on regional economic interests were also reflected in the interviews. According to one QS MNA, "cooperativism is very strong in Quebec ... It has marked the Quebec society and has allowed its development in many ways" (interview, 27 February 2013). She cites as evidence the Caisse de dépôt et placement du Québec, whose creation she sees as having been inspired by the French model of a socialist state. She goes on to explain why, in her view, having a strong state in Quebec is a necessary condition for guaranteeing individual freedom and emancipation: "A strong state provides most of our comfort so that we can spend our freed time and energy on things other than our survival in a sort of permanent battle of everyone against everyone." The PQ MNA also sees the interventionist state as necessary, particularly in guiding the development of the province's energy resources (interview, 15 August 2013).

That said, as was observed above with regard to social interests, we find that the other parties that lie on the centre-right of the ideological spectrum tend to disagree with the relevance of economic interventionism. Once again, the CAQ leads the charge and claims to be "the only party that has the courage to say that we must revise our state aid to companies" (interview, 22 February 2013). In broader terms, the PLQ and the CAQ each try to convince Quebecers that economic develop-

ment is their party's top priority. The CAQ is clearly seeking to contest
the Liberals' ownership of the economic issue: "We want people to recognize that we are the party of the economy in Quebec and that education is also our priority. There are other problems secondary to these,
like health care or child care, but first and foremost we want people to
recognize that we are the ones who can kick-start Quebec's economy"
(interview with CAQ MNA, 22 March 2013).

Thus, the substate picture with regard to economic interests is also one
of disagreement along ideological lines. Right-of-centre parties emphasize
economic development and wealth creation, whereas left-of-centre parties remain in favour of state intervention in Quebec' economy. But again,
these diverging views involve the definition of the nature of the Quebec
economic model, and not the question of whether they should promote
Quebec's autonomy in economic matters. On that point, most Quebec
parties are generally quick to note the long-standing vertical fiscal im-
balance within the Canadian federation, meaning that provincial governments do not have all the fiscal means to fulfill their important jurisdictional responsibilities – especially in the policy domains of health
care and education. This financial shortfall was notably the conclusion of
the nonpartisan Séguin Commission's report made public in 2002. Thus,
according to these parties, Quebec's growing deficit and debt problems
are to be attributed, at least in part, to the federal government, which
should be increasing the provinces' fiscal latitude and freedom.

Among statewide parties, the differences in viewpoints are similar,
although less pronounced than what we have observed in the substate
party system. Both the NDP and BQ agree that Quebec's economic
model is significantly different from other provincial models, and view
this distinction in a positive light. The Conservative Party disagrees, arguing that the Quebec government is faced with the exact same economic challenges as the other Canadian provinces and must address
them more or less in the same ways (interview with CPC MP, 6 December 2013). The Liberal MP we spoke with also tended to downplay the
differences between Quebec and the rest of Canada when it came to
their approach towards the economy (interview, 13 March 2013).

Supranational Interests

The final aspect of the regional interests dimension of the national
question involves supranational interests. In the particular context of
Quebec, supranationalism refers to the province's North American eco-

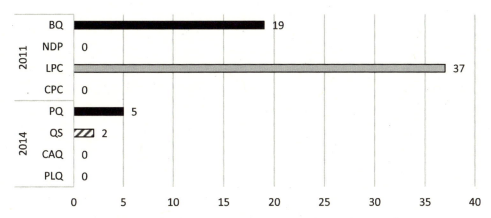

Figure 2.11 Salience of supranational interests in Quebec and statewide party manifestos

nomic integration. This integration has been pursued since 1994 via the North American Free Trade Agreement (NAFTA), which created a trilateral, rules-based trade bloc on the continent between Canada, the United States, and Mexico. North American integration has long been considered as an ideal economic empowerment strategy for Quebec society (e.g., Tremblay 1970). Supranationalism may also encompass the development of a foreign policy by the Quebec government. Having substate governments fostering both formal and informal links with foreign states has sometimes been called "paradiplomacy" (Aldecoa and Keating 1999; Kuznetsov 2015), and the case of Quebec has been a prime example of this phenomenon ever since the rise of nationalism during the 1960s and the adoption by the Quebec government of what came to be called the "Gérin-Lajoie doctrine," which justified Quebec's paradiplomacy efforts on constitutional grounds[11] (Bélanger 2002; Lachapelle and Paquin 2004).

According to the manifesto data, supranational interests, like social interests, did not receive a great deal of attention from parties (figure 2.11) although most statements made about it were in a positive direction, so towards more regional autonomy (figure 2.12). At the substate level, only the Parti Québécois and Québec Solidaire made references to supranationalism, with the former positively emphasizing the development of Quebec's foreign policy and cooperation (four of its five references). Québec Solidaire argued for the replacement of NAFTA by a new form of supranational integration that

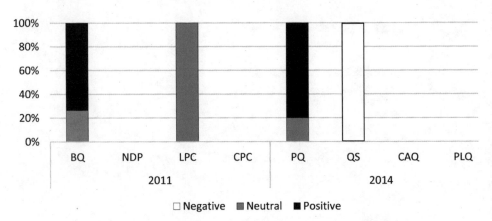

Figure 2.12 Direction on supranational interests in Quebec and statewide party manifestos

is more in line with what it perceives to be Quebec's interests, that is, more respectful of the environment and of democratic principles (two negative references). At the state level, a greater number of references were made but by only two parties: the Bloc Québécois (nineteen references, most of them involving foreign policy like the PQ) and the Liberals (thirty-seven references, most of them addressing continental integration and foreign cooperation). While the LPC is the statewide party that emphasized supranationalism the most, it was strictly in a neutral manner according to our directional coding. Meanwhile, the NDP and Conservatives made no references to this issue in their 2011 manifestos.

At the substate level, aside from Québec Solidaire – whose position we address below – none of the parties wish to pull out of NAFTA membership. Indeed, all parties see general benefits for Quebec from being a member of this free trade bloc. This inter-party consensus in Quebec is consistent with Martin's (1997) previous analysis. One CAQ MNA believes that "overall, NAFTA has been beneficial for Quebec. Quebec is a small market; we need to sustain our economic relations with the United States in order to effectively increase our gross domestic product" (interview, 22 March 2013). The PLQ MNA concurs and even sees a kind of inevitability in Quebec's economic integration: "There was not much choice to embark on this because isolated economies are less and less numerous ... I think that our domestic market is insufficient, so we need some form of integration with North America" (interview, 13 May

2013). In fact, another CAQ MNA underlines that the first Free Trade Agreement (FTA) negotiated in 1988 between Canada and the United States was made possible because of Quebec's strong support for it, coming as much from secessionists as from federalists (interview, 22 February 2013).

And indeed, the Parti Québécois remains firmly in favour of Quebec's North American economic integration, going so far as seeing in NAFTA a future strategic advantage for the independence movement. In the words of the PQ MNA, "Quebec, with its resources, is expected to play an increasingly important role in the geostrategic balance of the Americas ... Quebec energies, especially with the [hydroelectricity] surpluses that we have, will become – or once again become – attractive to the US economy. I think that Quebec has an interesting advantage there: clean energy that Americans are going to need more and more" (interview, 15 August 2013). In her view, this likely strengthening of economic and energy ties between Quebec and the USA may help secessionists gain the support of Americans in an eventual process of recognition of Quebec independence. It may also reassure Quebecers about their level of integration in the North American economy, possibly making them more immune to arguments of economic dislocation and fear that are often used by opponents of independence.

Québec Solidaire's position on Quebec's economic integration into NAFTA breaks with this inter-party consensus, however. This left-wing party's MNA states that QS is against trade agreements of the NAFTA type because Quebec's farmers and small entrepreneurs have not benefited as much from free trade as big businesses have. This view is consistent with Québec Solidaire's general ideology, according to which "the real opponent of Quebec's political independence is not the federal government; it is not the central state in Ottawa. It is the business community; it is the economic power in Canada, part of which is established in Quebec" (interview, 27 February 2013). The party's leadership came out against the more recent Trans-Pacific Partnership signed by Canada in 2016, citing a similar reason – that is, a possible loss of sovereignty for the Quebec state (Fontecilla 2016).

Among statewide parties, the issue of supranationalism is clearly a valence one since all four parties are in favour of NAFTA and believe that most of Quebec's economic sectors gain from being part of the agreement. But two additional viewpoints are expressed on this issue by some of the MPs we interviewed. First, both the Conservative and the Liberal MPs underline that being part of the Canadian domestic market provides Quebec with a strong insurance policy against possible economic turmoil coming from the American partner. Second, the BQ MP argues that the main strategic reason for why the United States is not in favour of Quebec secession is that the US establishment thinks an independent Quebec would be too unpredictable in terms of its foreign policy positions. For example, an independent Quebec might take on the defence of left-leaning Latin American governments at the United Nations, or might side with the Palestinians in the Arab-Israel conflict (interview with BQ MP, 22 March 2013).

MULTILEVEL DYNAMICS

An overarching aspect of the national debate is the multilevel context in which political parties and politicians compete in Quebec and Scotland. In this section we ask, Is there a clear territorial bloc in Quebec that opposes, or diverges from, state-level government policies? And if so, is this due to a stronger priming effect at the substate level (our fourth hypothesis), where many aspects of the national question incite agreement among Quebec parties?

To a large extent, there is a territorial bloc at the substate level in Quebec. Almost all of the substate parties emphasize the importance for Quebec of maintaining a balance of power (*un rapport de force*) vis-à-vis the federal government in Ottawa. In the period under study, the PQ's approach of sovereignist governance embodies this philosophy the most clearly. As one PQ MNA explains, "Sovereignist governance is a permanent balance-of-power posture; you need to constantly be in a situation of balance of power vis-à-vis the central government ... For an independentist who wants all of the powers – who seeks full sovereignty – the more new powers you obtain, the closer you get to your ultimate goal which is to have all the powers" (interview, 15 August 2013).

Several of the parties in Quebec have grievances against the 1960s–1970s era of state centralization under Prime Minister Pierre Trudeau. One CAQ MNA argues that Trudeau's approach, which she describes as one of provocation and confrontation, fuelled the independence movement (interview, 22 February 2013). The QS MNA agrees, claiming that Canada's centralizing tendency goes contrary to the true spirit of federalism and that it creates a significant gap between Canadian policies and the traditional policy aspirations of Quebecers (interview, 27 February 2013). As another CAQ representative puts it, "There are quite different views, opposing even, between Canada and Quebec" (interview,

22 March 2013). She mentions the example of the disagreements between Quebec and Ottawa over establishing a target for reducing greenhouse gases, which resulted in the industry having to obtain different permits – one federal and one provincial. These general grievances are largely shared by the federal-level independentist Bloc Québécois. The BQ MP we interviewed even went as far as to describe the central government's attitude vis-à-vis Quebec as a "colonialist" one whereby it seeks to "impose its vision through its policies and its money" (interview, 22 March 2013).

The only dissenting voice on this issue at the substate level is that of the PLQ. The provincial Liberals tend to break away from this territorial bloc, as they prefer to see the economic benefits of maintaining strong links with the provinces east and west of Quebec. At the very least, by emphasizing interprovincial trade, the Liberals somewhat downplay the centre-periphery tensions within the Canadian federation. The PLQ MNA we spoke to even praised the growing worldwide move towards the adoption of federal-type institutional arrangements, believing that "federalism is the most modern style of governance." She also claims that being part of a larger ensemble has provided Quebecers with a greater sense of security since the terrorist attacks of 9/11 south of the Canadian border (interview, 13 May 2013).

How have statewide parties reacted to this territorial bloc? Some of them understand, and even respect, the existence of such a centre-periphery cleavage. The Conservatives and the NDP try to accommodate it, to some degree, by proposing a collaborative approach with Quebec whereby areas of substate jurisdiction are better respected. No matter what it is called (the Conservatives use the expression "open federalism" while the NDP talks of asymmetrical federalism), the basic idea is to offer Quebecers a more flexible and pragmatic kind of federal-provincial relationship – and one that does not call for a formal renegotiation of the Canadian Constitution. For its part, the Liberal Party tends to adopt a dismissive attitude, viewing the *rapport de force* strategy more as a ploy for boosting independence support: "Those who want to push the nationalist mood towards political independence will use disagreements over the division of powers as proof that Canada doesn't work ... This has the effect of freeing supporters of independence from having to justify their project" (interview with LPC MP, 13 March 2013). The Liberal MP goes on to argue that substate federalist parties tend to fall into the trap of asking for more devolved powers because they hope that it will quash the independentists' arguments and assuage the Quebec population's nationalist fever, a strategy that the MP thinks is a miscalculation.

CONCLUSION

There is no denying that over the past half century, the national question has been at the heart of party politics in Quebec. Ever since the emergence of René Lévesque's Parti Québécois at the end of the 1960s, the issue has become a salient one for political parties competing at the substate and state levels. In that sense, it is safe to conclude that the rise of the secessionist PQ and the valence nature of the national question have had a significant effect on Quebec party competition. Every substate or statewide political party has had to position itself on this issue, and the national question regularly comes to the fore during election campaigns in Quebec. In other words, by establishing itself as the promoter and owner of the national question, the Parti Québécois has initiated a movement whereby the other parties have all tried to compete on the PQ's issue to one degree or another. For a time, this movement spilled over to the state-level scene when a federal-based secessionist party – the Bloc Québécois – was created at the beginning of the 1990s and claimed ownership of the national question within the statewide party system.

What our analysis of party behaviour in Quebec has been able to show is that the national question is clearly a multifaceted political issue, just as it is in Scotland as we shall see in chapter 3. Reducing the issue to the single question of whether Quebec ought to secede from the rest of Canada provides an incomplete picture of the strategic party dynamics at work. We have seen that beyond the general disagreement about the goal of secession itself, all substate parties are more or less in favour of more constitutional autonomy for Quebec. The picture is the reverse among statewide parties. With the exception of the secessionist Bloc Québécois, while all of the Canadian federal parties are against independence, they disagree on whether Quebec ought to have more autonomy or not. Indeed, two parties – the Liberals and Conservatives – actually argue that Quebec already enjoys enough autonomy within the Canadian federation. In short, on the question of constitutional autonomy we find a clear centre-periphery cleavage at play in the Quebec case.

The same kind of centre-periphery cleavage is also observed in the multilevel dynamics of the national question. With the exception of the Parti Libéral du Québec, all other parties at the substate level form a relatively strong territorial bloc that seeks greater autonomy for Quebec and opposes many Canadian policies in general (fourth hypothesis). To the exclusion of the Bloc Québécois, all of the statewide parties for their part tend to form a counter-bloc, although two of them (the NDP and the Conservatives) show some willingness to respect Quebec's jurisdictional authority, in what they call a spirit of collaboration.

The valence nature of the national question in statewide elections in Quebec (second and fourth hypotheses) is clearly observed in its two other key dimensions, identity and regional interests. Among state-level parties, there is virtual agreement regarding all three aspects of the regional interests dimension (albeit with some reservations on the part of the Liberals and Conservatives when it comes to defining the distinctive nature of Quebec's social and economic model of governance) as well as on the issue of French-language protection. However, on the issue of cosmopolitanism, only the Bloc Québécois does not support the multiculturalism model of integration, and thus finds itself an isolated issue owner on this aspect of the identity dimension. Meanwhile, at the substate level there is relative agreement on the language and supranational aspects. There is less consensus on cosmopolitanism and on the governance model, although disagreements here concern the definition of these models more so than the question of whether Quebec's autonomy in these areas should be defended and promoted.

In general, it appears that at the state level the national question is more of a "niche" issue exclusively associated with the Bloc Québécois, at least in the period under study. Meanwhile in the provincial party system, the Parti Québécois' ownership of the national question is contested by the Coalition Avenir Québec and Québec Solidaire, especially when it comes to issues of constitutional autonomy and regional identity. These substate dynamics seem in part to be the product of a priming effect whereby the PQ has encouraged other substate parties to more strongly defend Quebec's powers and language. On paper (i.e., in its manifesto) the Parti Libéral du Québec seems to resist this dynamic, especially on the autonomy issue, although the party does not hesitate to bring up the constitutional dimension in its campaign discourse so as to polarize the debate and distinguish itself from the PQ, all the while emphasizing the one issue that it does appear to own – the economy. The reason why the PLQ brings up the constitutional issue in these ways is clear: the party correctly perceives that the majority opinion in Quebec is not in favour of independence (see chapter 4).

In accordance with our first hypothesis, all parties in Quebec feel compelled to address the national question and to take a position on this issue. It is a super issue that structures party competition. One of the CAQ MNAs that we interviewed explained this dynamic by quoting from his party's 2012 manifesto: "Because of its magnitude and nature, this fundamental issue stands above all other partisan considerations and is rooted in the deepest layers of Quebec society" (interview, 22 March 2013). Even the most federalist party, the PLQ, is frequently reminded by political commentators (e.g., David 2015) of the dangers of leaving this issue unaddressed and the necessity to define a clear position, as well as offer a clear defence of that position.

3

Party Behaviour in Scotland

This chapter examines the nature and dynamics of party behaviour in Scotland. It begins from the starting point that traditional left-right (or class-based) understandings of party competition have limited application in Scottish politics unless they are considered in tandem with the strength of a "territorial" issue – otherwise known as the national question. Yet, rather than assume that territory only constitutes a divisive cleavage *between* parties in Scotland, we wish to examine the extent to which the national question is also a valence issue in Scottish politics, whereby few parties would oppose the political empowerment of the Scottish nation or the defence of its interests.

In this chapter we explore how parties have adopted a range of positions in favour of strengthening the Scottish nation, including support for fiscal autonomy, the creation of an inclusive cosmopolitan Scottish identity, and increased control over welfare and social services. These issues all came under the intense scrutiny of political parties during the referendum on Scottish independence in 2014. But beyond the binary positions of the Yes and the No camps in the referendum, one could argue that on the other dimensions of the national question all of the parties in Scotland have been recently moving in similar directions: towards greater self-determination and self-affirmation. This has not always been the case. As chapter 1 revealed, the national question has often proved a divisive issue in Scottish politics, with the leading UK mainstream parties – the Labour Party and the Conservative Party – taking bitterly opposing positions to Scottish home rule at different points in time.

Thus, the purpose of this chapter is to understand the extent to which the national question dominates party behaviour in Scotland, and to analyze the ways in which substate and statewide parties articulate their views on the national question and on its various dimensions. In so doing, we pay special attention to whether nationalist parties (essentially the Scottish National Party) act as owners of the territorial issue and whether the other parties' discourse is influenced by this issue, in part as a reaction to the behaviour and demands of nationalist parties but also as an effort to reach out to the median Scottish voter. We also pay attention to any differences in the behaviour of parties across the two levels of government, that is, the substate (Scottish) and state (UK) levels. To restate our hypotheses, which mirror those proposed in chapter 2 for the Quebec case:

1 Given its importance in Scotland, the national question is an issue on which all parties take a position that becomes a central component of their political positioning.
2 The most nationalist party in Scotland, the SNP, "owns" the valence dimensions of the national question and therefore emphasizes this issue the most.
3 The most nationalist party in Scotland, the SNP, and the least nationalist one, the Conservative Party, emphasize the constitutional dimension the most because they each stand to benefit the most from the polarization of the electorate on this dimension.
4 The priming of the national question by the parties dominating this issue, and the valence nature of some of its dimensions, exert pressure on other parties in the substate party system, inciting them to take stronger stances in this debate. This phenomenon is more marked at the substate level, leading substate parties to act as a territorial bloc in opposition to state-level parties and policies.

As in chapter 2, this empirical analysis draws on multiple data and methods to examine Scottish party positions on the national question. The first source of data comes from a content analysis of Scottish political party manifestos. The party manifestos of two recent Scottish and UK elections were selected: the 2010 UK general election (including the manifestos of the SNP, UK Labour Party, UK Conservative Party, and UK Liberal Democrats) and the 2011 Scottish parliamentary election (including the manifestos of the SNP, Scottish Labour Party, Scottish Conservative and Unionist Party, and Scottish Liberal Democrats). Thus a total of eight manifestos – covering substate and state elections – were subject to analysis. The coding scheme used (see appendix tables A1 and A2) is exactly the same as for the Quebec manifestos' analysis presented in chapter 2, and aims to determine the salience and positioning of Scottish political parties on each of the dimensions of the national question that we examine in this book.

The second source of information comes in the form of semi-structured elite interviews with senior party officials. Each participant was consistently asked the same series of interview questions that we asked participants in Quebec. Interviews were conducted in November 2012 with members from the four most important parties in Scotland: members of the Scottish Parliament (MSPs) for the SNP, Scottish Labour Party, Scottish Conservative and Unionist Party, and Scottish Liberal Democrats. At the statewide level, we interviewed Scottish members of the UK Parliament (MPs) for the SNP and Labour, for a total of twelve interviews.[1]

THE CONSTITUTIONAL DIMENSION

According to the data from our manifestos analysis for the 2010 UK general election and 2011 Scottish Parliament election, the SNP clearly owned the constitutional dimension. Looking at our data on issue salience, the SNP paid the greatest amount of attention to Scotland's constitutional status within the UK in both the Scottish Parliament and the UK general elections. As figure 3.1 reveals, the SNP made fifty-five references to constitutional issues in the 2010 election manifesto, and fifty-two references in the 2011 manifesto. In sharp contrast, the three unionist parties gave much less attention to constitutional concerns. The Conservatives came second place, by making twenty-two references to Scotland's place in the UK in their 2010 general election manifesto (alluding primarily to maintaining political union), and zero references in the 2011 Scottish election – similar to the Parti Libéral du Québec as seen in the last chapter. The Liberal Democrats came third, making sixteen references to constitutional issues (on transferring more competences to Scotland) in the 2010 general election, and only one reference in 2011. Labour came last, making nine references to Scotland's status (in particular fiscal autonomy) in its 2010 manifesto and only seven references in 2011. When looking at salience, then, we can surmise that our third hypothesis is supported, although it is more clearly so at the state level than the substate one. The SNP is the party that acted the most as the owner of the issue of Scotland's constitutional status, in both substate and statewide politics. The party most in favour of the constitutional status quo, the Conservatives, emphasized this

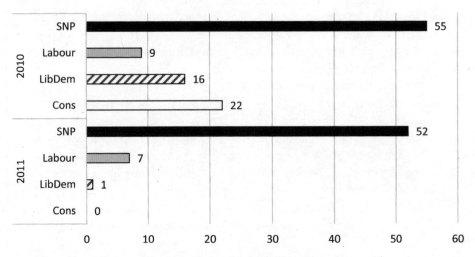

Figure 3.1 Salience of the constitutional issue in Scottish and statewide party manifestos

issue as well in statewide elections but remained silent on it in their substate election manifesto – although, as argued for the Parti Libéral du Québec, silence may be interpreted as support for the status quo.

It is the directional coding data, presented in figure 3.2, which allow us to determine whether the fourth hypothesis about the SNP's priming and the valence nature of some of the national question's dimensions exerting pressure on other parties holds any weight. Here, one finds evidence that none of the parties in Scotland are in favour of abolishing the Scottish Parliament, reversing Scotland's powers or supporting any other centralizing tendencies. Instead, each of the three unionist parties have – to varying degrees – advocated increased powers for Scotland during the period under study. The predominance of positive references to constitutional issues is illustrated in the bar charts. The majority (58 per cent) of the Conservative Party's references to the Constitution in its 2010 election manifesto were coded as +1 (representing positive statements about decentralization in the past or present); all of the Labour Party's constitutional references in 2010 were also coded as +1, and in 2011 these references were evenly split between neutral and +1; 58 per cent of the Liberal Democrats' constitutional references were coded as +1 in 2010, and 100 per cent of these references were coded as positive in 2011. As figure 3.2 illustrates, all three union-

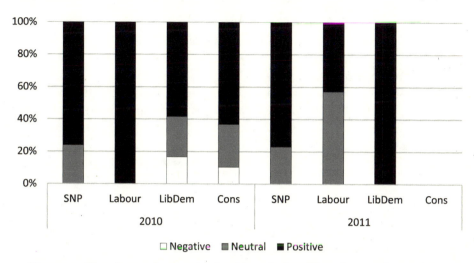

Figure 3.2 Direction on the constitutional issue in Scottish and statewide party manifestos

ist parties are wholly positive about further powers for Scotland, even if they emphasize this issue less than the SNP.

In contrast with the manifesto data, however, our interviews – undertaken at the start of the two-year independence referendum campaign in 2012 – revealed that the constitutional question was the most divisive issue for political parties. According to one of our Scottish Labour Party interviewees, "there isn't really any ideological divide apart from the Constitution" (interview, 13 November 2012).

Putting this remark into context, throughout the postwar period, but especially in the years since the SNP took power in 2007, all of the major parties in Scotland have sought to emphasize their differences over whether or not Scotland should become an independent country. This independence-unionism cleavage was cemented during the two-year-long referendum campaign, whereby the three "unionist" parties – Labour, Conservatives, and Liberal Democrats – despite their ideological differences collectively endorsed a "No" outcome, while the SNP and the Green Party campaigned for a "Yes" vote. This Yes-No question resulted in a very black-and-white perspective on constitutional politics.

However, as the manifestos data make clear, this cleavage on the constitutional question is "greyer" and more nuanced when the actual positions of parties are looked at. Far from constituting a clear divide between anti- and pro-independence supporters, the parties propose a range of constitutional solutions on self-determination. To begin with, the SNP has always advocated "degrees of independence for Scotland within larger political frameworks" (Hepburn 2009b, 190). Thus the party has articulated a vision of independence within the British Empire, then the Commonwealth, then the European Union, and now within the "social union" of the British Isles. The SNP's interpretation of independence is far from the nineteenth-century understanding of exclusive territorial sovereignty. Instead, the SNP has been forced to recognize its interdependence – not only on a global or European stage, but also within the United Kingdom.

To that end, former SNP leader Alex Salmond has stressed the continuation of a "social union" between the people of Scotland and the rest of the UK in a post-independence scenario (Cook 2013). In emphasizing that an independent Scotland could remain part of the United Kingdom, the SNP has stressed several "unions" with the rest of the UK in its vision of independence, including the social union, a currency union (keeping the pound sterling), and a monarchic union (keeping the Queen as head of state) in addition to the partnership it would continue with the UK within the European Union (pre-Brexit) and NATO. As one SNP MSP argued, "After independence, Scotland, assuming there is a Yes vote, would probably, with the rest of the UK, be the two most integrated countries anywhere in the world" (interview, 21 November 2012). Commentators have described this "unionist" nationalist position as "independence-lite." Indeed, the SNP itself embraced the goal of "devolution max" during its first term in government (2007–11), arguing for the devolution of all fiscal powers to the Scottish Parliament as a "softer" form of independence (see Hepburn 2009b). However, political opponents such as Labour have argued that this "unionist" strategy has been "part of the SNP agenda, you know, 'don't scare the horses: we're still going to be part of Britain'" (interview with Scottish Labour Party MSP, 13 November 2012).

While the SNP has been at pains to emphasize that independence will not be a big step away from the current devolved settlement, and that Scotland will still maintain the same cultural, social, economic, and monetary links to the rest of the UK, its competitors in the Scottish party system have been moving onto the same terrain. The parties supporting the No campaign argued that their constitutional proposals would also move beyond the devolution settlement but would allow Scotland to continue its strong partnership with the UK. According to one Scottish Labour MSP, "Our view is 'we're better together.' That is not, however, a defence of the status quo. It's certainly not really a defence of the Union and the way it's presented as it was signed in 1707. It is a defence of devolution, of a strong Scottish Parliament in a devolved UK ... I would like to see a greater degree of autonomy all around" (interview, 15 November 2012). Thus, while Labour in the early days of devolution refused to even consider granting the Scottish Parliament any more powers (see interviews with Labour MSPs conducted in Hepburn 2010b), the party has done a sharp U-turn in response to the SNP's entry into government in 2007. This policy reversal first manifested itself in the creation of the Calman Commission on Scottish Devolution in 2008, which was supported by Labour, the LibDems, and the Conservatives (and not the SNP), whose recommendations for Scotland's future – including more powers over revenue-raising and capital-borrowing – were included in the Scotland Act 2014 (see Commission on Scottish Devolution 2009).

But during the independence referendum campaign, Scottish Labour strategists realized that the Calman Commission had not gone far enough for Scottish voters. Indeed, as chapter 5 will reveal, there is clear majority support among the public for more powers to Scotland, even within the Labour constituency. The party attempted to address such concerns when it established a Devolution Commission in 2012, which recommended a raft of new powers, including making the Scottish Parliament indissoluble, increasing powers over income tax, and assuming control over housing benefits (Scottish Labour 2014a). Former Labour prime minister Gordon Brown confirmed this commitment to more devolution when he made a speech in support of the "vow" just two days before referendum day.

However, there is evidence that some party members disagree with, or wish to move beyond, this position of supporting an enhanced devolved settlement. One Scottish Labour MSP said that "in the long run [devolution] starts to become difficult when you have one part of the country [England] that is not devolved in any way ... That's why I'm kind of attracted to federalism" (interview, 15 November 2012). Another Scottish Labour MSP admitted, "I am not entirely optimistic about the commission, as someone who would want substantially more powers for the Scottish Parliament" (interview, 13 November 2012). It is quite unsurprising – given Labour's reticence on the constitutional issue – that a group of Labour MSPs broke from the party line to come out in favour of independence. "Labour for Independence" was formed in

2012 in response to polls that showed that approximately 30 per cent of Labour voters in Scotland favoured independence (although our opinion data presented in chapter 5 indicate that the proportion may have been lower than that).

No similar organization has broken away from the Scottish Conservative and Unionist Party (SCUP). While Labour and the SNP are both competing for the same broad electoral base – pro-autonomy, centre-left – the SCUP has a different following. Out of all the parties, it considers itself to be the most "unionist" and most in favour of a strong, United Kingdom (Aughey 2011). The opinion data that will be presented in chapter 5 certainly confirm this impression. According to one SCUP MSP, "We believe that Scotland has been very well served by being part of the Union of Nations of the UK" (interview, 14 November 2012). However, the party has also – grudgingly – supported the Scottish Parliament since losing all seats in Scotland in the 1997 general election. Yet it appears that support for devolution is strategic rather than principled. In the early days, the Conservatives needed to win back Scottish voters; in the present climate, they need to compete with the SNP: "The acid test of the transfer of powers to the Scottish Parliament has been a political judgment as to what would be the best way to stop the SNP from progressing further" (interview with SCUP MSP, 14 November 2012). With that goal in mind, the SCUP supported the UK Calman Commission and established its own party Commission on the Future Governance of Scotland. The commission's recommendations went even further than Labour's, proposing full powers over income tax, shared value-added tax (VAT) receipts, and control over housing benefit and attendance allowance. Some members of the party wish to take this a step forward and establish a federal UK, which would "create a much more stable constitutional settlement than what we currently have" (interview with SCUP MSP, 20 November 2012).

One party that has staunchly defended the federal model has been the Scottish Liberal Democrats. As a LibDem MSP explained, "What we want to have is permanent powers here, rather than powers on loan, which we currently have, which would make the Scottish Parliament a much more equal partner with the UK" (interview, 14 November 2012). However, as a federal solution to the UK's constitutional question was not on the table during the independence referendum, the Scottish Lib-Dems have instead focused their energy on proposing additional powers for the devolved Scottish Parliament by emphasizing the terminology of "Home Rule." Thus the Scottish LibDems also supported the

Calman Commission and created their own Home Rule and Community Rule Commission, which recommended granting the Scottish Parliament powers over almost all income tax, capital gains tax, and air passenger duty (Scottish Liberal Democrats 2012).

Thus, the three pro-UK parties have proposed variations on enhancing the Scottish Parliament's powers, which led to the three party leaders agreeing to a declaration of more powers for the Scottish Parliament: "The Scottish Labour Party, the SCUP and the Scottish Liberal Democrats have each produced our own visions of the new powers which the Scottish Parliament needs. We shall put those visions before the Scottish people at the next general election and all three parties guarantee to start delivering more powers for the Scottish Parliament as swiftly as possible in 2015" (BBC 2014). The declaration was later signed by the leaders of the UK Conservative, Labour, and Liberal Democrat parties. However, critics – including the SNP and civil society leaders – have voiced concerns that these proposals have been watered down since the referendum result. The Smith Commission on Further Devolution was established after the referendum to implement the "vow" made by unionist party leaders for more powers. The report of this cross-party commission recommended devolving significant tax and welfare powers to Scotland, in addition to making the Scottish Parliament permanent in UK legislation. However, the draft Scotland Bill that was based on the Smith Report (2014), and which was eventually passed in the UK Parliament in 2016, has been criticized for not implementing the full recommendations of the cross-party Smith Commission.

The perception that the legislation did not go far enough is one explanation for why the SNP experienced an unprecedented surge in electoral support during the 2015 UK general election. But even before the electoral wipeout of the unionist parties in the 2015 election and before the referendum vote, our interview data showed clear evidence that all of the pro-UK parties were vying to promise more powers for the Scottish Parliament. Taken together with the fact that the SNP also sought to moderate its position on independence – through a form of "independence-lite" whereby Scotland would retain its cultural, economic, and social links with the rest of the UK – it could be argued that the issue of self-determination, beyond the divisive question of whether Scotland should be an independent country, has in some ways become a valence issue, with all parties arguing for greater powers although with varying degrees of commitment.

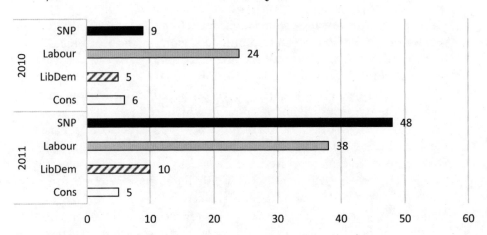

Figure 3.3 Salience of cosmopolitanism in Scottish and statewide party
manifestos

Cosmopolitanism

There is an assumption in the literature that a key aim of nationalist
parties is to enhance and protect their nation's distinct cultural or ethnic identity (Mueller-Rommell 1998; Hutchinson 1999). However, the
manifestos analysis for the 2010 UK general election and 2011 Scottish
Parliament election reveals that this is not the case in Scotland. In
contrast to the assumption that culture is the "property" of nationalist parties, our data indicate that the Scottish Labour Party has strongly focused on the issue of culture, at least through the angle of cosmopolitanism. As can be seen from figure 3.3, while the SNP made
forty-eight references to culture in its 2011 Scottish Parliament election manifesto and nine references in its 2010 general election one
(for a total of fifty-seven), the Labour Party made thirty-eight references to culture in 2011 and twenty-four in 2010 (for a total of sixty-
two). Therefore, Labour emphasized this issue almost to the same extent as the SNP, although the latter is the party that made the most
mentions of it in the substate election (in line with our second hypothesis). Yet there are differences in the content of references. For
Labour, the most numerous references were to pride, culture, and the
arts; for the SNP, the focus was on multiculturalism and heritage. In
contrast, the Liberal Democrats and Conservatives barely mentioned

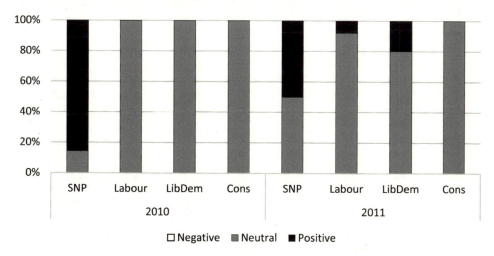

Figure 3.4 Direction on cosmopolitanism in Scottish and statewide party manifestos

cultural issues in their manifestos (with an average of seven references per manifesto).

Moving on to our directional data, the findings reveal that all of the parties favour a "status quo" position on Scottish culture. As we can see from figure 3.4, the vast majority of statements on culture made by unionist parties are neutral (coded as "0") – neither seeking to strengthen Scottish culture nor to reduce levels of protection. The SNP was the only party making positive statements, by seeking to strengthen multiculturalism in Scotland.

The generally neutral statements of Scottish political parties on culture, combined with their support for diversity, indicate (in line with our fourth hypothesis) that Scottish parties have achieved a degree of consensus on their definition of the Scottish nation as an open and multicultural place to live. While Scottish identity remains a central aspect of the national question, Scottish parties are reluctant to associate this with exclusive characteristics, such as birth, descent, or a shared religion (McCrone 1992; Calder 1994; Brown, McCrone, and Paterson 1996; Hamilton 1999).

Beyond our manifestos data, other sources of qualitative data – including our interviews – confirm that the Scottish National Party has been a staunch defender of a multicultural Scotland. For the SNP, newcomers to Scotland are seen to make up the "tartan tapestry" of Scottish culture (see Hepburn and Rosie 2014). In a Race Equality Statement issued in 2008, the SNP government set out its vision of a cosmopolitan Scotland as a place that "embraces diversity whilst also fostering a sense of common purpose and goals," and that supports multiculturalism and pluralism as ways of creating "a strong, fair and inclusive national identity" (Scottish Government 2008, 1, 8). The SNP is also a strong advocate of increasing levels of immigration to Scotland, an unusual stance in the increasingly restrictive UK political landscape (see Hepburn 2014b). The rationale for this is economic as well as cultural: the SNP wishes to increase immigration to grow Scotland's economy and population as well as benefit from the cultural enrichment that immigrants bring (Hepburn and Rosie 2014). These positive attitudes towards integration were evident not only in the manifesto data but also in our interviews. As one SNP MSP put it, "At a political level, we are always very keen to emphasize that this is a civic nationalist party, rather than an ethnic nationalist party; we are based on the community [rather than] some kind of strange ideal of what it means to be ethnically Scottish" (interview, 21 November 2012).

This position has received broad support across the political spectrum in Scotland. Indeed, the Scottish Labour Party and the Scottish Liberal Democrats, who formed a coalition government in the early years of devolution, preceded the SNP government in their desire to foster a plural, multicultural Scotland through their "One Scotland, Many Cultures" campaign that was launched in 2002. This campaign – which was intended to combat racism in Scotland – sought to emphasize how Scotland was a place of many cultures (Scottish Executive 2002), while the Labour-LibDem government's "Fresh Talent" policy initiative sought to attract immigrants to Scotland (Scottish Executive 2004). As one Labour MSP said, "I think we should be a multicultural society ... It's one area where Labour and the SNP have actually sung from the same song sheet" (interview, 13 November 2012). Similarly, an MSP for the Scottish Liberal Democrats thought that "we all have good story to tell; we are a welcoming and encouraging country and that's what we have to work very hard on" (interview, 14 November 2012).

Meanwhile, the SCUP – while not directly employing the terminology of multiculturalism – has given its support for the creation of an inclusive and tolerant nation. As one MSP revealed, "I would say that Scots have been demonstratively a more tolerant nation than England. I think that one of the things we bring to the Union is that tolerance" (interview with SCUP MSP, 14 November 2012). It is interesting to note that, while the cosmopolitan dimension of the national question has become a valence issue in Scotland, with all of the parties supporting the vision of a plural, multicultural Scotland, the views of their UK counterparts could not be more different. The UK Labour, Liberal Democrat, and Conservative parties have all rejected the multiculturalist model of immigrant integration, blaming it for the creation of segregated communities leading to "parallel lives" in the UK (Blair 2006; Cameron 2011), and have pursued a more assimilationist approach to immigrant integration (see Lewis and Craig 2014; Hepburn 2014c). Thus, while the multiculturalist model has become a valence issue in Scotland, the positions of Scottish parties lie in stark contrast to those of the UK parties.

Language

Contrary to what was seen for Quebec in chapter 2, the issue of language plays a very minor role in Scottish debates about the national question. This is because the most prominent minority language in Scotland – Gaelic – is spoken by only about 1 per cent of the population, with the majority of Gaelic speakers concentrated in the western isles and the northwest Highlands (Paterson et al. 2014). For most Scots, especially those living in the high-population "central belt" based around Edinburgh-Glasgow, the Gaelic language is as foreign as Flemish or Basque. As such, "Gaelic does not serve as a talisman of Scottish national identity" (McLeod 2001, 7) unlike many other nationalist movements in Europe and North America – although it is related to some extent to Scots' national identity attitudes as well as cross-level party identification (Chhim and Bélanger 2017). Moreover, Gaelic is only one language among many in Scotland; others, which have been given far less prominence in policy-making and are not recognized as official languages, include Doric (spoken in the northeast) and Scots or "Lallans" (spoken in the south).

How is the issue of language mobilized by parties in Scotland? All of our data suggest that language constitutes a valence issue in Scottish politics, with parties generally agreeing that enough has been done to protect its status in Scotland. This is confirmed in both our manifestos data analysis and our interviews with politicians. In the 2010 general election and 2011 Scottish parliamentary election manifestos, the issue of language received very little attention across the board. In terms of the salience of this issue, figure 3.5 shows that the greatest number of references to language was in Labour's 2010 general election manifesto

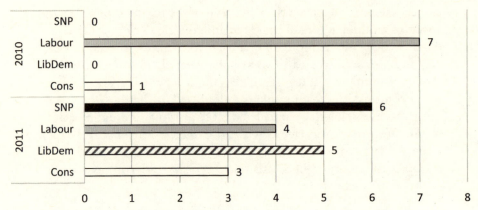

Figure 3.5 Salience of language in Scottish and statewide party manifestos

(seven); for that same election, the SNP made no references to language. Given that language is a devolved issue, it is not surprising that the parties made more references to language in the 2011 Scottish parliamentary election campaign. However, even then, all parties – including the SNP – only made a handful of references to this issue (SCUP, three; Labour, four; LibDems, five; SNP, six), underlining the low salience of this issue in Scottish party politics. Our second hypothesis that the SNP, as the most nationalist party, owns the valence dimensions is therefore not clearly confirmed in the case of the language issue. In terms of the direction of party positions on language, figure 3.6 shows that the Conservatives, Labour Party, LibDems, and SNP were cautiously positive, scoring between 0 and +2 in the 2011 Scottish parliamentary election. Surprisingly, of the parties making the most positive statements about language, we find the Conservatives and Labour, who are the most in favour of protecting the status of Gaelic in Scotland. These findings indicate that while the Constitution may be a polarizing issue in Scottish politics, unionist parties are happy to support Scotland's cultural autonomy, something that may be viewed as evidence in line with our fourth hypothesis.

The results of the manifestos data were also confirmed in our interviews. The general attitude among all parties is that Gaelic should be recognized and protected; however, it should not be imposed upon the Scottish population. Out of all the parties, SNP officials were the most pro-Gaelic. However, the party's general approach has been very cautious. When we asked one SNP MSP whether she thought that the Gael-

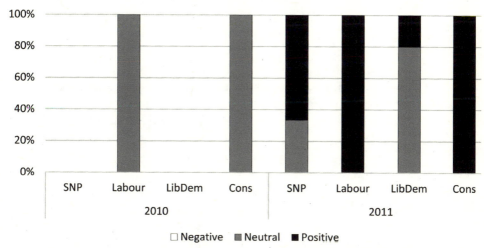

Figure 3.6 Direction on language in Scottish and statewide party manifestos

ic language should be strengthened in Scotland, she diplomatically replied, "It depends what you mean by 'strengthened.' Gaelic is a language that is indigenous to Scotland and is something that is part of our heritage and plays a role in our culture. The level of importance that we place on it, it's up to people" (interview, 21 November 2012).

Another SNP MSP recognized that "there are criticisms that we put too many resources in. Don't force feed a diet of Gaelic to people, but I think it has to be available" (interview, 12 November 2012). The SNP's stance is therefore to support the Gaelic language (as it must respond to concerns of its Gaelic-speaking supporters) but not to impose it as Scotland's national language (unlike, say, Welsh in Wales) as such a move would encounter widespread public opposition. Indeed, the SNP recognizes that Gaelic is one language among many, and is quite foreign to some Scots. Other party members believe that Scotland's other languages, or "dialects," should be promoted: "I also do live in a Scots-speaking part of Scotland and probably the richest vein of Scot speakers left in Scotland. I think that should be important to nurture too and give kids pride in their language" (interview with SNP MP, 15 November 2012).

Scotland's other parties also believe that Gaelic is a constituent part of Scotland's culture, although few argue that Gaelic is central to identity. One Scottish Labour MSP stated, "People should not be excluded from using it as a language. I think it's reasonable that there's some access to Gaelic-medium education, but I would be dubious about a massive increase. It is just not remotely the same as the French/English issue in Quebec" (interview, 15 November 2012). Meanwhile, a Scottish Liberal Democrat MSP, like the SNP MSP mentioned earlier, argued that "Gaelic is not the only language in Scotland. We have lots of dialects and I think we should celebrate them all. I think it's very disappointing that the Scottish government concentrates only on Gaelic and suggests that only Gaelic matters. Actually I think that Doric in the northeast, the Shetland dialect in my part of the world, and others around the country have the role that they want to play in our country" (interview, 14 November 2012).

Finally, the SCUP also acknowledges the place of Gaelic in Scotland's culture and history. As one SCUP MSP put it, "Whilst I don't wish to see it die because, I mean, in parts of Scotland it has a very natural heritage, there are other languages – Doric for example – in Scotland which are dying" (interview, 14 November 2012). However, the Conservatives are also the most concerned about the amount of money being spent on protecting Gaelic – including establishing bilingual road signs in parts of the country with no Gaelic heritage. As the SCUP MSP continued, "I just don't think it should be artificially strengthened. It's potentially a colossal waste of money." So while language is a valence issue in Scotland, with no party opposed to strengthening Gaelic and with support for protecting other languages or dialects, there is a small difference between the SCUP and others over the degree to which public funds should be spent on promoting the use of Gaelic.

REGIONAL INTERESTS

Social Interests

The Scottish model of governance is characterized by a commitment to universalism in public services and an interventionist state (Mooney, Scott, and Williams 2006; Keating 2007, 2010). Because party competition mostly takes place on the left of the political spectrum (with four parties out of five considering themselves as centre-left), Scottish parties tend to adopt a more social-democratic and welfarist approach to social policy. This tendency is even acknowledged by the SCUP, which often pursues more centrist positions on social policy than its UK counterpart. As one SCUP MSP admitted, "Undoubtedly [Scotland is] more social democratic than in England, and you see that in the makeup of Parliament and in the way the debates go" (interview, 20 November 2012).

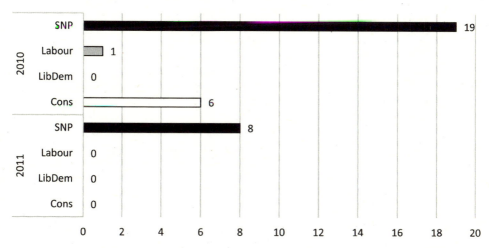

Figure 3.7 Salience of social interests in Scottish and statewide party manifestos

The two parties battling it out to be the "protector" of a Scottish social model are the Scottish National Party and the Scottish Labour Party. And since New Labour's move to the centre(-right), and its openness to the partial privatization of public services and to austerity reforms, the SNP appears to be winning that argument in the period under analysis. This was borne out in both the manifestos and the interview data.

To take the former, our manifestos analysis for the 2010 UK general election and 2011 Scottish Parliament election reveals that social interests – which we identify as distinct social values, shared solidarity, a "Scottish model," and distinct ways of governing – were emphasized most by the SNP as expected from our second hypothesis, and were often excluded altogether from the manifestos of the Liberal Democrats, Conservatives, and Labour Party. As shown in figure 3.7, the SNP emerged as the party claiming ownership of social interests in both election manifestos, with nineteen references in 2010 and eight references in 2011 to Scotland's distinct voice, interests, and social values. In contrast, the LibDems made zero references to social interests in either election; Labour made only one reference to a "new politics" in Scotland in 2010 and none in its 2011 election manifesto; and the Conservatives made six references to Scotland's values and new politics in 2010, but none in 2011. Clearly, "social interests" have been revealed to be the property of the SNP for these two elections, rather than the assumed Labour Party.

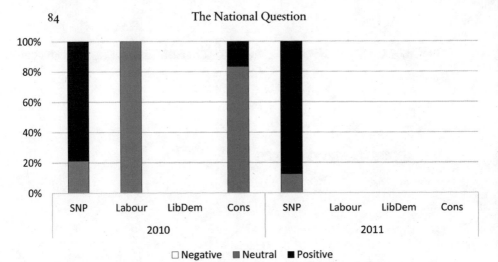

Figure 3.8 Direction on social interests in Scottish and statewide party manifestos

Looking at the directional data, these too offer confirmation of the SNP's ownership of the social interest dimension of the national question. However, in contrast to our fourth hypothesis, these data also indicate a relative lack of influence of the SNP on other party positions. As we can see from figure 3.8, while the SNP makes strongly positive statements about Scotland's distinct voice, values, and interests (approximately 80 per cent of coded statements for both the 2010 and 2011 elections), the only parties that make any reference to these issues – Labour and the Conservatives in 2010 – offer neutral statements, in particular on the "new politics" of Scotland following devolution.

The SNP's attempt to "own" the social interests dimension was also borne out in our interviews and qualitative analysis. This endeavour was clearest in relation to a concept called "the common weal," which was the name given to a pro-independence grouping during the referendum campaign, a movement that was broadly endorsed by the SNP. "I think we have a different ethos around the common weal. And I make no apologies for using a Scots word, because I don't know an English word for it" (interview with SNP MP, 15 November 2012). The closest word may be something akin to egalitarianism, with an emphasis on equal opportunity, inclusion, sustainability, and a strong welfare state. The common weal has been defined as "a distinctively Scottish version of the type of society that has been achieved in the Nordic area" (Reid Foundation 2013). In particular, the SNP has contrasted the social-democratic Nordic approach to social development with the market-driven approach of the UK government.

According to one SNP MSP, there is fertile ground for developing a common weal project in Scotland: "All issues have a more left-liberal consensus in the Scottish Parliament than in the UK Parliament. We have an unusual political party system in that the two main parties draw on centre-left social democratic traditions" (interview, 21 November 2012). The SNP made a particular point of trying to replace Labour as the protector of working-class interests when Scottish Labour leader Johann Lamont made a statement in which she was seen to be criticizing the welfare state. In a radical policy U-turn, she committed the party to ending the provision of free universal benefits in Scotland such as free prescriptions, free care for the elderly, and free tuition fees, which she viewed as "wrong" and "unaffordable" (quoted in Macdonell 2012). This created significant tensions within the party. As one Scottish Labour MSP admitted, "Labour's got a problem there because we've opened up the possibility of reviewing these things [like universal benefits], and if we come to any sort of conclusions we can be accused of abolishing all these things, which probably we would do in practice" (interview, 13 November 2012). The media frenzy following Lamont's admission that she would seek to review universal benefits indicates that these are equated with a strong welfare state that is tied to Scottish values. The SNP criticized Lamont's plans to destroy Scotland's "shared social bonds" (Macdonell 2012) and instead emphasized its commitment to more generous welfare provisions, a higher minimum wage, and the creation of workers' councils (Scottish Government 2013a).

In addition to challenging the Scottish Labour Party on the issue of who is best placed to protect the Scottish social model of egalitarianism, the SNP has been competing with the UK parties on social issues. For instance, the SNP has argued that independence is the only way to "protect" the British welfare state, and in particular the National Health Service (NHS), from the privatization plans of UK parties. The SNP has also strongly criticized the UK government's "austerity cuts" to social benefits, and has vowed to undo all of these policies in an independent Scotland. The SNP's competitors have acknowledged that this is a powerful strategy: "Bits of the welfare state seem to be disappearing, and that's a big issue in this [referendum] campaign ... I think that the SNP is going to run very strongly on the welfare cuts" (interview with Scottish Labour MSP, 13 November 2012).

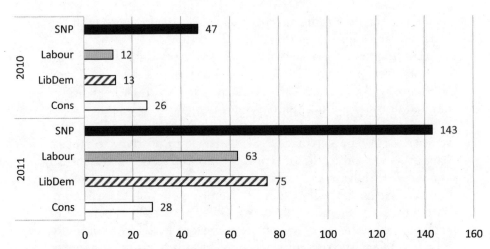

Figure 3.9 Salience of economic interests in Scottish and statewide party manifestos

However, the SNP has not been alone in its criticism of the UK parties. Scottish Labour has also vowed to end the austerity cuts of the Conservative government in Westminster. As one Scottish Labour MSP admitted, "I think the place where we as Labour politicians feel the most frustration around the division between devolved and reserved [powers] is those areas of the tax and welfare system" (interview, 15 November 2012). In response, Scottish Labour has sought to gain control over social security and housing benefits for the Scottish Parliament, to ensure a more progressive approach to housing that is in line with Scottish values. However, there are limitations to the extent to which Labour can pursue these aims within the UK party. In particular, while Labour has moved towards the right on many issues south of the border (for instance, in supporting limited austerity cuts and reducing child benefits), party members in Scotland have been seeking to move towards the left, revealing a very fragmented party across both ideological and territorial lines. In any case, there is evidence that while the "social model" in Scotland is largely a valence issue (with only moderate dissent from the Conservatives), it has become a strong cleavage between Scottish and UK parties, with the former seeking to protect Scotland from a purely market-driven approach to social development. Moreover, this cross-level divide on social issues is clearly reflected in Scottish public opinion (see chapter 5).

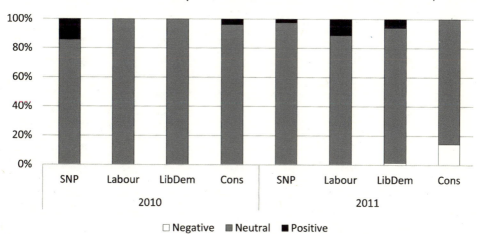

Figure 3.10 Direction on economic interests in Scottish and statewide party manifestos

Economic Interests

According to the data from the 2011 Scottish Parliament election, it was the SNP that emphasized regional economic interests more than any other party, in line with our second hypothesis. As figure 3.9 shows, the SNP made 143 references to the regional economy; the LibDems seventy-five references; Labour sixty-three references; and the Conservatives twenty-eight references. Interestingly, the SNP attached greater salience to economic issues than to the constitutional issue in its manifesto. As we may recall from figure 3.1, the SNP made only fifty-two references to Scotland's constitutional status, compared with 143 references to the Scottish economy (figure 3.9). In contrast, for the 2010 general election, economic issues were less salient for parties across the board: Labour emphasized regional economy the least in 2010, with only twelve references, and the SNP emphasized it the most with forty-seven references.

What of the policy direction of parties on regional economic issues? Here, as we can see from figure 3.10, all of the parties made overwhelmingly neutral statements about the regional economy, with approximately 90 per cent of statements by all parties for the 2011 election being coded as "0." However, there was support among the SNP, Labour, and LibDems to increase infrastructure for economic growth and make greater use of natural resources to grow the Scottish economy (with approximately ten statements per party being coded as +1); such support was absent in the Conservative manifesto. In terms of our fourth hypothesis, these results from our manifesto content analysis show that while the SNP made a clear bid to own the economic territorial issue, it has had limited influence on the positions of other parties.

Let us now put the manifestos analysis into context. While there is general agreement that Scotland is a more left-of-centre country, which is reflected in the more universalist approach to social policies in the Scottish Parliament, there is less consensus on the economic dimension of the "Scottish model of governance." While the SNP claims to be a broadly social democratic party, this is evident only in its social policies. On economic policies, the SNP embraces a more market-oriented approach that some commentators have described as "flirting with economic liberalism" (*Spectator* 2013). For instance, the SNP supports lowering levels of corporation tax "to counterbalance the pull of London and the South-East," increasing private sector investment (especially into renewable energy), cutting air passenger duty, reducing national insurance contributions, and diversifying the business base (Scottish Government 2013b). In these respects, the SNP's economic position is closer to that of the Scottish Conservative Party, which commends the SNP's "willingness to be more entrepreneurial with respect to business" (interview with SCUP MSP, 14 November 2012). This commonality was clear during the SNP's first government from 2007 to 2011, when it relied heavily on the Conservative Party to support its budget, and both parties found agreement on many economic policy and taxation issues. One SNP MSP sought to describe the party's ideology with regard to economic policy: "I understand it as a kind of amalgamation of Robert Burns and Adam Smith, a kind of good economics and prudent business allied to a social conscience" (interview, 12 November 2012).

Meanwhile, the Scottish Labour Party has attacked the SNP's economic policy, portraying the then SNP leader Alex Salmond as a "tax-cutting friend of big business" (Carrell 2014). Instead, Scottish Labour has articulated a more interventionist approach to the economy, emphasizing its commitment to taxing bankers' bonuses, ending tax cuts for hedge funds, introducing a new 50 pence top rate of income tax, and extending the living wage to more public sector agencies (Scottish Labour 2014b). The economic division between Labour and the SNP is echoed in the two parties' bases of support: while Labour relies heavily on trade union funding, the SNP has been able to entice donations from wealthy benefactors and business owners in Scotland (see Mitchell, Bennie, and Johns 2011; Hassan and Shaw 2012).

However, the main debates on economic policy in Scotland during the period of analysis were undoubtedly linked to the constitutional issue. As one Scottish Labour MSP maintained, "In terms of more powers for the Parliament, the economic area is probably the key area that people are talking about. And a lot of the debate is around fiscal powers" (interview, 13 November 2012). While the SNP seeks full fiscal control in an independent Scottish state, the pro-UK parties are all suggesting various degrees of fiscal autonomy for a devolved Scottish Parliament. As another Scottish Labour MSP stated, "Our party's position is that Scotland is stronger as part of that larger national unit and a lot of the arguments for that are economic. They are around the pooling of both risk and opportunity" (interview, 15 November 2012). The Scottish Conservatives and Liberal Democrats both agreed – as part of their collective "Better Together" campaign – that Scotland's economy would be better protected as part of the union, benefiting from the "UK's economic strength, stability and international reputation" (Better Together 2014).

Some politicians indeed underline that there are fewer economic divisions between Scottish parties than the rhetoric suggests: "The general approach is a bit more social-democratic. There's probably more consensus around the deficit reduction … going too far too fast, that kind of thing … and probably more hostility to the [then UK Conservative-LibDem] coalition government" (interview with SNP MSP, 13 November 2012). Furthermore, there are other areas of consensus among Scottish parties on economic issues – for instance, putting immigration at the centre of Scotland's economic development policy as we discussed earlier (Scottish Government 2008). Also, there is support across Scottish parties for reinstituting the "Fresh Talent" scheme, which had been abolished in 2008, to encourage migration to Scotland. While there may be some degree of disagreement on the definition of the parties' left-right economic policy positions, we do find greater cross-partisan consensus on the notion of defending and reinforcing the economic capacities of the Scottish region.

Supranational Interests

Although European integration once provided a bone of contention between parties in Scotland – most notably with the Conservatives being pro–single market but hostile to political and social integration,

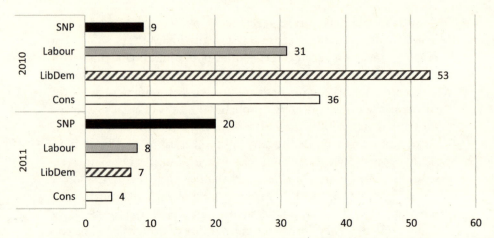

Figure 3.11 Salience of supranational interests in Scottish and statewide party manifestos

and the centre-left parties such as Labour, the SNP, and LibDems strongly supporting the European social model – in the current period of study there was more consensus on supranational issues (for a detailed analysis of Scottish party responses to European integration, see Hepburn 2006, 2010c). At the time of writing, all of the parties have become critical of the lack of political accountability in the European Union (especially since the Greek crisis) and wary of the European single currency (especially since the eurozone crisis). However, none of the parties in Scotland wish to exit the EU and withdraw their membership, in contrast to some of the UK parties. Instead, European integration is still viewed as a generally positive development for Scotland. The only real divide on the European issue is whether parties want Scotland to have its own seat on the European Council as a small, independent member state (SNP), or if Scottish interests are best represented through being part of the UK (see Jeffery 2005; Bulmer et al. 2006; Hepburn 2010c).

The manifestos data – illustrated in figure 3.11 – indicate that the Liberal Democrats were the clear owner of the European issue in the 2010 general election with fifty-three references in their manifesto, compared with thirty-six references in the Conservative manifesto, thirty-one by Labour, and only nine in the SNP manifesto. The data also reveal that the issue of Europe was of greater importance to unionist parties in the general election of 2010 than in the devolved 2011 election (which is to be expected given that "European integration" is an area reserved to Westminster). Meanwhile, Europe was more important to the

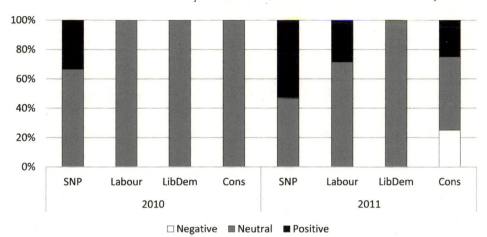

Figure 3.12 Direction on supranational interests in Scottish and statewide party manifestos

SNP in the Scottish election of 2011, presumably as it wishes the Scottish Parliament to have more control over EU matters. Thus, while on average the unionist parties mentioned Europe six times each in their 2011 manifestos, the SNP emphasized this issue the most out of all parties in the Scottish Parliament election, with twenty references. Based on these data, while the LibDems act as the owner of the EU issue in UK general elections, the SNP appears to seek ownership of it at the Scottish substate level.

Looking at the directional data in figure 3.12, we can see that the unionist parties were generally neutral on the issue of Europe. The only exception was the Conservative Party: 28 per cent of its statements were coded as negative (-1), as it seeks to reduce the UK's political participation in the EU. Meanwhile, the SNP took a slightly more positive direction, supporting increased representation and greater autonomy for Scotland within Europe (thus rendering 50 per cent of its statements about Europe as +1). In terms of our second and fourth hypotheses, these data therefore present a complex picture: while all parties are generally in favour of integration with Europe (with the SNP the most positive and the Conservatives the least positive), unionist parties (especially the LibDems) emphasize this issue more in the general election, while the SNP seeks to own this issue in Scottish elections.

How can we explain the positioning of Scottish parties on Europe? Putting this analysis into context, the SNP moved to a position of supporting European integration in the late 1980s, which coincided with the period of structural funding reform and Jacques Delors's vision of a "social Europe." The SNP also adopted its position of "independence in Europe" in 1988, whereby Europe was portrayed as an external economic and political framework for Scottish independence that could replace the structure of the UK. However, the SNP's position on Europe became more cautious in the early 2000s, and moved to open criticism by the end of that decade (see Hepburn 2008, 2010c, 2011). During the period under analysis, the SNP took the position of "critical friend" of Europe. One SNP MP put it this way: "We've been very keen to work with our neighbours. We're very pro-democratic Europe and pro-cooperative Europe. [But] many folks in the SNP have a problem with the current integrationist direction of travel … with the Lisbon Treaty and the way in which it was never really put to any kind of democratic mandate" (interview, 15 November 2012).

As well as criticizing the lack of democratic accountability in the EU and the weakness of European parliamentarians, the SNP has condemned the Common Fisheries Policy and its consequences for the Scottish fishing industry: "The fisheries management over the past three decades has been catastrophic for the communities I represent. It just hasn't worked" (interview, 15 November 2012). On the issue of the single currency, while the SNP was once wholly in favour of adopting the euro (albeit subject to referendum), the party did a U-turn after the euro currency crisis and it now favours keeping the pound sterling until "the economic conditions … [are] right for Scotland" (interview, 21 November 2012).

Scottish Labour's position isn't too dissimilar from the SNP's. It also wishes to see a reformed Europe with more democratic governance. As one Scottish Labour MSP intimated, "No doubt, the EU has been a good thing both for the UK and for Scotland. In the early days of Europe, Scotland did very well in terms of things like European Structural Funds. That's less true now simply because of how Europe is meant to work … One way or another we would be likely to remain in the EU, if that's what we wanted. All the major parties in Scotland do want that" (interview, 15 November 2012). This view was echoed by another Scottish Labour MSP who stated, "As far as it is going, I'm not particularly supporting it going a lot further and I'm not enthusiastic in the present circumstances about joining the euro, and I think that's probably got a degree of consensus in Scotland, including the SNP. But I am comfortable with where Europe has got to" (interview, 13 November 2012). Scottish Labour's position has clearly become much more critical since its peak in pro-Europeanism in the mid-1990s.

The Scottish LibDems have followed a similar trajectory. While they once unconditionally supported European integration and the creation of a federal Europe, and to that extent have been the traditional "owners" of the European issue, they too are more cautious now. As one Scottish LibDem MSP argued, "Overall, it has been a very successful institution, if you take off the recent and past experiences that have been chaotic. But it does actually pose a challenge for Scotland and the United Kingdom, and even for pro-Europeans like myself, if there is a requirement for fiscal and political control" (interview, 14 November 2012). The Scottish LibDems have clearly been going through a period of soul-searching on their support for European integration.

Less so the SCUP, which has always been critical of the noneconomic aspects of European integration. One SCUP MSP's views are fairly representative of those of the party: "I'm just one of those who believe that we have joined an economic union, not a political union, and that the broader interference of the European Union in all other aspects of national sovereignty has been unhealthy" (interview, 14 November 2012). But this more critical view does not mean that the Scottish Conservatives want to leave the EU, unlike sections of the UK Conservative Party: "I don't think I favour pulling out. It's one of these issues where I would like to find some sort of middle ground ... We're members of the EU, but we're not part of the eurozone. I think that would be the best place for us to be, as part of a free trade area, but not part of this ever-closer political union" (interview, 20 November 2012).

Thus European integration has become a valence issue in Scottish politics, with all parties moving towards a more cautious position, but still remaining broadly positive about the benefits that the EU offers Scotland. This situation is in line with our fourth hypothesis, and it contrasts sharply with political debates taking place south of the Scottish border, where there is a strong strain of anti-Europeanism – evident in sections of the UK Conservative Party and the anti-EU United Kingdom Independence Party, which became the biggest party in England in the 2014 European elections. Scottish parties are very much aware of the different tone of European debates in England. As one former Labour MP and MSP stated, "I am a big fan of Europe. I don't like the drift of anti-Europeanism that we see in Westminster, the danger that the Labour Party could be a bit opportunistic on that" (interview, 16 November 2012). Another Scottish Labour MP pointed out that "the little England aspect we do get doesn't apply in the same way [in Scotland]" (interview, 15 November 2012). Finally, the SNP is scathing in its criticism of UK parties' anti-Europeanism, and in that context seeks to position itself as much more sympathetic towards integration: "The UK government has mercilessly used it [Europe] as a bogeyman. You get all these stories of straight bananas and stuff" (interview with SNP MSP, 12 November 2012). The SNP's desire to distance itself from the UK government's position on Europe is very similar to its strategy on multiculturalism, seeking to present Scotland as a much more progressive, outward-looking, and tolerant nation than the rest of the UK.

The interest in fostering strong links with the EU on the part of many Scottish party elites is a good illustration of that region's paradiplomacy drive (Paquin 2001; Irvine and Nossal 2005). Like for Quebec, supranational integration is seen by the substate nation of Scotland as a way for it to radiate on the international scene. Of course, the question of Scotland's integration within the EU has become even more salient in the wake of the Brexit vote in 2016. Given that a majority of Scots voted in favour of the UK remaining in the EU, the fact that the Leave option nonetheless prevailed makes the supranational argument in favour of Scotland's independence all the more potent. However, at the time of writing, it remains to be seen whether the EU issue will open the door to holding a second Scottish independence referendum in the short to medium term. The setback experienced by the SNP in the June 2017 general election certainly calls this possibility into question.

MULTILEVEL DYNAMICS

The primary focus of this chapter so far has been on the impact of the national question on party behaviour in Scotland. Our next question is, What has been the impact of the Scottish question on multilevel politics in the UK? In particular, do we see a reinforcement of a territorial cleavage between the UK "centre" and the Scottish "periphery"? Moreover, if some aspects of the national question have become valence issues in Scotland, with all parties agreeing on the direction that certain territorial policies should take, what effect has that had on multilevel politics?

At the outset of the chapter, we put forward the hypothesis that cross-party consensus on the national question will be more likely to occur at the substate level than at the state level, and consequently, that substate parties will be more likely to act as a territorial bloc in opposition to central-government policies. Based on the data collected, we believe that this fourth hypothesis has been clearly confirmed in the case of Scotland. The distinctive nationalist characteristics of Scottish public opinion have had a much stronger influence on the stances of Scottish parties (or branches of statewide parties) – that is, the Scottish Labour Party, scUP, Scottish LibDems, and Scottish Greens – than on the UK parties themselves. This is clearly the case on the issue of language (where all parties in Scotland endorse Gaelic protection, but where none of the UK parties mention it in their manifestos), on cosmopolitanism (where all substate parties support a multicultural Scotland, in contrast to the UK parties), and on European integration (where Scottish parties are generally more favourable than their UK counterparts). The one area where we have seen a similar priming effect on both substate and statewide parties was on the issue of further powers for Scotland. Here, parties at both levels have recently increased their support for further constitutional devolution to Scotland. However, judging from the recommendations of the Smith Commission compared with the provisions of the UK government's Scotland Act 2016, Scottish parties more strongly support constitutional autonomy than the UK parties.

The increasing salience of the national question at the substate level has strengthened the centre-periphery cleavage on this issue. But here, rather than the SNP being a lone voice in representing the "periphery" against the centre, we have witnessed Scottish parties across the spectrum seeking to "stand up for Scotland's interests." The data have shown that Scottish and UK parties (regardless of their political persuasion) are taking increasingly diverging positions on key issues surrounding the national question, and on occasion Scottish parties from across the ideological spectrum have acted as a territorial bloc in defence of Scottish interests against the UK government/parties. We witnessed, for instance, how all of Scotland's parties have supported increased levels of immigration to Scotland and seek to foster an open and tolerant society that is respectful of different cultures – in sharp contrast to the increasingly restrictive immigration and integration policies being endorsed by all of the major UK parties. We also saw that on social policy, there has been some consensus among parties on Scotland's distinct policy style and an emphasis on welfarism and universalism in contrast to the marketization measures being pursued in Whitehall – something that unites the SNP, LibDems, and Labour, while the scUP is less antagonistic to these policies (which it acknowledges win much public support in Scotland) than its UK counterparts.

Clearly, then, when Scottish parties believe that their distinct Scottish interests (such as social benefits) are under threat from measures taken in London, or when there is a particular policy that would clearly favour Scotland's interests (such as moderate increases in immigration to fill labour market gaps), they present a united front against Westminster. And some of the SNP's competitors, despite their differences on some issues, even admit that having the nationalists in power at Holyrood may be the best way to get Scotland's voice heard in London. As one Scottish Liberal Democrat MSP intimated, "While I might not agree with a nationalist government in Edinburgh on issues, there is no question that they make a Scottish argument. I don't think there's been a time when Scottish issues haven't been more understood at the top of [the UK] government than now" (interview, 14 November 2012).

CONCLUSION

We set out the hypothesis at the start of this chapter that parties in Scotland must take a stance on the national question, which has become a primary dimension of party competition in the region. Taken as a whole, the findings presented in this chapter clearly support this first hypothesis. All political parties in Scotland are addressing the national question and are taking clear positions on most of its dimensions, and these stances constitute a central component of their political positioning and aim at mobilizing voter support. We also hypothesized that the "owner" of the national question, which we assumed was the leading nationalist party operating in the territory – the Scottish National Party – has pushed the other political parties to adopt stronger positions in the debate. To what extent has the latter expectation been met?

Our findings have indicated that the SNP has been the successful owner of several dimensions of the national question. In particular, the SNP has – during the period of analysis – led on the issues of constitutional change, language, cosmopolitanism, social policy, and the economy. Taking these subcategories separately, we saw that the SNP's demands for independence directly encouraged other parties in Scotland to adopt stronger regional autonomy demands, in particular eliciting a commitment from all three pro-UK parties – Scottish Labour, the Scottish Conservatives, and the Scottish Liberal Democrats – to guarantee enhanced powers for the Scottish Parliament after a No vote in the 2014 referendum. While the constitutional dimension has provided the greatest source of contestation – especially during the referendum campaign that pitted pro-independence campaigners against pro-unionists –

when one looks in greater detail at the parties' positions regarding autonomy, there is actually less difference between them than one might expect. The SNP has advanced a vision of "independence-lite" that retains most of the links that Scotland currently shares with the rest of the UK, and the parties endorsing the Better Together camp have all supported enhanced powers for the Scottish Parliament.

On the issue of language, while it was the Scottish Labour–Liberal Democrat government that passed the landmark legislation on recognizing Gaelic as an official language in 2005, the SNP is now the strongest advocate of Gaelic language protection. However, the issue of language protection is not central to the national question in Scotland, as only a small percentage of the population of Scotland speaks Gaelic, and many others speak one or another regional dialect. As one Scottish Labour MSP admitted, "The SNP would be quite supportive of the Gaelic, but we can't really criticize that or be very enthusiastic about it. It is still very marginal, so language in that sense is not so important" (interview, 13 November 2012). As well as lacking any centrality to the national question, the issue of language is a valence one in Scotland, with all parties supporting the protection of the Gaelic language, as well as some regional dialects, although parties are clear that any minority language uptake should be voluntary and not imposed on old or new inhabitants of Scotland.

Equally, on the issue of cosmopolitanism, the SNP is leading on the "multicultural" dimension of the national question. Even though the Scottish multiculturalist approach was initiated by the Scottish Labour–Liberal Democrat coalition government with the launch of the One Scotland, Many Cultures campaign, the SNP has extended this approach to integration, most notably in its Race Equality Statement and its position on immigration. The SNP has sought to encourage the creation of a plural Scottish identity that all newcomers to Scotland can share, a policy strongly supported by all of Scotland's parties, but which goes against the current views of most of the statewide political parties regarding multiculturalism in the UK. Similarly, the SNP has – building upon the previous Labour-LibDem government's Fresh Talent initiative – argued that Scotland must have increased levels of immigration to satisfy labour market demand and to offset population aging and decline. Again, none of the parties have disagreed with this position (unlike parties in Westminster), with even the Conservatives proclaiming that "where we have an expanding economy and skill needs, yes, of course we should bring people in. We have plenty of space!" (interview with SCUP MSP, 20 November 2012).

In terms of issue ownership, the SNP has faced the greatest competition over the social dimension. The Scottish Labour Party, as noted in chapter 1, once held the lead on this issue by presenting itself as the party representing the social values of Scotland. However, with criticisms of Labour moving to the centre(-right) under Tony Blair and the recent announcements of Labour support for (albeit more limited) austerity cuts, in addition to Scottish Labour's recent difficulties in explaining its withdrawal of commitment to universalism, the SNP has sought to portray itself as the party to the left of Labour. This positioning has involved promises to protect Scotland's social model from threats of marketization and privatization emanating from Westminster. Indeed, the SNP has presented its position as seeking to protect the "British welfare state" in Scotland – in particular the NHS and social benefits – from a Conservative government in London that is bent on privatizing public services in the UK. The SNP's opponents have had a difficult time criticizing this position. Indeed, it appears that there is a broad consensus in Scotland over a generally welfarist, interventionist state in social matters, with support for maintaining public services such as health care and education free at the point of use.

On the economic dimension, the Scottish Labour Party's ownership of this issue has been challenged by the SNP. However, the SNP's proposed tax cuts for business have concerned and sometimes alienated many Labour voters who would otherwise support the SNP. Scottish Labour has also committed itself to the economic dimension of the Scottish model of governance – in increasing the top rate of income tax and taxing bankers' bonuses – even if it is having difficulty positioning itself on the social dimension.

Finally, with respect to the supranational dimension, while the Lib-Dems have sought to lead on this issue in UK elections, it is the SNP that claims ownership of this issue within the substate party system. But here it is more difficult to disentangle the party competition dynamics: in some ways the SNP has moved to a more Eurocritical position (following the lead of the Conservatives), but in other ways, the other parties in Scotland have followed the SNP's lead in demanding more Scottish influence in Europe. In any case, it is clear that in Scotland – unlike the rest of the UK – European integration is generally a valence issue, with all parties seeking the benefits of EU membership. The debate that surrounded the Brexit referendum in 2016 only underlined further the existence of this centre-periphery cleavage within the UK on the issue of Europe.

As was pointed out in chapter 1, it may be one thing for a political party to emphasize issues in its manifestos and campaign discourse, and hence to claim ownership over them, and another for a party to actually succeed in inducing voters to support it based on its issue ownership. This outcome depends on how voters perceive party competition on the national question, and on whether they are willing to cast their ballot on the basis of this multidimensional issue beyond other voting considerations. The next two chapters will examine whether, and to what extent, party positionings on the national question are linked to the behaviour of Quebec and Scottish voters.

4

Voter Behaviour in Quebec

Whereas the two previous chapters focused extensively on the strategic behaviour of political parties, this chapter and the next one seek to determine to what extent the "national question" is at the heart of electoral dynamics in Quebec and Scotland, respectively. By the national question, we mean the debates surrounding not only the political status of these two territories in the greater Canadian and UK ensemble, but also the protection and promotion of the identity and interests of these regions' majority population. By electoral dynamics, we mean the link between Quebecers' and Scots' opinions on the future of their respective nation and the protection of their culture, and support for one of the four largest political parties competing in their territory in substate and statewide elections.

There has been much work done on the relationship between Quebecers' constitutional preferences and the political choices they have made over the past few decades (see chapter 1 for an overview). This book intends to contribute to this body of scholarly literature by pushing theoretical reflection and empirical analysis a little further with regard to the meaning of the national question in Quebec and its impact on partisan dynamics within the province. In this chapter, we examine the link between Quebecers' constitutional preferences and their vote choice in the 7 April 2014 election. The results of these analyses clearly show that the national question is very much at the heart of the political game in Quebec and that all parties must position themselves on this issue in order to be electorally competitive.

What can we conclude from our overview of the role that the national question plays in electoral dynamics in Quebec presented in chapters 1 and 2? The first conclusion is that this question is a "super issue" in Quebec. That means that, more so than left-right divides or partisan identification, it is the main factor that structures electoral behaviour in Quebec (Bélanger and Nadeau 2009) – effectively making these substate elections "first order." Second, the national question is in and of itself multidimensional, having both valence and positional characteristics. Defending regional interests and affirming a distinct identity are dimensions around which there largely exists a consensus; political parties differentiate themselves not by taking radically different positions, but rather by showing varying degrees of commitment and determination to achieve these objectives. The logic that prevails in the case of these two dimensions is closer to the one proposed by saliency and ownership theories of issue voting as seen in chapter 1. As such, the Parti Libéral du Québec, which is the most federalist party in the province, will declare its willingness to defend Quebec and its culture, but will generally do so with less vigour than the other parties (the Parti Québécois in particular). Thus, each party should subscribe to the consensus surrounding these questions without straying too far from the position of the median voter, who in Quebec has nationalist tendencies. The political game in Quebec on these dimensions of the national question is clear. It is in the strategic interest of the most nationalist party in Quebec that questions of identity and language remain at the forefront during an election campaign, and it is in the interest of the other parties that these same concerns take up less space on the political agenda.

The political dynamic is entirely different for the third dimension of the national question: constitutional preferences. For the past few years, Quebec public opinion has been on the side of the federalists. For this reason the Parti Libéral du Québec, otherwise discreet on the question of defending Quebec's interests and identity, has put constitutional issues at the heart of its electoral campaigns (even though the party remained silent on this dimension in its manifestos, as seen in chapter 2). For this same reason the Parti Québécois, who often brandishes defending Quebec's interests and identity during electoral campaigns, has said relatively little about sovereignty – even though, on paper and in principle, it remains the party's premier policy goal (see chapter 2). The other parties, less engaged in the opposition between federalism and sovereignty, would benefit from this question being removed from the political debate altogether and voters' attention being drawn to other issues.

The preceding recapitulation of our theoretical framework and of our core political party findings for Quebec allows us to suggest some hypotheses that will be tested using data from an online survey that we carried out in Quebec in the week following the 7 April 2014 provincial (substate) election that brought the Parti Libéral du Québec into power. The opinion survey was administered to 1,517 adult Quebecers by Canadian polling firm Léger Marketing through web-based interviews between 9 April 2014 and 16 April 2014, thus immediately after the election. The survey respondents were recruited from Léger Marketing's LégerWeb online panel of Canadian households.[1] A list of all the survey items used in our analyses is presented in appendix table B1, together with information on how the answers were coded into variables. The hypotheses are the following:

1 Given its importance in Quebec, the national question dominates over all other cleavages, including that of traditional left-right.
2 The priming of the national question by the parties dominating this issue, and the valence nature of some of its dimensions, exert pressure on each party to take a side on this debate. This phenomenon is more marked in Quebec on the left and should be more visible for the left-wing Québec Solidaire than for the right-wing Coalition Avenir Québec.
3 The national question has a greater impact on substate vote choice (provincial elections) than on state-level vote choice (federal elections).
4 The most nationalist party in Quebec, the Parti Québécois, is perceived as being the most adept at defending Quebec's interests, language, and culture. This advantage results from the majority of the population, especially francophone voters, having nationalist sensibilities.
5 The party most opposed to Quebec independence, the Parti Libéral du Québec, will dominate the constitutional preferences dimension of the national question. This advantage arises because the majority of the population favours keeping the province within the Canadian federation, and the PLQ is the sole party clearly articulating this position.
6 Support for parties (the PQ or the PLQ) dominating one of the dimensions of the national question is linked to this issue more so than is support for any other party. Thus, support for the PQ and the PLQ is tied to (a) the importance voters themselves give to the national question, (b) their feelings of attachment and identification towards Quebec and Canada, (c) their evaluations of the costs

and benefits of the various constitutional options, and (d) their own constitutional preferences.

The first three hypotheses offer different ways of testing the general idea that the national question is a mainstream issue – even a super issue – in substate politics. The last three hypotheses serve to test the ideas that the national question is a multidimensional issue, and that specific parties benefit electorally from being viewed as the issue owner on some of these dimensions. We believe that the best way to estimate the impact of the ownership of the national question on parties' support in Quebec is to establish a link between opinions and attitudes related to this issue (identity, attachment towards Quebec and Canada, support for independence and devolution, etc.) and respondents' inclination to vote for these parties. The contribution of these opinions and attitudes to an explanation of vote choice is thus expected to be more important for the parties that dominate on one or more of the dimensions of the national question.[2]

QUEBEC VOTERS AND THE NATIONAL QUESTION

The hypotheses are tested via a survey carried out in the context of the April 2014 Quebec provincial election. This election lends itself quite well to a study of the electoral impact of the national question. The Parti Québécois minority government called the election on the basis of favourable polls amidst the debate surrounding the adoption of the Charter of Quebec Values, which aimed to affirm the secular nature of Quebec society (see chapter 2). However, the electoral campaign quickly became centred on the theme of Quebec independence after the addition of well-known businessman Pierre Karl Péladeau to the ranks of the PQ candidates.[3] Upon announcing his candidacy, Péladeau unequivocally expressed his support for Quebec sovereignty. This announcement unintentionally derailed the campaign from its focus on issues favourable for the PQ, such as defending Quebec identity, to ground that was more favourable for the Parti Libéral du Québec, such as constitutional preferences.

We will first examine in a descriptive way Quebec's political landscape before testing our various hypotheses with the help of bivariate and multivariate analyses. The first thing we need to establish is the importance of the national question in Quebec. Quebec is the only province in Canada where a majority of the population is French-

speaking. Debates over the place of Quebec within the Canadian federation and the status of the French language have been a recurrent
theme in Quebec's history. As a result, partisan divisions are largely a
function of individuals' attitudes on these questions.

In order to shed light on how central a role the national question
plays in electoral preferences, we first asked survey participants how
important the following three considerations were in casting their ballot in the 7 April 2014 provincial election: how well the party defends
Quebec's current and future interests; how well the party understands
Quebec's history and culture; and the party's constitutional preferences.

The figures in table 4.1 clearly show that a large majority of voters at-
tribute great importance to these questions. As much as 93 per cent of
respondents see defending Quebec's interests as important; on this
issue, there is a general consensus and political parties position themselves accordingly, as was seen in chapter 2. That a party can defend
Quebec's culture and history is also important for three out of every
four respondents (75 per cent). A similar level of importance is given to
the constitutional positioning of the party, at 77 per cent of the respondents. It is not surprising to see that voters for the two parties most
engaged in the constitutional debate, the Parti Libéral du Québec and
the Parti Québécois, give more importance to this question (87 per cent
for the PLQ and 83 per cent for the PQ) than supporters of other parties
such as Québec Solidaire (65 per cent) or Coalition Avenir Québec (59
per cent). These third parties seek to move the political debate in Quebec towards economic and social questions. However, the importance
of the national question, in spite of these differences, is still obvious.

The second important element for understanding the influence of
the national question has to do with the state of public opinion in Quebec. Quebecers' nationalist sensibilities can be illustrated in two ways.
First, as shown in table 4.2, is Quebecers' greater attachment to Quebec than to Canada. While 90 per cent of Quebecers report being "very"
or "somewhat" attached to their province, this proportion is only 66
per cent when it comes to attachment to Canada. This gap is even wider
among francophones, who make up about 80 per cent of Quebec's population: 94 per cent of francophone respondents in our sample report
being attached to Quebec versus 60 per cent for being attached to Canada (75 per cent of nonfrancophones report being attached to Quebec
whereas 92 per cent of them report being attached to Canada).

A look at the distribution of these feelings along partisan lines is revealing (see table 4.3). The Liberal clientele, largely due to the larger

Table 4.1
Importance attached to various issues in the 2014 election in Quebec (%)

	All	PQ	QS	CAQ	PLQ
Party stands up for Quebec interests	93	97	92	93	90
Party understands Quebec history and culture	75	90	88	66	65
Party constitutional position	77	83	65	59	87

Question: How important are the following questions in your decision to vote for this party in the provincial election of April 7 in Quebec?

Table 4.2
Level of attachment to Quebec and Canada (%)

	Quebec	Canada
Very	59	36
Somewhat	32	30
Not very	8	23
Not at all	2	11

Question: Would you say that you are very attached, somewhat attached, not very attached, or not attached at all to Quebec? Canada?

Table 4.3
Attachment to Quebec and Canada by party identification (%)

	PQ	QS	CAQ	PLQ
Very attached to Quebec	85	59	48	48
Very attached to Canada	6	7	26	72

Question: Would you say that you are very attached, somewhat attached, not very attached, or not attached at all to Quebec? Canada?

proportion of nonfrancophones in its ranks, shows a higher level of attachment to Canada than other partisan groups. The difference between Liberal voters' degree of attachment to Canada and the levels of attachment observed in the population overall explains the PLQ's relative discomfort on language and identity matters. Stuck between a less nationalist electoral base and a more nationalist general population, the PLQ, unlike the Parti Québécois, tends to avoid these questions, even if the party subscribes to the general goals of preserving and promoting Quebec identity (see chapter 2).

The third notable aspect of Quebec public opinion on the national question stems from the second. To the extent that Quebecers are more attached to Quebec than to Canada, they also give particular importance to the role that their provincial government plays. For many Quebecers, their provincial government should have more powers within the Canadian federation. In order to measure the pervasiveness of this attitude, we asked the following question: "If there were a referendum that asked you whether you want the Quebec National Assembly to have more powers from Ottawa, would you vote Yes or No?"

The responses to this question are revealing. As shown in table 4.4, approximately two-thirds of Quebecers (64 per cent) would vote in favour of this option. Furthermore, the separation of respondents along partisan lines is quite informative. Support for this option either reaches or surpasses 80 per cent among PQ and QS voters, receives majority support from the mostly federalist supporters of the CAQ (57 per cent), and is backed by only one in four PLQ supporters. Therefore, the question of repatriating powers is a delicate matter for the Liberals. It is also a touchy subject for the PQ, as its hard-core supporters would not be happy if their party of choice seemingly abandoned its raison d'être by limiting itself to merely pursuing more powers within the federation.

The perspective changes completely when one measures support for Quebec independence. Although support for independence is currently at a low compared with decades past, it seems that independence never really had clear and widespread support within the population (with the exception of a few points in history; see Pinard 2002; Yale and Durand 2011). Table 4.5 shows that at the time of the 2014 provincial election, barely one in three voters would have supported Quebec independence. Interestingly, this constitutional option is also rejected by about one in four PQ voters (25 per cent) and almost one out of every two QS voters, two parties that actually support sovereignty. Unsurprisingly, supporters of federalist parties reject independence in even greater proportions. About 82 per cent of CAQ voters and no less than 97 per cent of PLQ supporters would vote against Quebec independence.

Thus, the picture is clear. Quebec voters have nationalist sensibilities while being in favour of keeping Quebec within the Canadian federation. These voters want their provincial government to defend Quebec's interests and protect its identity and culture. Along these questions, it would seem natural that voters have confidence in a nationalist party such as the Parti Québécois. However, although nationalists, Que-

Table 4.4
Opinions about transferring more powers to the Quebec government (%)

	All	PQ	QS	CAQ	PLQ
Favourable	64	83	80	57	25
Opposed	36	17	20	43	75

Question: If there were a referendum that asked you whether you want the Quebec National Assembly to have more powers from Ottawa, would you vote YES or NO?

Table 4.5
Opinions about the independence of Quebec (%)

	All	PQ	QS	CAQ	PLQ
Favourable	34	75	52	18	3
Opposed	66	25	48	82	97

Question: If there were a referendum that asked whether Quebec should be an independent country, would you vote YES or NO?

Table 4.6
Party images in Quebec (%)

Best party:	PQ	QS	CAQ	PLQ
To defend Quebec's identity and culture	43	7	8	16
To defend Quebec' interests	33	7	14	25
To manage the economy	14	3	22	32
To cut taxes	7	5	30	15
To fight poverty	12	26	11	18

Question: Which party is best able to handle the following issues?

becers also favour the federalist option in greater numbers. Thus, it would also seem natural that they have confidence in the most federalist party, the Parti Libéral du Québec, in order to keep Quebec within Canada.

As a first cut at our hypothesis tests, we asked respondents which party they thought was the best at handling certain issues such as defending Quebec's interests, protecting Quebec's language and culture, and making policies on the economy, taxes, and poverty. The figures in table 4.6 go in the direction of our fourth hypothesis and show that the most nationalist party, the PQ, has the advantage when it comes to "valence" dimensions of the national question (i.e., defending Quebec's interests and protecting its identity and culture). This advantage is even clearer among francophone respondents in our sample. Within this group, the PQ is perceived as being the most adept at protecting Quebec identity (49 per cent of respondents versus 11 per cent for the PLQ, 10 per cent for QS, and 9 per cent for the CAQ). These figures, along with the data showing relatively weak support for Quebec independence, confirm that the Parti Québécois dominates the valence dimensions of the national question in Quebec and that the Liberals have a clear advantage when it comes to the "positional" aspect of this question (i.e., the choice between independence or remaining within Canada).

Moreover, it is interesting to note that there is a certain degree of coherence to voters' perceptions of parties on issues. Québec Solidaire, the most leftist party, is most highly ranked for tackling poverty; the Coalition Avenir Québec, which focused on public finances in the 2014 electoral campaign, is ranked most highly for lowering taxes; and the Parti Libéral du Québec scores highly on the economy, which has been the party's trademark issue for a while. This coherence shows that the data we have on how the parties are viewed by the Quebec electorate paint an accurate portrait of issue ownership in Quebec, notably on the dimensions of the national question.

Multivariate analyses of support for the four largest political parties in Quebec will allow us to test more rigorously and thoroughly our hypotheses about issue ownership of the national question in Quebec. They will also allow us to evaluate the degree to which the national question in Quebec is a "super issue" whose influence is greater than that of any other political cleavage.

A MULTIVARIATE ANALYSIS OF SUPPORT
FOR QUEBEC POLITICAL PARTIES

We continue our analysis of the impact of the national question on voting behaviour by looking at the determinants of vote choice in Quebec during provincial elections. To do this, we examine the explanatory factors behind voter support for the four main political parties in Quebec: the Parti Libéral du Québec, the Parti Québécois, the Coalition Avenir Québec, and Québec Solidaire. These four parties won 42 per cent, 25 per cent, 23 per cent, and 8 per cent of the vote, respectively, during the 7 April 2014 election (recall table 1.1). In the end, the PLQ won a majority of seats (seventy) in the Quebec National Assembly, followed by the PQ who formed the official opposition with thirty seats. Finally, the CAQ and QS managed to have twenty-two and three representatives elected, respectively.

The dependent variable takes a value of 1 when a survey respondent reports having voted for a party and 0 otherwise (nonresponses are excluded). We use binomial logistic regression analyses performed separately for each political party, as well as a "bloc-recursive" approach (e.g., Miller and Shanks 1996; Blais et al. 2002; Nadeau et al. 2012), which means that the independent variables are introduced into the model in successive blocs. The first bloc contains long-term factors (other than the national question) that weigh on political choices in Quebec, such as sociodemographic variables (age, gender, language, education, income) and political attitudes (ideological positioning on a left-right axis, moral liberalism, political cynicism; a more detailed presentation of the variables and their coding is presented in appendix B). The second bloc includes measures of attachment to Quebec and to Canada, as well as a variable on identification (dominant, exclusive, or shared) with both Quebec and Canada – also known as the Linz-Moreno measure. The third bloc contains two variables. The first takes its maximum value when the respondent says that Quebec society's values are different from those of the rest of Canada. The second measure taps how individuals view the trade-offs between political sovereignty (even if it means belonging to a smaller market) and the benefits of belonging to a larger market (even if it means a loss of political sovereignty). The fourth bloc measures the effect of constitutional preferences (about independence and about having more powers) on vote choice in Quebec. The fifth and final bloc includes a variable that has a clear short-term component: the importance given by the respondent to the constitutional position of the parties during the April 2014 election. This variable is first included separately to assess its impact on voters' preferences. It is then interacted with constitutional options to determine how the priming of these preferences may have impacted the vote at the last election in Quebec.

Before delving into the multivariate analyses of public opinion, we should finally note that each of these blocs of determinants (except the first) is associated with one of our three dimensions of the national question: the second bloc relates to regional identity, the third refers to aspects associated with regional social and economic interests, and the fourth and fifth blocs tap the dimension linked to constitutional preferences.

Table 4.7
Change in probabilities for voting models of provincial election in Quebec:
Sociodemographic and attitudinal variables

	PQ	QS	CAQ	PLQ
Age	0.24**	−0.17**	−0.08	0.08
Female	−0.02	0.00	−0.05*	0.07**
Language	0.43**	0.11**	0.37**	−0.49**
Education	−0.15**	0.12**	−0.08	0.08
Income	−0.13**	−0.01	0.10*	0.05
Left-right	−0.34**	−0.20**	0.15*	0.36**
Moral liberalism	0.15**	0.13**	−0.13**	−0.11**
Cynicism	−0.10*	0.06*	0.15**	−0.13**
N	1,127	1,127	1,127	1,127

$**p \leq 0.01$; $*p \leq 0.05$ (two-tailed tests).

Long-Term Factors

The effect of long-term factors on vote choice is presented both in appendix C (table C1) and in table 4.7 (we present changes in probabilities in the text, but provide the raw results of the regression analyses in the appendix). The sociodemographic variable that has the biggest impact on vote choice in Quebec is language. The probability of voting for the PLQ drops 49 percentage points when a respondent is francophone, while their probability of voting for the PQ, the CAQ, or QS rises by 43, 37, and 11 percentage points, respectively. Moreover, this linguistic cleavage translates into constitutional preferences: nonfrancophones, strongly federalist, massively support the Liberals while francophones, more nationalist, tend to split their votes between the four main parties in Quebec. The other significant cleavage is age: the PQ receives more support from older voters (essentially the "baby boom" generation) while the QS, an emerging party, draws upon younger and more educated voters for its support.

The effect of political attitudes is also significant. The Parti Québécois and Québec Solidaire, both centre-left parties, receive more support from individuals who position themselves on the left and who have more liberal opinions on morality questions. The opposite trend is observed for more rightist parties such as the Coalition Avenir Québec and the Parti Libéral du Québec. Interestingly, individuals who are more cynical towards politics tend to support emergent parties such as the QS and the CAQ rather than traditional parties such as the PLQ and the PQ.

The results show that vote choice in Quebec is structured by two important determinants: voters' language and their positioning on ideological and moral questions. But as we will see in the next sections, these cleavages overlap to a large extent with the individuals' constitutional preferences. Nonfrancophones largely support the Liberals, and individuals who are more conservative economically and socially are more favourable to maintaining the constitutional status quo.

Identity and Vote Choice in Quebec

Two variables can help us measure the intensity of respondents' opinions towards the national question in Quebec. The first is an indicator of their degree of attachment towards the two national communities of Quebec and Canada. As we have seen previously (in table 4.2), Quebecers are massively attached to Quebec and more divided in their attachment to Canada. Another frequently used indicator looks at individuals' exclusive, dominant, or shared identification with these national communities. In this case, the question asks respondents if they view themselves as only Quebecer, first Quebecer then Canadian, equally Quebecer and Canadian, first Canadian then Quebecer, or only Canadian. The figures show that Quebecers are split in terms of how they identify with both Quebec and Canada. A little less than 40 per cent of them identify first with Quebec (10 per cent exclusively and 27 per cent primarily), and about the same proportion identifies first with Canada (9 per cent exclusively and 30 per cent primarily). About a quarter equally identifies with both national communities.

The results of the regression analyses for the model that includes these variables are presented in appendix C (table C2) and in table 4.8. Three clear conclusions can be drawn from these results. First, including these variables considerably weakens the effect of two variables: language of daily use and, especially, left-right ideological positioning. In fact, the latter variable remains strong and significant for only one party: Québec Solidaire, a small leftist party that won 8 per cent of the vote in this election. These results already offer some kind of confirmation of our first hypothesis that the national question in Quebec dominates all other cleavages, including left-right.

The second conclusion relates to the relative effect of the indicators measuring attachment to and identification with Quebec and Canada.

Table 4.8
Change in probabilities for voting models of provincial election in Quebec:
Attachment and identification variables

	PQ	QS	CAQ	PLQ
Age	0.20*	−0.15**	−0.04	0.06
Female	0.00	0.01	−0.06*	0.05*
Language	0.11	0.09*	0.40**	−0.24**
Education	−0.19**	0.10**	−0.08	0.09
Income	−0.07	−0.01	0.09	0.00
Left-right	−0.03	−0.17**	0.07	0.10
Moral liberalism	0.05	0.12**	−0.11**	−0.03
Cynicism	−0.11**	0.05	0.14**	−0.09**
Identity	0.42**	−0.05	0.05	−0.19**
AttachQC	0.25**	−0.05	−0.19**	−0.08
AttachCAN	−0.29**	−0.11**	0.12*	0.49**
N	1,127	1,127	1,127	1,127

**$p \leq 0.01$; *$p \leq 0.05$ (two-tailed tests).

In most studies on nationalist movements, it is the variable measuring identification with national communities that is most often used. However, the results show that the variable measuring not *identification*, but rather *attachment* to the national communities performs clearly better for three of the four parties in Quebec (PLQ, CAQ, and QS), the exception being with the supporters of the Parti Québécois for whom both dimensions play an important role.[4]

The third conclusion has to do more specifically with the effect of feelings of attachment on support for political parties. From the data, two ideal types emerge. The first consists of voters for parties that are clearly involved in the debate over the national question in Quebec: the Parti Québécois and the Parti Libéral du Québec. For these voters, identity and relative attachment to Quebec and Canada play a large role in their support for these respective parties. By contrast, supporters of Québec Solidaire and Coalition Avenir Québec – parties that are on the sidelines of this debate – are much more divided in their feelings of attachment towards Quebec and Canada. The increases in the levels of explained variance for the different party models are telling. Whereas including these variables produces a significant increase in the level of the pseudo-R^2 for the Liberal and the PQ models (+0.22 for the PLQ and +0.25 for the PQ), the same figures are almost negligible for the CAQ and QS (+0.02 in each case). Taken together, the results provide some degree of confirmation for our sixth hypothesis, which stipulated that the two parties most directly engaged in the national debate in Quebec (i.e., the PQ and the PLQ) would dominate this issue and profit electorally from it.

Cost-Benefit Evaluations

As seen in chapter 2, the debate over the national question in Quebec often tends to revolve around two questions. The first, most often put forward by independentists, says that a sovereign Quebec would be better able to correspond to Quebecers' values and aspirations. This argument assumes that Quebecers' values differ from those of other Canadians and that nothing short of full control of a nation-state would allow Quebec to act upon these supposedly different policy preferences. The second argument, often made by federalists, states that in the modern era, it is preferable to be part of a larger economic entity, even if that means giving up a little bit of national sovereignty.

We tested the impact of these two arguments, which are central to the national debate in Quebec, by including two variables in our models. The first sees whether Quebecers think their values and aspirations differ from those of other Canadians. It is a scale variable where 0 means that the respondent believes Quebecers have exactly the same values as other Canadians and 10 means that the respondent believes Quebecers have very distinct values. The other variable is also a scale variable where 0 means that the respondent believes it is better to belong to a larger market even if this means a loss of sovereignty, and a 10 means that he or she prefers sovereignty, even if this means belonging to a smaller market.

The distribution of these variables is interesting. With regard to values, Quebecers are rather split. Slightly more of them believe that they share the same values as other Canadians (44 per cent answered between 0 and 4 on the scale) than those who believe that they do not (40 per cent answered between 6 and 10 on the scale; 12 per cent chose the middle value and 4 per cent refused to answer). Regarding the other question, Quebecers show a clear preference for a larger market, even at the cost of autonomy: 42 per cent of respondents expressed their support for this view (by responding from 0 to 4 on the scale), which contrasts with only 24 per cent who chose the opposite perspective (by responding from 6 to 10 on the scale; 19 per cent chose the median score and 15 per cent refused to respond).

Table 4.9
Change in probabilities for voting models of provincial election in Quebec:
Cost-benefit variables

	PQ	QS	CAQ	PLQ
Age	0.21**	−0.15**	−0.05	0.05
Female	0.01	0.01	−0.06*	0.04*
Language	0.11	0.09*	0.40**	−0.23**
Education	−0.19**	0.10**	−0.08	0.09*
Income	−0.06	−0.01	0.08	−0.01
Left–right	−0.02	−0.17**	0.07	0.08
Moral liberalism	0.04	0.12**	−0.11**	−0.02
Cynicism	−0.11**	0.05	0.15**	−0.09**
Identity	0.37**	−0.06	0.08	−0.14*
AttachQC	0.19**	−0.06	−0.16*	−0.05
AttachCAN	−0.20**	−0.09*	0.08	0.41**
Values	0.04	0.00	−0.02	−0.05
Market	0.22**	0.05	−0.11*	−0.15**
N	1,127	1,127	1,127	1,127

$**p \leq 0.01$; $*p \leq 0.05$ (two-tailed tests).

The effect of these variables in our multivariate vote models is presented in appendix C (table C3) and in table 4.9. The results are clear. The notion that Quebecers' and other Canadians' values are different does not seem to be an important factor dividing partisan groups. Belonging to a larger market, even if it translates into a loss of sovereignty, has a larger impact than perceived common shared values on Quebecers' vote choice. The impact of these variables related to the national question is once again much larger for the parties at the centre of this debate, the PQ and the PLQ, than for more peripheral parties. Preferences are divided along partisan lines. Voters of the PQ opt for more sovereignty, whereas PLQ supporters put more value in belonging to a larger market. The data confirm again that the PQ and the PLQ dominate, for the time being, the debate over the national question and that their electoral support depends on it more so than for Québec Solidaire or the Coalition Avenir Québec.

Constitutional Preferences and Vote Choice

A crucial dimension of the debate over the national question is the parties' constitutional positioning. For the past forty years, two positions

Table 4.10
Change in probabilities for voting models of provincial election in Quebec:
Constitutional preferences

	PQ	*QS*	*CAQ*	*PLQ*
Age	0.19**	−0.16**	−0.06	0.09
Female	0.02	−0.00	−0.07**	0.04
Language	0.11	0.07	0.36**	−0.23**
Education	−0.15**	0.10**	−0.10	0.08
Income	−0.04	−0.01	0.07	−0.03
Left-right	−0.01	−0.19**	0.05	0.07
Moral liberalism	0.02	0.12**	−0.11**	−0.02
Cynicism	−0.10**	0.05	0.14**	−0.09*
Identity	0.23**	−0.06	0.11	−0.07
AttachQC	0.11	−0.04	−0.11	−0.04
AttachCAN	−0.10*	−0.11**	−0.01	0.34**
Values	0.01	0.00	−0.00	−0.02
Market	0.12*	0.06	−0.05	−0.10*
Independence	0.16**	−0.05*	−0.20**	−0.14**
More powers	0.07*	0.04	0.04	−0.08**
N	1,127	1,127	1,127	1,127

**$p ≤ 0.01$; *$p ≤ 0.05$ (two-tailed tests).

have dominated the Quebec scene: remaining within Canada – the federalist option; or acceding to the status of an independent state – the sovereignty option. As stated before in chapter 2, the sovereignist stance is advocated by the Parti Québécois and that of the federalists by the Parti Libéral du Québec. After some intense internal debate, Québec Solidaire decided to join the sovereignist cause, even if this question was not at the centre of its political discourse. The position adopted by the Coalition Avenir Québec is more ambiguous. Until recently, this party expressed the view that the constitutional debate should be left aside and that the focus should be on strengthening the province's political and economic position. Tellingly, in the fall of 2015 this party adopted a more explicit constitutional position that puts forth a series of devolution demands in an effort to expand its electoral base. That said, the party remains in the federalist camp, even if it takes a more nationalist stance than the PLQ does when it comes to defending Quebec's interests and promoting its identity and even if it uses the label "nationalist" rather than "federalist" to describe its position. In this sense, the CAQ's new orientation could be associated with the quest for more powers for Quebec. This middle-of-the-road position has long had support in the province, although many Quebecers have expressed skepticism in the past about the feasibility of devolution since its implementation depends on the federal government's openness to transfer additional powers to their province.

Two variables are introduced into the model to measure the impact of constitutional positions on vote choice: support (or not) for the independence of Quebec and support (or not) for transferring more powers from the federal to the Quebec government (recall tables 4.4 and 4.5). The results for the vote models including these variables are presented in appendix C (table C4) and in table 4.10. Support for independence and for more powers for Quebec contributes to increasing the chances of supporting the PQ. Rejecting the independence option contributes significantly to increasing the chances of supporting the CAQ (by 20 percentage points) and a bit less for the Liberals (14 percentage points). The somewhat superficial way in which QS supports independence can be seen quite clearly. First, this party is the only one for which the left-right dimension is more important than the federalism-sovereignty dimension. In fact, if respondents position themselves on the right, their probability of voting for this party decreases by 19 percentage points. What is more, being supportive of independence does not have a positive, but rather a negative, effect on the probability of voting for this party (a decrease of 5 percentage points). Also, the data show that the PLQ receives support not only from opponents of independence, but also from those who oppose further transfer of powers to the Quebec government. This result suggests that the PLQ is not only a federalist party, but also one in favour of the constitutional status quo.

Two additional results are worth mentioning. First, the most popular position in Quebec – repatriation of more powers – has not been systematically associated with any party in recent decades. For PQ voters, this is a fallback position that is less interesting than that of independence. The Liberal clientele rejects this position. Voters of the CAQ and QS have not seemed strongly attracted to this constitutional option in the past (although see next section). Thus, gaining more powers for Quebec is the most popular position, but also one that has not found a durable and viable political home. Second, constitutional preferences are more strongly linked to support for the PQ and the PLQ than for other parties. This finding underscores the domination of these parties on this issue, along with the relatively superficial nature of QS's support for the sovereignist option.

Table 4.11
Change in probabilities for voting models of provincial election in Quebec:
Salience of the national question

	PQ	*QS*	*CAQ*	*PLQ*
Age	0.19**	−0.15**	−0.07	0.10*
Female	0.02	0.00	−0.06*	0.03
Language	0.12*	0.06	0.31**	−0.20**
Education	−0.16**	0.10**	−0.11*	0.09
Income	−0.03	−0.02	0.05	−0.02
Left-right	−0.00	−0.20**	0.05	0.05
Moral liberalism	0.02	0.11**	−0.12**	−0.01
Cynicism	−0.09*	0.04	0.12**	−0.07*
Identity	0.24**	−0.07	0.07	−0.04
AttachQC	0.09	−0.03	−0.08	−0.06
AttachCAN	−0.11*	−0.11*	0.01	0.30**
Values	0.00	0.00	0.00	−0.02
Market	0.11*	0.07	−0.04	−0.10*
Independence	0.15**	−0.04	−0.17**	−0.15**
More powers	0.07**	0.03	0.04	−0.08**
IMPCONST	0.09*	−0.07**	−0.22**	0.18**
N	1,127	1,127	1,127	1,127

**$p \leq 0.01$; *$p \leq 0.05$ (two-tailed tests).

The Saliency Effect

The saliency effect can be assessed in two ways. The first mechanism is additive and is the most simple. A party that projects a proactive image on a certain issue will receive increased support among voters who view this issue as important. The second mechanism is interactive and stipulates that opinion on an issue will have more weight among people who attach a greater importance to this issue (Bélanger and Meguid 2008).

We first examine the additive effect of voters' priorities on their vote choice. To do this, we add to the preceding model a variable that measures how important a respondent believes a party's constitutional position is to their vote decision. The results of including this variable are shown in appendix C (table C5) and in table 4.11. The results are telling. They allow us to see that the two parties that profit the most from the constitutional cleavage in Quebec are the Parti Libéral du Québec and the Parti Québécois. These are also the two parties that have the most diametrically opposed positions on the constitutional question. Parties that give less importance to the issue, such as Québec Solidaire and especially Coalition Avenir Québec, get significantly less support from voters who view party positions on the national question as being very important.

These findings confirm and nuance the bivariate analyses previously presented. They clearly show that attributing ownership of the national question to the most nationalist parties is far too simple a hypothesis to correspond to reality. In fact, the two parties most radically opposed to each other, the PQ (the most nationalist party in Quebec) and the PLQ (the least nationalist party), both benefit from this issue. The Parti Québécois wins votes because it is sovereignist, but also because voters view it as being the most determined to defend the province's interests and identity. The Parti Libéral du Québec largely profits from the national question because it is perceived as being the best protector of the constitutional status quo.

Thus, the PQ and the Liberals are both protagonists in the constitutional debate. The more heated this debate, the more both parties benefit. If the debate centres more on Quebec's interests or identity, the Parti Québécois will come out on top. However, if the debate is more about Quebec independence, as it was in the 2014 election campaign, then the Parti Libéral du Québec will come out ahead. The other parties excluded from this dynamic must somehow insert themselves into the debate. The leftist party, Québec Solidaire, decided to portray itself as a party favourable to Quebec independence. The Coalition Avenir Québec decided, in a more explicit fashion recently, to take a middle-ground position by claiming to be a nationalist party but not in favour of going so far as independence.

The gains made by the PQ and the PLQ through the constitutional debate show how both parties, for different reasons, benefit from keeping this issue at the top of the agenda. Moreover, some dimensions of the national question are valence, which implies that every party in Quebec should appear sensitive vis-à-vis this issue. The positions adopted by QS and the CAQ reflect a kind of priming effect, whereby each political party in a substate party system where the national question is important is compelled to take a stance on the issue. As seen with our second hypothesis at the outset, we argue that this phenomenon is more obvious for the leftist QS (favourable to independence) than for the rightist CAQ (favourable to federalism). However, the results in table 4.11 bring nuances to this characterization. While it is true that such pressure affects the official positions of the parties (as seen in chapter

2), this same phenomenon cannot be observed among voters who choose a party at the periphery of the national debate, such as Québec Solidaire. The data show, to the contrary, that voters for this party are less interested in the national question (see also table 4.1) and that their support for QS stems from the desire to see the political debate focus on other issues. Thus, a priming effect can be observed at the level of the party leadership, but it has not reached the majority of QS voters.

Another way of examining the effect of constitutional preferences is to see if the link between these preferences and vote choice varies as a function of the importance given to the issue of Quebec's political future. To do this, we added interaction variables that allow us to more precisely study the effect of constitutional preferences as a function of how important survey respondents viewed the issue. For example, the variable IMPCONSTIND allows us to discern the effect of support for Quebec independence on vote choice based on the importance that individuals give to constitutional questions. The variable IMPCONSTPWRS looks at the same effect, but among those who support only a greater devolution of powers to Quebec.

Table 4.12 presents the results for the model including interaction variables (see also table C6 in appendix C). These results are interesting for several reasons. The most revealing finding is that the link between support for sovereignty and support for the PQ is strongest among voters who attach more importance to constitutional issues. This result shows that, for some individuals, support for Quebec sovereignty is a necessary but not sufficient reason to support Quebec's most nationalist party. This result also means that some voters support Quebec sovereignty without seeing it as a priority. These people are less likely to support the PQ and will be more likely to support another party whose positions on other issues are closer to their own. For example, this could be the case for pro-sovereignty voters who choose to support QS (a leftist party) or the CAQ (a rightist party), depending on which issues dominate the campaign. It seems that this dynamic was at work in the 2014 election and that support for the PQ, which was at its lowest level in forty years, was limited to only the most assertive advocates of Quebec independence.

Another interesting result in table 4.12 relates to support for the Coalition Avenir Québec. While the party takes nationalist positions, it is opposed to outright Quebec independence. In the past, this more moderate version of Quebec nationalism was expressed through demands for greater political autonomy. Thus, support for the CAQ can

Table 4.12
Change in probabilities for voting models of provincial election in Quebec:
Interactive variables

	PQ	QS	CAQ	PLQ
Age	0.17**	−0.15**	−0.07	0.10*
Female	0.02	0.00	−0.06*	0.03
Language	0.10	0.06	0.31**	−0.20**
Education	−0.17**	0.10**	−0.10	0.09
Income	−0.03	−0.02	0.06	−0.02
Left-right	0.02	−0.20**	0.04	0.05
Moral liberalism	0.02	0.11**	−0.12**	−0.01
Cynicism	−0.09*	0.04	0.12**	−0.07*
Identity	0.18*	−0.07	0.08	−0.03
AttachQC	0.10	−0.03	−0.08	−0.06
AttachCAN	−0.11*	−0.11**	0.01	0.31**
Values	−0.01	0.00	0.02	−0.02
Market	0.11*	0.07	−0.04	−0.10*
Independence	−0.11*	−0.01	0.01	0.02
More powers	0.08	0.04	−0.06	−0.06
IMPCONST	−0.11	−0.04	−0.23**	0.21**
IMPCONSTIND	0.42**	−0.05	−0.31**	−0.23
IMPCONSTPWRS	−0.01	−0.01	0.16	−0.04
N	1,127	1,127	1,127	1,127

$**p \leq 0.01$; $*p \leq 0.05$ (two-tailed tests).

be seen as both a firm rejection of independence and support for more powers for Quebec within the Canadian federation. The results also show that CAQ voters who attach more importance to the issue of Quebec's future seem to be driven by this dichotomy. The negative coefficient for IMPCONSTIND and the positive coefficient for IMPCONSTPWRS clearly show that separatists are less willing to support the CAQ, but autonomists are more willing to support it.[5] The negative sign for the variable IMPCONSTIND for the Liberal vote is not surprising, although its smaller impact than for the PQ and CAQ voting models likely reflects the massive opposition (almost unanimous in the case of independence) of this party's supporters to constitutional change. Finally, the absence of significant interaction terms for the QS vote model seems to reflect once again the low impact of this issue on support for that party.

The results of this section are clear. The two parties that benefit the most from the constitutional issue are the Parti Libéral du Québec and the Parti Québécois. The Liberals draw their support from individuals who are firmly and almost unanimously opposed to Quebec independence. On the other side, the PQ can count on hard-core separatists. The other parties, the CAQ and QS, struggle to win votes and to make their voices heard in between the two main parties. As a result, the CAQ and QS have developed both similar and different strategies in order to try to break into the electorate, in spite of the national question being so central to the political debate in Quebec. The first element of this strategy – and common to both parties – was to attempt to shift the political debate in Quebec to issues other than the Constitution. For Québec Solidaire, this meant social issues, and for the CAQ it meant economic and fiscal issues. However, since the 2014 election the CAQ has tried another strategy, which is to take on the label of being a nationalist party by speaking out more assertively about defending Quebec's interests and the French language. It remains to be seen whether this nationalist positioning of "more autonomy, but not sovereignty" will allow the CAQ to decisively undermine the PQ-PLQ duopoly and its several decades-old control over the national question in Quebec.

CANADIAN FEDERAL ELECTIONS IN QUEBEC: SAME BATTLE, DIFFERENT BATTLEGROUND

The debate over the national question in Quebec has always weighed significantly on electoral dynamics at the state level. As seen in chapter 1, the Liberal Party of Canada has long taken advantage of this issue by presenting itself as a defender of both Quebec interests and national unity (Dion 1975). However, debates surrounding the unilateral repatriation of the Canadian Constitution in 1982 and the failure of the Meech Lake Accord in the late 1980s changed the situation. In the wake of these events, a sovereignist party on the federal level was created: the Bloc Québécois. This party dominated Quebec's votes in federal elections from 1993 to 2008. Table 1.2 in chapter 1 showed that over this period, the BQ won about 43 per cent of the vote in Quebec (versus 32 per cent for its nearest rival, the LPC). Furthermore, the party has been able to elect a majority of Quebec MPs at each of these elections (it is important to note that, like the Scottish National Party in the UK, the Bloc Québécois does not present candidates anywhere else in Canada).

From this point of view, the 2011 federal election was a resounding failure for the Bloc Québécois. The party's support crumbled to 23 per cent of the Quebec votes, and the BQ was able to secure only four out of a total of seventy-five Quebec seats in the Canadian House of Commons. This defeat was largely due to the charismatic personality of Jack Layton, the New Democratic Party's (since deceased) leader. His popularity allowed his party to soar to a record score for the NDP in Quebec: 43 per cent of the province's votes and fifty-nine MPs from Quebec elected to the federal Parliament (on the 2011 federal election in Quebec, see Fournier et al. 2013; on support for the Bloc since 1993, see Nevitte et al. 2000; Blais et al. 2002; Young and Bélanger 2008; Gidengil et al. 2012).

In this section, we examine the determinants of Quebecers' support for political parties in Canadian federal elections. More specifically, we look at the 2011 election, which pitted four main political parties against each other: the Bloc Québécois, the Liberal Party of Canada, the Conservative Party of Canada, and the New Democratic Party. In other words, in this election a regional separatist party competed against three statewide federal parties. In the previous six elections (1993 through 2008), the Bloc had come to dominate federal elections in Quebec, by not only mobilizing sovereignists but also rallying the nationalist vote under the theme of defending Quebec's interests. The nationalist vote has largely deserted the Liberal Party since the early 1980s, a disaffection that benefited the Conservative Party in the 1984 and 1988 elections. Beginning in 1993, the Bloc Québécois appeared on the scene to snatch up this nationalist vote. However, its string of successes was interrupted in 2011 when the NDP, a party previously seen as centralizing and having few chances in Quebec, shook the Bloc's fortress. The 2015 election confirmed the decline of the BQ. The Liberals secured 36 per cent of the vote in Quebec, NDP support fell to 25 per cent, the Conservative Party held at 17 per cent, and support for the Bloc dropped even further to 19 per cent (Bélanger and Nadeau 2016).[6]

Therefore, we can say that the 2011 election was a break with voting trends in Quebec. Our interest in this particular election is twofold. First, it provides us with the opportunity to study the profile of those most motivated by the national question, that is, the 23 per cent of Quebec voters who remained loyal to the Bloc Québécois. Second, this election could be the sign of a durable realignment of the Quebec electorate at the federal level.

We will first analyze the profiles of BQ loyalists and supporters of the three federalist parties. In this section, the dependent variable used is recalled vote choice. Our data come from an opinion survey we conducted in Quebec in September 2012, a little over a year after the May

Table 4.13

Change in probabilities for voting models of federal election in Quebec:
Sociodemographic and attitudinal variables

	BQ	NDP	LPC	CPC
Age	0.06	−0.18**	0.12**	0.01
Female	−0.06*	0.11**	0.01	−0.03
Language	0.72**	0.05	−0.17**	−0.04
Education	0.11	−0.14*	0.13**	−0.12**
Income	0.01	−0.03	−0.02	0.03
Left-right	−0.46**	−0.02	0.21**	0.33**
Moral liberalism	0.12**	0.01	0.05	−0.15**
Cynicism	0.13**	0.12**	−0.05*	−0.15**
N	1,091	1,091	1,091	1,091

**$p < 0.01$; *$p \leq 0.05$ (two-tailed tests).

2011 federal election.[7] This relative proximity of the survey to the previous election provides relatively reliable data.[8] In addition, this survey contains the same battery of items about the national question that we used in the previous section to study Quebec provincial voting behaviour, and that we will be using in the next chapter to examine voting behaviour in Scotland.[9] We were therefore able to code the variables for the 2012 and 2014 surveys in the exact same way (as detailed in appendix B).

The results of the analyses are presented in tables 4.13 to 4.17 using changes in probabilities and in appendix tables C8 to C12 using regression coefficients. We use the same models as when we studied the 2014 Quebec provincial election in the previous section. For example, table 4.13 presents the results for the long-term variables. The profile of Bloc Québécois voters is clear: its clientele consists mainly of left-leaning francophone voters who are liberal on moral issues and show a cynical attitude towards politics. These features contrast sharply with the moral and economic conservatism of Conservative Party voters. This profile is also different from that of Liberal Party supporters, who are older, less francophone, more conservative, and less cynical about politics than the Bloc partisans. The results also help explain why a certain number of voters defected to the NDP in 2011. The party, which was a novelty in Quebec, captured the support of younger voters, who traditionally voted Bloc. NDP support was also higher among voters who believed that those elected to the federal Parliament were not very sensi-

Table 4.14
Change in probabilities for voting models of federal election in Quebec:
Identity and attachment

	BQ	NDP	LPC	CPC
Age	0.09	−0.21**	0.08*	0.02
Female	−0.04	0.10**	0.00	−0.02
Language	0.29*	0.13**	−0.07**	0.03
Education	0.10*	−0.14*	0.13**	−0.11**
Income	0.03	−0.045	−0.05	0.02
Left-right	−0.13*	−0.12	0.09	0.25**
Moral liberalism	0.02	0.03	0.08*	−0.12**
Cynicism	0.05	0.14**	−0.03	−0.13**
Identity	0.72**	−0.11	−0.13*	−0.08
AttachQC	0.09	0.07	0.02	−0.17**
AttachCAN	−0.14**	0.15*	0.21**	0.08
N	1,091	1,091	1,091	1,091

**$p \leq 0.01$; *$p \leq 0.05$ (two-tailed tests).

tive to their needs. In the past, this group expressed their dissatisfaction by voting for the sovereignist party in state-level elections. Finally, the NDP clientele is the one that displays the greatest ideological proximity to the voters of the BQ. In short, while the Bloc held onto the support of its most loyal partisans in 2011, the party suffered heavy losses among its younger followers, who were more moderate and looking for a new vehicle to express their dissatisfaction with the political dynamic in Quebec.

Table 4.14 presents the results when identification and attachment variables are included. These findings confirm the previous results. Bloc supporters identify more as Quebecer than other voters and also have a weaker attachment to Canada. The reverse pattern can be seen for LPC voters. They are less likely to identify as Quebecer, but are more likely to express an attachment to Canada. Conservative voters are less attached to Quebec and have more positive feelings towards Canada. New Democratic voters, who are mainly francophone, are a bit in-between these two portraits. They are certainly more attached to Canada, but also have positive feelings towards Quebec.[10] It is from this clientele that the NDP managed to pick up voters from the Bloc Québécois.

The other variables in the models presented in tables 4.15 and 4.16 support the preceding interpretations. It is not surprising that Bloc vot-

Table 4.15
Change in probabilities for voting models of federal election in Quebec:
Cost-benefit variables

	BQ	NDP	LPC	CPC
Age	0.09	−0.21**	0.09*	0.01
Female	−0.03	0.10**	−0.00	−0.04*
Language	0.28*	0.13*	−0.07**	0.03
Education	0.11*	−0.14*	0.13**	−0.10*
Income	0.04	−0.04	−0.06	0.00
Left-right	−0.08	−0.12	0.07	0.21**
Moral liberalism	0.01	0.03	0.08*	−0.11**
Cynicism	0.05	0.14**	−0.03	−0.13**
Identity	0.67**	−0.11	−0.12*	−0.03
AttachQC	0.05	0.07	0.03	−0.15**
AttachCAN	−0.07	0.16*	0.18**	−0.01
Values	0.08	−0.02	−0.02	−0.10**
Market	0.11*	0.04	−0.07	−0.15**
N	1,091	1,091	1,091	1,091

**$p \leq 0.01$; *$p \leq 0.05$ (two-tailed tests).

ers are the only ones who are sensitive to the idea that Quebecers' and other Canadians' values are different and that they would rather see their province gain more powers instead of remaining part of a larger economic unit. Supporters of the federalist parties (most notably the Conservatives and Liberals) reject these arguments, but once again NDP voters' mixed views on these issues seem to reflect the gains made by the party at this election among former BQ supporters. However, the most noteworthy findings concern the relationship between constitutional preferences and vote choice (see table 4.16). Unsurprisingly, the data show that BQ voters are more sovereignist, with the reverse being true for LPC and NDP supporters (Conservative voters are opposed to devolving more powers to Quebec). Here, the profile of NDP voters is particularly interesting. Those who vote for this party are certainly opposed to the independence of Quebec, but they are also the most favourable to devolving more powers to Quebec. This double disposition can be seen as the expression of a moderate nationalism, that is to say, a political position marked by an opposition to independence but support for greater constitutional autonomy within the Canadian federation. It is among this moderately nationalist group, which has long supported

Table 4.16
Change in probabilities for voting models of federal election in Quebec: Constitutional options

	BQ	NDP	LPC	CPC
Age	0.08	−0.22**	0.10*	0.03
Female	−0.02	0.09**	−0.01	−0.04*
Language	0.26*	0.07	−0.06**	0.04
Education	0.11*	−0.13*	0.13**	−0.12**
Income	0.04	−0.04	−0.06	0.01
Left-right	−0.07	−0.12	0.06	0.20**
Moral liberalism	0.01	0.03	0.08**	−0.11**
Cynicism	0.05	0.12**	−0.02	−0.12**
Identity	0.63**	−0.12	−0.10	−0.01
AttachQC	0.02	0.07	0.05	−0.13**
AttachCAN	−0.03	0.10	0.12*	−0.04
Values	0.06	−0.02	−0.01	−0.08*
Market	0.07	0.08	−0.05	−0.13**
Independence	0.08*	−0.17**	−0.11**	−0.01
More powers	0.04	0.16**	−0.03	−0.07**
N	1,091	1,091	1,091	1,091

**$p \leq 0.01$; *$p \leq 0.05$ (two-tailed tests).

the Bloc and its defence of Quebec interests, that the NDP made its biggest gains in 2011 (the models including interactive variables support this interpretation overall).

Finally, the data in table 4.17, which presents the models that include the variable measuring the importance given to the national question by respondents, are revealing. First, these findings show that the likelihood of voting for the BQ is greatest among those who attach more importance to this issue. The results also indicate that those who vote for the LPC, traditionally the party most opposed to Quebec independence and increased autonomy for the province, stand out for their interest in this issue. But it is mainly the results for NDP voters that speak for themselves. These results clearly show that the likelihood of supporting this party was significantly greater among those less concerned about the national question in Quebec during the 2011 federal election. Thus, the NDP was able to significantly increase its support by attracting more moderate voters on this issue, or at least those least likely to make it a priority. The NDP in 2011 seems to have been able to succeed on the federal level in the way that the CAQ and Québec Solidaire failed on

Table 4.17
Change in probabilities for voting models of federal election in Quebec:
Salience of the national question

	BQ	NDP	LPC	CPC
Age	0.07	−0.20**	0.09*	0.03
Female	−0.02	0.10**	−0.02	−0.04*
Language	0.25*	0.08	−0.07**	0.04
Education	0.11*	−0.15*	0.13**	−0.11**
Income	0.04	−0.04	−0.06	0.01
Left-right	−0.06	−0.12	0.05	0.20**
Moral liberalism	0.01	0.04	0.08*	−0.11**
Cynicism	0.05	0.12**	−0.02	−0.12**
Identity	0.63**	−0.14	−0.10	−0.01
AttachQC	−0.00	0.11	0.05	−0.13**
AttachCAN	−0.03	0.12	0.10	−0.04
Values	0.05	−0.00	−0.00	−0.08*
Market	0.06	0.09	−0.05	−0.13**
Independence	0.08*	−0.15**	−0.12**	−0.01
More powers	0.04	0.15**	−0.02	−0.07**
IMPCONST	0.06	−0.21**	0.06	0.02
N	1,091	1,091	1,091	1,091

**$p \leq 0.01$; *$p \leq 0.05$ (two-tailed tests).

the provincial level, that is to say, in channelling the support of moderate nationalists.[11]

The national question as a whole does not contribute as much to an explanation of federal vote choice as was observed for provincial elections in the previous section (third hypothesis). Indeed, the increase in the value of the pseudo-R^2 when the blocs of variables relating to the national question are added to the vote models is smaller for federal elections: +0.24 for the BQ (compared to +0.34 for the PQ in substate elections) and +0.11 for the LPC (compared to +0.27 for the PLQ in substate elections), with no real cross-level difference for the other political parties (which are difficult to compare across levels anyway since they are very different parties). On average, the increase in the proportion of explained variance that is observed with the inclusion of the national question variables is nearly 1.5 times greater for provincial elections compared with federal ones.

The results of this section have clearly highlighted the very distinctive profile of Bloc voters in the 2011 federal election. This profile is generally similar to that of the Parti Québécois voters in substate elections. This is not surprising – not only because of the constitutional preferences of their supporters, but also because of the parties' similar levels of support in 2011 (23 per cent for the BQ) and 2014 (25 per cent for the PQ). This analysis of voter characteristics for these sovereignist parties helps us to understand the various parties' positioning on the national question in Quebec that we examined back in chapter 2.

But this section's findings also provided some insight into the federalist parties' struggle to capture the support of a segment of the Quebec electorate that has nationalist sensibilities, but is opposed to independence. This group of voters, long faithful to the Bloc Québécois on the federal scene, decided to support the NDP in 2011. Similarly, at the substate level the rise of the CAQ, a party claiming to be in the autonomist tradition in Quebec, contributed to limit the PQ's victory in 2012 and accentuate its defeat in 2014. The issue of the national question has long shaped Quebec politics, both on the provincial scene and in state-level elections. If the impact of the national question remains uncertain in the immediate future for federal elections, it is reasonable to believe that it will continue to be central to Quebec substate elections in the foreseeable future.

SUPPORT FOR CONSTITUTIONAL OPTIONS

We have thus far analyzed the determinants of support for political parties in Quebec with particular attention to the national question. However, we have seen that constitutional preferences play an important role among these vote choice determinants. Therefore, it is necessary to complete the analysis of the role of the national question on Quebecers' political choices by examining whether the variables that significantly influence their voting behaviour have a similar effect on preferences about the constitutional future of Quebec.

Tables 4.18 and 4.19 (appendix tables C13 and C14) present results from analyses of support (in 2014) for the two options of Quebec independence or greater constitutional autonomy within the Canadian federation. In each case, the dependent variable takes the value of 1 if the respondent stated his or her intention to support these options if referendums were to be held on these issues, and 0 otherwise (nonresponses were excluded from the analysis). The models used to explain these choices are the same as those used previously. The first bloc of factors in these models includes long-term variables, to which are succes-

Table 4.18
Change in probabilities for regression models of support for Quebec independence

	(1)	(2)	(3)	(4)
Age	0.08	−0.01	−0.00	−0.00
Female	−0.09**	−0.04*	−0.03	−0.03*
Language	0.42**	−0.02	−0.05	−0.05
Education	−0.07	−0.14**	−0.13**	−0.12**
Income	−0.09	−0.01	−0.00	0.00
Left-right	−0.51**	−0.09*	−0.06	−0.06
Moral liberalism	0.15**	0.05	0.03	0.04
Cynicism	−0.01	−0.02	−0.03	−0.02
Identity	–	0.45**	0.38**	0.39**
AttachQC	–	0.37**	0.27**	0.24**
AttachCAN	–	−0.43**	−0.29**	−0.29**
Values	–	–	0.06	0.05
Market	–	–	0.35**	0.33**
IMPCONST	–	–	–	0.09**
N	1,323	1,323	1,323	1,323

**$p \leq 0.01$; *$p \leq 0.05$ (two-tailed tests).

sively added indicators measuring the respondents' identity and degree of attachment to Quebec and Canada, their cost-benefit considerations about distinct values and economic integration, and the importance that they give to the national question.

The data in table 4.18 allow us to draw a portrait of the supporters of the constitutional option – namely, the province's accession to the status of a sovereign state – that has been at the heart of the political debate in Quebec for several decades. Here, the very distinctive profile of independence supporters comes to the fore. A typical supporter of independence is male, francophone, liberal on moral issues, and positioned to the left of the political spectrum (see column 1). These voters primarily define themselves as Quebecers and express a much stronger attachment to Quebec than to Canada (column 2). A perception that Quebecers have different values, but above all, a preference for greater political autonomy over remaining within a larger economic market also weigh significantly on the likelihood to support Quebec independence (column 3). Finally, and unsurprisingly, partisans of independence attach a lot of importance to constitutional questions (column 4).

Table 4.19
Change in probabilities for regression models of support for more powers
for Quebec

	(1)	(2)	(3)	(4)
Age	0.31**	0.27**	0.27**	0.27**
Female	−0.06	−0.03	−0.02	−0.02
Language	0.38**	0.10**	0.09**	0.09**
Education	0.05	0.03	0.01	0.00
Income	−0.10	−0.05	−0.04	−0.04
Left-right	−0.35**	−0.09	−0.05	−0.05
Moral liberalism	0.19**	0.12**	0.11**	0.11**
Cynicism	0.05	0.05	0.05	0.05
Identity	–	0.41**	0.35**	0.34**
AttachQC	–	0.22**	0.16**	0.17**
AttachCAN	–	−0.32**	−0.20**	−0.20**
Values	–	–	0.17**	0.17**
Market	–	–	0.14**	0.14**
IMPCONST	–	–	–	−0.01
N	1,323	1,323	1,323	1,323

$**p \leq 0.01$; $*p \leq 0.05$ (two-tailed tests).

The results in table 4.19 examine the support for a less radical option, that of transferring more federal powers to Quebec. The autonomist (or devolutionist) profile resembles that of the pro-independence, but with some notable differences. The autonomist option is supported by men, francophones, and those with leftist values (column 1), although the latter trait is less pronounced in this group than among the sovereignists. The most notable difference between the two groups is the age of the supporters. Proponents of greater constitutional autonomy for Quebec are significantly older than those supporting political independence. That support for sovereignty is not more pronounced among young voters is in itself a revealing finding, since this group in the past has tended to support the idea of an independent Quebec in greater numbers (Blais and Nadeau 1984b; Pinard 2002).

The results also highlight some other interesting similarities and differences between sovereignists and autonomists. Both groups report a strong sense of identification and attachment to Quebec (see column 2 of tables 4.18 and 4.19). However, autonomists seem more sensitive than sovereignists to the differences in values between Quebecers and other Canadians, and somewhat less concerned by the debate on the relative merits of political sovereignty versus economic integration (see columns 3 of tables 4.18 and 4.19). Finally, it is revealing that the variable measuring the importance given to constitutional issues is not tied to support for transferring more powers to Quebec. This means that for many autonomists, devolution is desirable but not a priority (see column 4 of tables 4.18 and 4.19).[12]

The results highlight interesting differences in how preferences for various constitutional options relate to support for political parties in Quebec. This link in and of itself is not surprising, given the differing levels of support for devolution (64 per cent), sovereignty (36 per cent), and the Parti Québécois (25 per cent) during the 2014 Quebec provincial election. That said, it is clear from the results that those who support devolution are older, more moderate, and less concerned with the national question than sovereignists are. They are also more sensitive to perceived differences in values between Quebecers and other Canadians. Supporters of the PQ are also older and more moderate than pro-sovereignty individuals. They attach as much importance to the national question as sovereignists do, but the variables directly related to constitutional options (attachment, values, and political independence vs. economic integration) have less impact on their decision to actually vote for the PQ than on their predisposition to support that party's constitutional option.

These findings paint a rich picture of the impact of the national question on Quebecers' political choices. The profile of the typical PQ voter compared with that of a sovereignist shows that, as previously observed in chapter 2, this party has tried to maximize its support by rallying moderate nationalists. For example, no less than a quarter of PQ voters were opposed to Quebec independence in the 2014 election (see table 4.5). This proportion could become even higher as support for this party increases. During an election, the PQ must mobilize an inner core of sovereignty activists and sympathizers while attracting moderate nationalists who will support the party because it is perceived to be most capable of defending Quebec's language and culture. Simply put, the PQ's strategy is to form a winning electoral coalition by combining a high proportion of separatists with moderate nationalists. Therefore, it is not surprising that the profile of the typical PQ voter is different from that of the typical sovereignty supporter.

The difficulty for the PQ is to arrive at a balanced policy position that will appeal to voters with different positions on the national question.

This balancing act is less of a challenge for other parties such as the Parti Libéral du Québec, whose voters are almost unanimously opposed to Quebec independence (97 per cent) and massively opposed to devolution (75 per cent). Of course, the PLQ must also seek out a certain number of francophone voters with nationalist tendencies. But reaching for some kind of policy compromise to appeal to these target voters is less risky for the PLQ than it is for the PQ since the Liberals represent the party with the clearest and most unequivocal federalist position on the constitutional dimension in Quebec. In that sense, the PLQ's support base is more "captive" of its party than it is in the case of the PQ.[13]

The Parti Québécois is not alone in facing this challenge; the other Quebec political parties, Coalition Avenir Québec and Québec Solidaire, must also deal with the problem of voters in their ranks having different positions on the national question. Just over half of QS voters are in favour of sovereignty (52 per cent), and four out of five QS supporters (80 per cent) approve of more powers for Quebec. Thus, the party must take a political stance on constitutional issues that allows it to maintain its cohesion and eventually enlarge its support base, even if the primary motivation of the party is not the national question. Québec Solidaire's support for political independence is part of this logic. While the issue is not central for the party, its stance is enough to satisfy its more nationalist wing. Moreover, this positioning allows QS to appeal to left-leaning PQ voters.

The Coalition Avenir Québec must also deal with the need to find a balance between its more nationalist supporters (18 per cent of them are in favour of independence, and 57 per cent support more powers for Quebec) and the high proportion of federalists in its ranks. In positioning itself on the national question, the CAQ, like its competitors, is trying to simultaneously appease its base while attracting new voters. To do so, Québec Solidaire has chosen to support Quebec sovereignty, whereas the CAQ presents itself as a resolutely nationalist party.

This section has shown that support for political parties in Quebec depends largely, but not exclusively, on these parties' positions on the national question. For example, half of QS voters and a quarter of PQ voters are opposed to sovereignty, while about one in five CAQ supporters are favourable. The coexistence of these trends within each of the parties explains why the profile of various electoral clienteles in Quebec is not as typical as that of someone supporting a radical option such as Quebec independence. It also explains why the political game in Quebec mostly consists of finding a position on the national question that allows each party to mobilize its electoral base while attracting new voters.

A few remarks are in order regarding the profile of those who support devolution, which is the modal preference in Quebec. Three features characterize these supporters. They are older, less interested in the constitutional question, and sensitive to the possible differences between the values of Quebecers and other Canadians. These characteristics highlight certain features of Quebec *autonomisme*. This policy stance has been part of Quebec's political landscape for a long time. It is perceived as a moderate compromise between the status quo and sovereignty, by virtue of its claim that Quebec should have special powers in order to take into account its uniqueness in the Canadian federation. The attractiveness of this option for older and more moderate individuals who are sensitive to the distinctiveness of Quebec's values seems understandable. However, the vagueness of the autonomist option, and the poor mobilization so far around this political goal – which is seen as desirable but perhaps neither a feasible policy nor a priority – probably explain its smaller impact on political dynamics in Quebec.

A final result, which is related to the relationship between respondent age and support for sovereignty and the PQ, deserves some comment. Historically, support for the PQ and for sovereignty has been highest among younger voters (Blais and Nadeau 1984a, 1984b; Martin and Nadeau 2002; Piroth 2004), and the lack of any relationship between this variable and support for sovereignty in table 4.18 is revealing. Even more telling is that in 2014 the PQ drew its support from older voters, as seen in table 4.7. These two developments seem to indicate a certain disconnect between Quebec's youth and the independence project; however, it is too early to conclude that Quebec sovereignty is a fading project of the baby-boomer generation (Mahéo and Bélanger, forthcoming). Similar arguments were made after the 1980 referendum, then came the overwhelming support among youth for the Yes option in the second referendum held fifteen years later. In the past, support for Quebec independence has followed a cyclical pattern, especially among young people (Pinard 2002; Richez and Bodet 2012). Therefore, only the future can tell if the current drop in support for sovereignty among young voters is the sign of an enduring decline or just a temporary low point that could be followed by a significant resurgence. If this decline proves to be enduring and future generations of voters become less and less attracted to the PQ and its constitutional option, then the impact of the national question on Quebec's electoral politics will progressively diminish, or transform itself. Such a change would likely lead, in the end, to some kind of reconfiguration of the Quebec party system.

CONCLUSION

In this chapter, we have focused on the impact of the national question on support for the main political parties competing in Quebec. On this issue, we have discerned three dimensions: the parties' defence of Quebec's interests, affirmation of Quebec's identity, and constitutional preferences. We have concluded that there is a large consensus within the province over the first two dimensions. This consensus reflects the nationalist sensibilities of the province, thereby giving a valence issue character to these dimensions of the national question. However, constitutional options, and particularly the opposition between federalists and sovereignists, polarize Quebec voters. Unlike the first two dimensions, this aspect of the national question has the typical characteristics of a positional issue in the electorate.

Our theoretical framework led us to formulate six hypotheses. The last three directly relate to the notion of issue ownership and the idea that the national question is a multifaceted issue. Contrary to what might be commonly believed, we hypothesize that the national question does not necessarily belong to the most nationalist party in the substate unit of a state. We argue that the more consensual aspects of this question will indeed be dominated by the most nationalist party, but that the more adversarial aspects (such as seeking political independence) can also benefit the party that opposes these stances with the most vigour, to the extent that its position is congruent with the majority opinion and that it is the only party occupying that position.

The data show that this characterization adequately describes Quebec's electoral dynamics. The issue of the national question is dominated both by the most nationalist party, the Parti Québécois, which seems the most determined and able to defend Quebec's interests, and by the least nationalist party, the Parti Libéral du Québec, which represents the main opposition to the sovereignist project. Both parties have benefited from the national question being at the centre of the political debate for the past few decades.

The key position occupied by the PQ and the PLQ is explained by the importance of the national question in Quebec. Here, the national question is a "super issue" that supersedes all other cleavages in the province, including left and right. In fact, the only party in Quebec able to distinguish itself on the left-right issue is Québec Solidaire, a relatively small leftist party. In this context, and in accordance with our first hypothesis, the national question is clearly the dominant cleavage in Quebec. By contrast, the left-right division represents an almost niche issue.

As expected from our second hypothesis, the central role that the national question occupies in Quebec forces parties to adopt a stance regarding this question, while taking into account public opinion. Two parties are directly involved in the debate. The PQ focuses on Quebecers' nationalist sensibilities in order to maximize its votes, and the PLQ uses voters' federalist inclinations to build winning electoral coalitions. Any other party must find a way to insert itself into the debate if it wants to remain relevant. "Outsider" parties that are faced with such a dominant issue basically have two options. The first one, exemplified by Québec Solidaire, is to officially take a side in the debate – in this case, supporting independence – while priming other issues along the left-right spectrum. The second option is to take a middle-ground position or, at least for a short period of time, offer voters a kind of truce in the debate in order to focus on other issues. This was the strategy initially pursued by the Coalition Avenir Québec, whose clientele has a nationalist but nonsovereignist profile. At the time of its creation, the party wanted the national question to be put aside so that the province could work on consolidating its finances and jumpstarting its economy. This nationalist position had a fair share of ambiguity built into it. It reflected the need for all parties in Quebec to take a position on the national question, under threat of being perceived by the public as not being sensitive enough to Quebec's aspirations – even if this positioning was superficial, as in the case of QS, or ambiguous, as in the case of the CAQ. The CAQ's adoption of a more assertive nationalist position in the fall of 2015 and Québec Solidaire's 2017 plan of merging with the small independentist Option Nationale party are indicative of the pressure that the national debate puts on political parties in substate systems where this issue is dominant.

In this chapter, we also examined the determinants of Quebecers' support for political parties in federal elections, along with the factors linked to supporting the two most prominent constitutional options in Quebec: political independence and the devolution of some federal powers to the Quebec National Assembly (sometimes called *autonomisme*). We were able to show that the national question also played an important role in Quebecers' voting behaviour in state-level elections, particularly since the Bloc Québécois' breakthrough in 1993. However, our results also indicated that the national question has less of an impact on Quebecers' voting decisions in federal elections as opposed to provincial ones, at least in the current period (third hypothesis). In particular, the significant setback suffered by the BQ in the 2011 federal election suggests that this issue might occupy less space in the political debate at the state level over the coming years.

Looking at the factors underlying support for different constitutional options has led to some interesting observations. We were able to see that the factors behind support for (as well as opposition to) independence overlapped to a large extent with those that differentiate the electoral clientele of Quebec's provincial political parties. That said, the profile of these various electoral clienteles remains less "typified" than the profile of those who support various constitutional options. This result highlights the heterogeneity of the parties' supporters, where voters with different sensibilities regarding the national question cohabitate. This combination motivates parties to adopt a position on the national question that allows them to maintain cohesion among their current supporters while attracting those from competitor parties.

On the basis of these Quebec findings, it seems clear that the question of autonomist demands in substate national entities cannot be reduced to the simple category of "niche issues." On the contrary, this question is a mainstream issue in Quebec whose influence on the electoral dynamics is complex. Unravelling this complexity is useful and important for better understanding Quebec politics. Furthermore, the analysis presented in this chapter can be extended beyond the borders of Quebec and applied to other substate nations, like we do for Scotland in the next chapter.

5

Voter Behaviour in Scotland

It is often claimed that Scottish voters are different from voters in the rest of the United Kingdom. These are in fact two different but related claims. The first is that Scottish partisan preferences are different from partisan preferences in the rest of the UK. Scots, it is argued, back parties who better express a sense of being able to stand up for Scotland's interests (see, for example, Brown, McCrone, and Paterson 1996; Brown et al. 1999). In this case, "Scotland's interests" are assumed to be distinct from the interests of the other constituent parts of the UK. This relates to the second claim about difference, namely that Scottish values are distinct, and therefore these values, and the demographic context in which Scottish policy is created, further distance the Scottish electorate from the wider electorate in the UK.[1] Central to both claims is a belief in the distinctiveness of the Scottish polity.

Less explored, however, is whether this is a difference of outcome or process. Put simply, when Scots make their voting decisions, are different factors relevant – in other words, is there evidence of a distinctively Scottish decision-making calculus on the part of Scottish voters? If different things mattered to Scottish voters, then this difference would be construed as one of process. The alternative is a difference of outcome: the Scottish decision-making process might be the same – the same things matter to Scots as matter to Welsh and English voters – but these priorities lead them to back different parties. A voter with one set of values in England might vote for the Labour party, whereas the same person in Scotland might well support the Scottish National Party.

This chapter focuses on the decision-making calculus of Scottish voters, and more specifically on identifying the role that the "national question" plays within it. The first research question concerns the centrality of this issue in Scotland's electoral politics. Is the national question in Scotland a niche issue for one party or an issue of larger significance, perhaps even a "super issue" as in Quebec, that serves to structure party competition in Scotland? Certainly, we would expect that national identity and constitutional preferences might explain support for the Scottish National Party, but equally worth knowing is whether British identity or preferences for the constitutional status quo exert an influence on support for other parties and, if so, other parties equally. If the national question is found to be of central importance, it would certainly offer one piece of evidence in favour of a "different process" interpretation of Scottish voters' distinctiveness. Another key question concerns the multidimensionality of this issue. Is it also true for Scotland that the national issue has both valence (i.e., the defence of Scotland's interests and identity) and positional (the decision for Scotland to remain or not within the UK) characteristics?

How the positional axes on the left-right divide and the national question interact with voter preferences can be seen in both UK and Scottish elections. In UK general elections, for example, the first-past-the-post electoral system typically produces majority governments and so the capacity of smaller parties to play decisive roles in coalitions is minimized. This is one constraining effect on SNP support in UK elections. The other has been a general desire to keep the Conservative Party out of government because it was deemed to be "bad" for Scotland, and so voters who might under other circumstances have voted SNP voted for the other party best likely to defeat the Conservatives, whether Labour or the Liberal Democrats (see, for example, Carman and Johns 2010). This antipathy towards the Conservative Party stems from the fact that it is perceived to be out of step with Scottish values on both the left-right axis and majority constitutional preferences. Both, in a way, are tied to the national question, for one relates explicitly to constitutional arrangements for the polity and another to its perceived "national" values. Voters who in other polities might consider themselves to be right-wing believe themselves in Scotland to be left-wing, not because the median voter is to the right and therefore those in the centre are in fact on the left of the spectrum in the polity, but because voters perceive themselves to be more left-wing than they are and therefore rule out voting for a right-wing party (Wyn Jones, Lodge, Henderson et al. 2012; Wyn Jones, Lodge, Jeffery et al. 2013).

With the advent of devolution we see three changes. First, the use of the Additional Member System means that smaller parties have the capacity to influence coalition governments. Second, the territorial frame of government made voting for a party competing for seats only in Scotland a more viable option. Third, coincident with the arrival of devolution is a repositioning of the Labour Party under New Labour towards the centre of the political spectrum, which left the SNP to the left of new Labour (see chapter 1). This is not a static position, and we know that the SNP itself has shifted from the right to the left over time. Therefore, just as the axis of constitutional preferences has been more or less crowded at different times, the same can be said of the left-right spectrum, which has been arguably less crowded on the left than it once was. As a result we can see how these two axes have come to dominate the political debate in Scotland at different times. In particular, the constitutional issue rises and falls in salience, so that while the SNP always portrays itself as a pro-independence party, it sometimes also stresses its social-democratic credentials, positioning itself to the left of Labour and the Liberal Democrats (see chapter 1).

The fact, revealed by chapter 3, that the only remaining cleavage on the valence dimensions opposes a party with relatively limited support in Scotland, the Conservatives, to all the other parties (including the Greens and the Scottish Socialist Party) is telling. It signals that there is a broad agreement in Scotland about the desirability to extend the powers of the region's government. Scottish parties broadly agree on this goal but differ in their commitment about it. The party positionings on the issue of Scotland's independence are revealing as well. Here, the split pits a dominant party, the SNP, against the other three major parties (see chapter 3). This binary opposition suggests another cleavage between parties with more radical and moderate positions on the constitutional future of Scotland. The "radical" parties, the SNP and the Conservatives, should benefit from a rise of the independence issue on the political agenda because this question ranks high among their supporters' motivations. Such is not the case for the more moderate parties, Labour and the Liberal Democrats, whose supporters appear more inclined to cast their votes based on social and economic issues.

These remarks about the role of the national question in Scotland allow us to suggest some hypotheses that will be tested using data from an online survey that we carried out in Scotland in September 2012, a little over a year after the devolved election of 5 May 2011 during which the SNP secured 45 per cent of the constituency vote and was able to form afterwards a single-party majority government. This opinion survey was administered to 1,503 adult residents of Scotland by

UK-based polling firm Research Interactive (in collaboration with Quebec's Léger Marketing) through web-based interviews between 12 September 2012 and 25 September 2012. Survey respondents were recruited from Research Interactive's online panel of UK households.[2] The list of all the survey items used and information on how the answers were coded into variables are presented in appendix table B2. The hypotheses are as follows:

1 Given its importance in Scotland, the national question dominates over all other cleavages, including the traditional left-right one.
2 The priming of the national question by the party (SNP) dominating this issue, and the valence nature of some of its dimensions, exert pressure on each party to take a side in this debate. This phenomenon is more marked in Scotland on the left and should be more visible for the Labour Party than for the LibDems.
3 The national question has a greater impact on substate vote choice (devolved elections) than on state-level vote choice (general elections).
4 The most nationalist party in Scotland, the SNP, is perceived as being more adept at defending Scotland's interests and culture. This advantage arises because the majority of the Scottish population has nationalist sensibilities.
5 The party most favourable to Scotland's independence, the SNP, will dominate the constitutional preference dimension of the national question. This advantage arises not because the majority of the population agrees with this option but because opponents divide their support among three major political parties.
6 Support for parties with more radical views on the national question, the SNP and the Conservatives, is linked to this issue more than is the case for the moderate parties, Labour and the LibDems. Thus, support for the SNP and the Conservatives is more closely tied to (a) the importance voters themselves give to the national question, (b) their feelings of attachment and identification towards Scotland and the UK, (c) their evaluations of the costs and benefits of the various constitutional options, and (d) their own constitutional preferences.

As in the previous chapter, it is important to note here that the first three hypotheses relate to the idea of the national question being a mainstream issue (as opposed to a niche issue) in substate politics, and

Table 5.1
Level of attachment to Scotland and the UK (%)

	Scotland	UK
Very	60	33
Somewhat	32	43
Not very	6	18
Not at all	2	5

Question: Would you say that you are very attached, somewhat attached, not very attached, or not attached at all to Scotland? UK?

that the last three hypotheses allow us to test expectations about issue ownership effects and the multidimensionality of the national question as an electoral issue.[3]

SCOTTISH VOTERS AND THE NATIONAL QUESTION

For our study of voter behaviour in Scotland, we operationalize the national question as we did for Quebec in chapter 4 by analyzing three elements: national interests, national identity, and constitutional preferences. National interests include the perception that the polity as a whole has values and interests that are distinct from those in other parts of the state. As was previously noted, a second dimension of the national question has to do with promoting the specific identity of a particular region. National identity thus includes embracing separate identities for Scotland and the UK as well as deliberatively comparative identities (more Scottish than British, equally Scottish and British). Our third dimension relates to preferences regarding constitutional arrangements for the UK. Attitudes here may be located along a spectrum running from the status quo to full independence for Scotland, with various interim options in between such as enhanced fiscal autonomy, devolution max, or full fiscal autonomy.

We start our descriptive analysis of Scottish opinion survey data with our classic valence issue, namely, national identity. The results in table 5.1 show the strength of attachment to Scotland and the United Kingdom, with more than nine out of ten respondents either somewhat or very attached to Scotland. This drops, slightly, to three out of four voters somewhat or very attached to the UK, but it is at the poles of the scale where we see variation. Sixty per cent of those in our sample said they were very attached to Scotland, whereas just a third of them felt the

Table 5.2
Attachment to Scotland and the UK by party identification (%)

	SNP	Labour	LibDem	Cons
Very attached to Scotland	75	59	64	43
Very attached to the UK	16	39	61	66

Question: Would you say that you are very attached, somewhat attached, not very attached, or not attached at all to Scotland? UK?

Table 5.3
Importance attached to various issues in the 2011 election in Scotland (%)

	All	SNP	Labour	LibDem	Cons
Party defends Scotland's interests	87	98	89	84	80
Party understands Scotland's history and culture	80	95	76	81	67
Party constitutional position	83	89	85	82	87

Question: How important are the following questions in your decision to vote for this party in the 2011 election in Scotland?

same about the UK. In general we see a more even, or a less skewed, distribution of attachment to the UK. Such results mirror what we have long seen in Canada. Quebecers have not necessarily displayed higher than average attachment to their own province when compared with other Canadians, but have shown significantly less attachment to Canada (Mendelsohn 2002; see also chapter 4).

The results in table 5.2 show variations in levels of attachment according to partisan identification, and we see here that no group of supporters displays a profile similar to what was observed above for Scotland taken as a whole. Labour supporters come the closest, with approximately 60 per cent of them very attached to Scotland, but a greater proportion are very attached to the UK than is true for Scotland as a whole. The Liberal Democrats appear very attached to Scotland and the UK in roughly equal proportions. Predictably, the SNP sees the greatest gap between the proportion attached to Scotland and the proportion attached to the UK. The Conservatives, by contrast, are the only partisan group where a greater proportion is very attached to the UK.

We asked respondents to indicate how important the following issues were to their voting decision in devolved elections: the ability of

Table 5.4
Opinions about Scottish independence, by 2011 vote (%)

	All	SNP	Labour	LibDem	Cons
Favourable	37	71	17	7	6
Opposed	63	29	83	93	94

Question: If there were a referendum on independence that asked whether Scotland should be an independent country, would you vote YES or NO?

parties to defend the interests of Scotland; the capacity of the party to understand the history and culture of Scotland; and the constitutional preferences of the party. The results in table 5.3 show that more than 80 per cent of Scots believe each of these features to be important. Perhaps most interesting is the variation across supporters of different parties. The results also indicate that an overwhelming majority of respondents believe that a ballot cast for a Scottish party rests on its positioning on these various dimensions of the national question. Over four-fifths in each case believe that the party's ability to defend Scotland's interests, the party's understanding of history and culture, and its constitutional preferences are important determinants of vote choice. The lowest figures are observed for the party's understanding of Scotland's history and culture, but even two-thirds of Conservative supporters indicate that this dimension is important to their vote decision. Perhaps predictably, the constitutional preferences of parties appear more important for SNP and Conservative voters – the two parties that stand at the extremities of the spatial distribution of constitutional preferences – than for the two parties in the middle.

We can see the legacies of this link between the national question and voting decision when we look at how attitudes to the Constitution, one of the areas where the Scottish electorate shows itself to be distinct, and partisan identification correlate in table 5.4. On the issue of independence, we see clear variation, with supporters of the three parties that would later form part of the Better Together referendum campaign demonstrating majority support for constitutional options other than independence (over 90 per cent on the part of Conservative and LibDem identifiers, and 83 per cent on the part of Labour). Among SNP supporters, however, there is majority support for independence (71 per cent).

We see a predictably different pattern when we look at support for the idea of transferring more powers to the Scottish Parliament. In table

Table 5.5
Opinions about transferring more powers to the Scottish Parliament,
by 2011 vote (%)

	All	SNP	Labour	LibDem	Cons
Favourable	67	89	53	55	32
Opposed	33	11	47	45	68

Question: How would you vote in a referendum that asked whether the Scottish Parliament should
have much more powers, an option often described as "devolution max" or simply "devo max"; would
you vote YES or NO?

5.5, we see clear opposition among Conservative voters, overwhelming
support among the SNP, and sharp division among Labour and Liberal Democrat supporters. What this suggests is that constitutional preferences themselves serve as positional issues while there is greater consensus on national identity. These results provide a preliminary
confirmation of the notion that the national question is multidimensional, composed of both valence and positional issues. The results also
help explain in good part the various positions taken by the Scottish
parties that we analyzed back in chapter 3, with perhaps the nuance
that the relative consensus observed among parties on the question of
more constitutional autonomy is not as well reflected in the opinion
data as we might have expected, with greater partisan variation found
in Scots' views regarding the transfer of more powers to Scotland.

We also asked respondents which party they thought was best able to
perform certain roles. Each question formulated how a party might act
in the best interests of Scotland to defend Scottish identity and culture;
stand up for Scotland's interests, including at Westminster; improve education; and manage the economy or fight poverty. As Clarke et al.
(2011, 244) note, "Judgements about which party is best able to handle
a particular issue is what gives that issue its political clout."

The findings presented in table 5.6 confirm our fourth hypothesis.
The most nationalist party, in this case the SNP, benefits across the valence dimensions of the national question. It is perceived to be the party
best able to stand up for Scotland, particularly with respect to identity
and culture. Interestingly, this domination is less pronounced when it
comes to standing up to Westminster; on this role, Labour and the Conservative Party have a relatively positive image. A key result is the relatively strong showing of the SNP at managing the economy. All in all,
the results show that the SNP's recent electoral strength derives from

Table 5.6
Party images in Scotland (%)

Best party:	SNP	Labour	LibDem	Cons
To defend Scotland's identity and culture	52	11	3	5
To stand up for Scotland's interests	42	17	4	7
To stand up to Westminster	28	19	3	13
To manage the economy	27	16	3	9
To improve education	27	17	3	9
To fight poverty	22	21	4	4

Question: Which party is best able to handle the following issues?

its ability to present itself both as the most "Scottish" party and as a competent manager of the economy.

Unsurprisingly, Labour does better on the issue of fighting poverty.[4] That party also receives relatively good evaluations when it comes to the economy, education, and standing up to Westminster. The results suggest that Labour's positioning appears as a mix of soft nationalism and traditional left-right politics. This explains why Labour does well in Scotland when the circumstances are right (good economic performance when it is in power or bad economic conditions when it is in the opposition, national question lower on the political agenda, etc.). For its part, the Conservative Party is not the worst performer on many of these competence measures, despite the common perception that voters find it out of touch on both "Scottish" values and majority constitutional preferences. While the Conservatives are clearly not perceived to perform best on these valence issues, it is actually the Liberal Democrats who fare worst, and the gap between these two parties varies. Indeed, while there is less than a 3 percentage point gap between the two on standing up for Scotland's interests, defending its identity and culture, or fighting poverty, three times as many believe the Conservative Party is better able to manage the economy and improve education, and four times as many perceive it as the better party to deal with Westminster. By these measures at least, it is the Liberal Democrats rather than the Conservative Party that appear to be the sick man of Scottish politics, a situation that might be partly attributable to disenchantment (at the time of our data collection in 2012) with the UK coalition government that the LibDems and their then-leader Nick Clegg joined in the aftermath of the 2010 general election.

In the next section, multivariate analyses of support for the four largest political parties in Scotland will allow to test more rigorously and thoroughly our hypotheses about the influence of the national question on the vote decision in Scotland. These analyses will allow to establish if this issue is, like in Quebec, a "super issue" surpassing any other political cleavage including the left-right divide.

A MULTIVARIATE ANALYSIS OF SUPPORT FOR SCOTTISH POLITICAL PARTIES

We continue our study of the impact of the national question on voting behaviour by looking at the determinants of vote choice for elections to the Scottish Parliament. To do this, we examine the explanatory factors behind the support for the four main political parties in Scotland: the Scottish National Party, the Scottish Labour Party, the Scottish Conservative and Unionist Party, and the Scottish Liberal Democrats. These four parties respectively won 45 per cent, 32 per cent, 14 per cent, and 8 per cent of the constituency vote in the 5 May 2011 election. In the end, the SNP won a majority of seats in the Scottish Parliament (i.e., sixty-nine seats), followed by Labour (thirty-seven), the Conservatives (fifteen), and the LibDems (five).

As in the preceding chapter, the dependent variable takes a value of 1 when a survey respondent reports having voted for a given party, and 0 otherwise (nonresponses are excluded).[5] We consider the constituency vote only for these analyses. We use the binomial logistic regression as our statistical estimation technique, and we adopt a bloc-recursive approach including, one at a time and successively, the following: (a) long-term factors (other than the national question), (b) attachment to and identification with Scotland and the UK, (c) cost-benefit considerations (values of Scotland different from the rest of the UK, trade-off between political sovereignty and access to a larger market), (d) constitutional preferences (independence, more powers), and (e) salience of the national question (measured by the importance given to the parties' constitutional position by voters in the May 2011 election). As in chapter 4, the effect of the saliency of the national question on the vote is first considered separately, and then in interaction with constitutional preferences in order to determine how the priming of these attitudes may have influenced the vote decision at the 2011 Scottish Parliament election. Finally, recall that these blocs of explanatory variables are associated with each of our three dimensions of the national question: the

Table 5.7
Change in probabilities for voting models of devolved election in Scotland:
Sociodemographic and attitudinal variables

	SNP	Labour	LibDem	Cons
Age	0.02	−0.21**	0.12**	0.05
Female	−0.09**	0.05	0.06**	−0.00
Education	−0.04	−0.21**	0.18**	0.05
Income	−0.24**	0.03	−0.03	0.25**
Left-right	−0.19*	−0.34**	0.10	0.41**
Moral liberalism	−0.11*	0.14**	0.08*	−0.10**
Cynicism	−0.47**	0.25**	0.08**	0.15**
N	893	893	893	893

**$p \leq 0.01$; *$p \leq 0.05$ (two-tailed tests).

second bloc refers to identity, the third taps concerns over regional interests, and the fourth relates to the constitutional dimension.

Long-Term Factors

The results for the first set of regressions measuring the impact of long-term factors are presented in table 5.7 (changes in probabilities) and in appendix D (table D1, regression coefficients). The proportions of explained variance for these models are relatively low, except for the Conservative vote model (0.11, 0.08, 0.07, and 0.25 for the SNP, Labour, Lib-Dems, and Conservatives, respectively). The sociodemographic variables that seem to have the largest impact on vote choice in Scottish devolved elections are education and income. Not surprisingly, supporters of more left-wing oriented parties tend to be less affluent and educated. The probability of voting for Labour decreases by 21 percentage points for highly educated voters while the probability of voting for the SNP drops by 24 percentage points among wealthier respondents. On the other hand, support for the LibDems is higher among more educated respondents (+18 percentage points), and the vote for the Conservatives increases sharply (+25 percentage points) among the more affluent respondents.

The effect of political attitudes is also significant. Two variables stand out. First, the traditional left-right divide. The profile of partisans on this dimension is clear, with Labour and Conservative voters locating themselves on opposite ends of the ideological spectrum, and SNP and

LibDem voters displaying moderate attitudes (centre-left for the former and centre-right for the latter).[6] The second important finding is related to respondents' attitudes about the way the Scottish political system responds to their needs. The idea that the Scottish Parliament is the only one that is truly attentive to Scotland's specificities has been at the core of the SNP's rhetoric for a long time. Unsurprisingly, sharing this view (that is, scoring low on the cynicism scale) is strongly linked to SNP support. Tellingly, the impact of this variable is the strongest of all the long-term factors examined in this section. Fully agreeing with the view that the Scottish Parliament is not responsive to voters' demands (that is, scoring high on the cynicism scale) decreases the probability of supporting the SNP by no less than 47 percentage points. Also revealing is that the same belief is positively linked to support for the three unionist parties, and especially Labour.[7]

These results indicate that vote choice in Scotland is structured by three important factors: the voters' socioeconomic status, their positioning on the left-right divide, and whether they think that the Parliament in Edinburgh is responsive to the needs of Scotland's citizens. The results show that two clienteles, those of Labour and the Conservative Party, hold polarized ideological views whereas SNP and LibDem voters display more moderate attitudes. Also interesting is the fact that SNP voters express progressive opinions on socioeconomic questions while adopting a more conservative outlook on moral issues. Finally, the impact of cynicism strongly demarcates SNP supporters from the three other partisan groups in Scotland.

Identity and Vote Choice in Scotland

The variables measuring voters' feelings towards Scotland and the UK are included in the model presented in table 5.8 and in appendix table D2. When we turn to our national identity variables, we see that prioritizing Scottish over British identity increases the probability of voting for the SNP by 25 percentage points while decreasing the likelihood of supporting the Conservatives by 14 points. Interestingly, this variable is not linked to Labour and LibDem support, a point to which we will return below.

The other variables used to tap nationalist sentiments are scales measuring voters' level of attachment (from very attached to not at all attached) towards Scotland and the UK. One result stands out: attachment to Scotland does not seem to be a crucial factor here, being not signif-

Table 5.8
Change in probabilities for voting models of devolved election in Scotland: Attachment and identification variables

	SNP	*Labour*	*LibDem*	*Cons*
Age	0.10	−0.25**	0.08	0.05
Female	−0.08**	0.04	0.06**	0.00
Education	−0.03	−0.21**	0.19**	0.02
Income	−0.20**	0.00	−0.04	0.25**
Left-right	−0.01	−0.40**	0.04	0.32**
Moral liberalism	−0.08	0.14**	0.06	−0.10**
Cynicism	−0.32**	0.20**	0.05	0.08**
Identity	0.25**	−0.01	−0.03	−0.14**
AttachSC	0.11	0.01	0.01	−0.08
AttachUK	−0.37**	0.23**	0.19**	0.12*
N	883	883	883	883

$**p \leq 0.01$; $*p \leq 0.05$ (two-tailed tests).

icantly linked to the vote for any of the four parties. This result in itself is not surprising given the ubiquity of positive feelings towards Scotland among voters in this region (recall table 5.2). Feelings of attachment towards the UK are more polarizing, however. Indeed, we can see that a high degree of attachment towards the UK reduces the probability of backing the SNP by 37 percentage points while increasing the likelihood of voting for Labour, the LibDems, and the Conservatives by 23, 19, and 12 points, respectively.

Three clear conclusions can be drawn from the results in table 5.8. First, contrary to the situation in Quebec, adding variables tapping voters' feelings of attachment towards their region and the state does not contribute in Scotland to weaken significantly the effects of the long-term variables previously noted. The impact of individuals' socioeconomic status and left-right ideological orientations on their vote decision remains virtually as strong after the inclusion of this second bloc of explanatory variables. Hence, our first hypothesis about the domination of the national question in Scotland does not seem to be as strongly supported as it is in Quebec.

The second conclusion concerns the relative effect of indicators measuring nationalist sentiments in Scotland. In most studies on nationalist movements, it is the variable measuring identification with national communities that is most frequently used. However, as in

Quebec, our findings suggest that it is the variable measuring attachment towards the UK, not identification, that really matters for vote choice in Scotland.

The third conclusion, which also parallels a finding in Quebec but with some nuances, has to do with the effect of feelings of attachment on support for political parties. Two patterns emerge in Scotland on this question. The first one typifies the group of partisans more polarized on the national question, namely, the supporters of the SNP and the Conservatives. Voters of both parties prioritize a particular identity (Scottish or British) *and* also link their feelings towards the UK (negative or positive) to their vote choice. Both variables have a more important influence on the vote decision of SNP supporters than on that of Conservative supporters. The second pattern characterizes Labour and LibDem voters. Among both groups, the only significant determinant of the vote is the degree of attachment to the UK. Overall, in line with our sixth hypothesis, the impact of national sentiments on the vote appears stronger for parties with more radical views on the national question, the SNP and the Conservatives, than for the moderate parties on this issue, Labour and the LibDems. The increase in the proportion of explained variance when measures of attachment and identity are added to the different voting models is revealing, although the observed contrasts are not as marked as in Quebec. Whereas including these variables increases the value of the pseudo-R^2 for the SNP and the Conservative regression models by 0.11 and 0.07, respectively, the same increase is more modest for the LibDem (0.04) and the Labour (0.02) models. All in all, these results provide some degree of support for the notion that the parties more directly engaged in the national debate in Scotland – the SNP and the Conservative Party – are bound to dominate on this issue and profit electorally from it.

Cost-Benefit Evaluations

The debate over the national question in Scotland and Quebec seems to follow a common pattern (Atikcan 2015). As seen in chapter 3, a central argument promoted by the SNP claims that Scotland would be better able to respond to Scottish values and aspirations if it were an independent state. This argument assumes that Scottish values differ from those elsewhere in the UK and that having full control of the nation-state would allow the Parliament at Holyrood to act upon these distinctive policy preferences. A counterargument, shared by the unionist parties, states that in today's world, it is preferable to belong to a larger economic market, even if it means some loss of political sovereignty.

To test these two cost-benefit arguments, we include in our vote models the same two variables previously used in chapter 4 for the Quebec case. The first variable measures whether Scots believe their values and aspirations differ from those of people living elsewhere in the UK, where 0 means thinking that Scottish people have similar priorities as other Britons and 10 means that they have vastly different values. The other variable is a scale where 0 means a strong preference for belonging to a larger market even if it means a loss of sovereignty and 10 means full agreement with the opposite view.

The distribution of these variables is interesting. With regard to values, Scottish voters are quite split. Slightly more of them believe that they share the same values as other citizens of the UK (43 per cent answered between 0 and 4 on the scale) than those who think that they do not (41 per cent answered between 6 and 10 on the same scale; 13 per cent chose the middle value and 3 per cent refused to answer). Regarding the other question, our respondents are almost equally divided between those preferring a larger economic market and those favouring more sovereignty: 33 per cent of the respondents (0 to 4 on the scale) prioritized access to a larger market, 33 per cent expressed a preference for more political autonomy (6 to 10 on the scale), and 34 per cent picked the middle category (none of the respondents refused to answer).

The results when the cost-benefit components of the voting models are included are presented in table 5.9 and in appendix table D3. As can be seen, the values and market variables allow us to distinguish SNP and Labour supporters, with SNP supporters more likely to believe that Scotland has distinct values and to favour sovereignty at the expense of a larger market, and Labour supporters believing the exact opposite. The results are thus loud and clear. Thinking that Scottish values differ from those of the rest of the UK increases the odds of voting for the SNP by 14 percentage points while decreasing the probability of supporting Labour by 15 points. Favouring sovereignty over having access to a larger economic market boosts the probability of backing the SNP by 22 points while decreasing the likelihood of voting for Labour by 18 points.

Two main conclusions can be drawn from the results obtained with the inclusion of the cost-benefit variables. First, it is interesting to note that these variables do not contribute to the explanation of the vote for

Table 5.9
Change in probabilities for voting models of devolved election in Scotland:
Cost-benefit variables

	SNP	Labour	LibDem	Cons
Age	0.07	−0.22**	0.09	0.05
Female	−0.08**	0.04	0.06**	0.00
Education	−0.05	−0.18*	0.19**	0.02
Income	−0.21**	0.02	−0.05	0.25**
Left-right	−0.00	−0.40**	0.04	0.32**
Moral liberalism	−0.07	0.13**	0.06	−0.10**
Cynicism	−0.30**	0.18**	0.04	0.08**
Identity	0.22**	0.01	−0.03	−0.14**
AttachSC	0.11	0.013	0.01	−0.08
AttachUK	−0.31**	0.17**	0.19**	0.12*
Values	0.14**	−0.15**	−0.01	0.01
Market	0.22**	−0.18**	−0.05	0.00
N	883	883	883	883

$**p \leq 0.01$; $*p \leq 0.05$ (two-tailed tests).

the LibDems and the Conservatives. This finding contrasts with the results from the previous section showing that the cleavage on nationalist sentiments in Scotland mainly opposes SNP and Conservative voters. This result calls for a more nuanced characterization of the relationship between the national question and party support in Scotland than the one expressed in our sixth hypothesis. To recall, this hypothesis stated that support for parties with more radical views on the national question, the SNP and the Conservatives, will be linked to this issue more so than support for the moderate parties, Labour and the LibDems. Now, this hypothesis seems only partly true. If feelings of identification and attachment towards Scotland and the UK polarize SNP and Conservative voters, the main demarcation on the cost-benefit aspects of the national question opposes Labour and SNP supporters. Apparently, the LibDems are the only party in Scotland that is totally relegated to the sidelines in the debate surrounding the national question.

A second interesting finding, which also contrasts with what has been observed in Quebec, is that both cost-benefit variables – the clash of values and the market-sovereignty trade-off – play a significant role in explaining the vote in Scotland (recall that only the former variable is significant in Quebec). This result suggests that the SNP has been successful at priming perceptions that Scottish egalitarian values collide

Table 5.10
Change in probabilities for voting models of devolved election in Scotland:
Constitutional preferences

	SNP	Labour	LibDem	Cons
Age	0.08	−0.22**	0.08	0.04
Female	−0.05	0.01	0.05*	−0.00
Education	0.02	−0.20**	0.16**	0.00
Income	−0.14*	0.01	−0.08	0.21**
Left-right	0.02	−0.43**	0.03	0.33**
Moral liberalism	−0.10*	0.12**	0.05	−0.09*
Cynicism	−0.14**	0.08	0.02	0.05
Identity	0.12	0.05	−0.00	−0.10*
AttachSC	−0.04	0.11	−0.02	−0.05
AttachUK	−0.09	−0.02	0.12	0.11
Values	0.07	−0.13*	0.03	0.02
Market	0.05	−0.07	−0.05	0.04
Independence	0.28**	−0.27**	−0.13**	−0.14**
More powers	0.12**	−0.05	0.01	−0.03
N	752	752	752	752

**$p \leq 0.01$; *$p \leq 0.05$ (two-tailed tests).

with the liberal policies promoted at the UK level. Labour supporters, whose statewide party held power at Westminster from 1997 to 2010, tend to believe to the contrary that Scottish values are not necessarily at odds with the policies enacted by the UK Parliament. Consequently, they prefer the option of maintaining full access to the UK market for Scotland's economy since doing so is not incompatible with the promotion of Scottish values, nor perhaps with the very nature of these "Scottish" values. An SNP voter tends to think otherwise and would have a preference for more political sovereignty, even if it means belonging to a smaller market.[8]

Constitutional Preferences and Vote Choice

We have shown previously that the option of an independent Scotland is largely backed by SNP voters (71 per cent) but massively rejected by the partisans of the Labour Party (83 per cent), the LibDems (93 per cent), and the Conservatives (94 per cent). The other option, transferring more powers to the Scottish Parliament, receives massive support from SNP voters (89 per cent) but is also favoured by a majority of

Labour (53 per cent) and LibDem voters (55 per cent; recall table 5.5). The question now is to establish the extent to which individuals' constitutional preferences actually contribute to their voting decision.

The results for the models including these preferences are displayed in table 5.10 and in appendix table D4. Two results stand out. First, opinions about Scotland's independence clearly polarize the electorate between the SNP on the one hand and the three unionist parties on the other hand. Being favourable to this option increases the probability of voting for the SNP by 28 percentage points while decreasing the odds of supporting Labour, the LibDems, and the Conservatives by 27, 13, and 14 points, respectively. The other constitutional option – the devolution of more powers to the Scottish Parliament – has a more limited impact. Supporting this idea increases the chances of voting for the SNP by 12 percentage points but does not contribute to the explanation of the other parties' support.

Two main conclusions can be drawn from these regression results. First, the impact of constitutional preferences on the vote is clearly greater in the case of the SNP. The pseudo-R^2 value for the different voting models jumps 15 percentage points for this party (from 0.22 to 0.37) compared with only 7, 5, and 3 points for Labour, the Conservatives, and the LibDems, respectively. Once again, the idea that the LibDems are pushed to the sidelines of the national debate in Scotland seems to be supported by the data.

A second conclusion, in contrast with the Quebec case, is that for the most part constitutional preferences do not obliterate the socioeconomic and political cleavages that distinguish the partisan groups in Scotland. Besides being opposed to Scotland's independence, Labour voters in this region are older, less educated, firmly on the left, and liberal on moral issues. On the other hand, Conservative supporters, besides being strongly attached to the UK and being against Scotland's independence, have their own profile: wealthier, firmly on the right, and conservative on moral issues. The profile of LibDem voters is not as neatly defined (they are a bit older and more educated), but this lack of characterization has also been observed elsewhere in the UK (Clarke et al. 2004). Finally, the notion that the cleavage on the national question dominates all other determinants of the vote (first hypothesis) seems to apply for only one party, the SNP. In this case, and contrary to the other three parties, the variables having the largest influence on the vote are the constitutional preferences.

Table 5.11

Change in probabilities for voting models of devolved election in Scotland:
Salience of the national question

	SNP	Labour	LibDem	Cons
Age	0.11	−0.23**	0.09	0.03
Female	−0.03	−0.01	0.05*	0.00
Education	0.02	−0.18*	0.16**	−0.01
Income	−0.14*	0.01	−0.08	0.21**
Left-right	−0.03	−0.39**	0.05	0.33**
Moral liberalism	−0.11*	0.14**	0.06	−0.09*
Cynicism	−0.14**	0.08	0.03	0.05
Identity	0.12	0.04	0.01	−0.10*
AttachSC	−0.03	0.11	−0.01	−0.04
AttachUK	−0.08	−0.05	0.14*	0.12
Values	0.06	−0.13*	0.02	0.03
Market	0.07	−0.09	−0.05	0.02
Independence	0.28**	−0.29**	−0.13**	−0.12**
More powers	0.11**	−0.04	0.01	−0.04
IMPCONST	0.04	0.07	−0.12**	−0.04
N	718	718	718	718

**$p \leq 0.01$; *$p \leq 0.05$ (two-tailed tests).

The Saliency Effect

As mentioned in the preceding chapter, the saliency effect can be assessed in two ways. It can first be seen as a projection effect. A party
that is perceived as being strongly committed to a certain issue is expected to receive more support among voters who view this issue as
being important. Second, one might also expect that opinions on an
issue will have more weight among voters who attach a greater importance to this issue. We examine the first idea by adding to the previous vote model a variable measuring how important respondents
believe a party's favoured constitutional option is to their vote choice.
The results including this variable are shown in appendix table D5
and in table 5.11. They show that the saliency variable is only significant for the LibDems. The probability of supporting this party decreases by 12 percentage points among voters who view the national
question as being important. This result is not surprising in light of
our other findings above (and the party discourse analysis in chapter
3) that showed that the LibDems, contrary to the other parties, seem

Table 5.12
Change in probabilities for voting models of devolved election in Scotland:
Interactive variables

	SNP	Labour	LibDem	Cons
Age	0.11	−0.23**	0.08	0.02
Female	−0.03	−0.01	0.05*	0.00
Education	0.02	−0.17*	0.16**	−0.03
Income	−0.14*	0.01	−0.08	0.21**
Left-right	−0.03	−0.40**	0.04	0.35**
Moral liberalism	−0.11*	0.12*	0.06	−0.09*
Cynicism	−0.14**	0.07	0.03	0.05
Identity	0.12	0.04	0.01	−0.10*
AttachSC	−0.03	0.12	−0.01	−0.05
AttachUK	−0.08	−0.05	0.14*	0.11
Values	0.06	−0.13*	0.02	0.03
Market	0.07	−0.10	−0.05	0.03
Independence	0.29**	−0.11	−0.05	−0.68*
More powers	0.11	−0.20*	0.01	0.14*
IMPCONST	0.04	0.01	−0.11	0.02
IMPCONSTIND	−0.01	−0.09	−0.04	0.23*
IMPCONSTPWRS	0.00	0.08	0.00	−0.09**
N	718	718	718	718

$**p \leq 0.01$; $*p \leq 0.05$ (two-tailed tests).

to have a hard time finding a place in the debate about Scotland's political future.

Another way of examining the effect of constitutional preferences is to see if the link between these preferences and the vote varies as a function of the importance attached to this issue. To do this, we add two interaction variables, IMPCONSTIND and IMPCONSTPWRS, to estimate whether the impact of respondents' constitutional preference on their voting decision increases among those giving more importance to the national question. The results including these interaction variables are shown in appendix table D6 and in table 5.12. The findings are somewhat mixed.[9] But one interesting result relates to support for the Labour Party, which is opposed to Scotland's independence but favourable to the devolution of additional powers to its regional Parliament. The results in table 5.12 indicate that Labour voters who are giving more importance to the issue of Scotland's future seem to be driven by this dichotomy. Although the coefficients fall just short of

Table 5.13
Change in probabilities for voting models of general election in Scotland:
Sociodemographic and attitudinal variables

	SNPUK	LabourUK	LibDemUK	ConsUK
Age	0.13*	−0.19**	0.05	0.08
Female	−0.05	0.05	0.00	−0.01
Education	−0.03	−0.20**	0.19**	0.00
Income	−0.20**	0.01	−0.03	0.26**
Left-right	−0.05	−0.39**	−0.07	0.49**
Moral liberalism	−0.09*	0.03	0.14**	−0.09*
Cynicism	−0.37**	0.04	0.05	0.17**
N	1,047	1,047	1,047	1,047

$**p \leq 0.01$; $*p \leq 0.05$ (two-tailed tests).

reaching standard statistical significance levels, the negative coefficient
for the variable IMPCONSTIND and positive coefficient for the variable
IMPCONSTPWRS suggest that opposition to independence and support
for more devolution for Scotland exert a stronger impact on the decision to support the Labour Party among the group of voters giving a
greater importance to the national question.

UK GENERAL ELECTIONS IN SCOTLAND: SAME BATTLE, DIFFERENT BATTLEGROUND

In this section, we examine the determinants of Scots' support for
statewide political parties in the context of UK general elections. To
do so, we use a recalled vote question asking the respondents which
party they supported at the 2010 general election. This amounts to examining the predictors of vote choice only for those casting ballots
in Scottish constituencies. Despite some limitations,[10] the analyses presented below offer interesting insights about the impact of
the national question on Scottish voting behaviour during UK general elections.

The results for vote models attempting to explain Scots' voting decision in UK general elections are presented in tables 5.13 to 5.17 and in
D8 to D12 in the appendix. We have broadly the same expectations as
for devolved elections, namely, that ideology should matter more for
the Labour and the Conservative parties and that national identity and
constitutional preferences should matter more for those parties adopt-

Table 5.14
Change in probabilities for voting models of general election in Scotland:
Identity and attachment

	SNPUK	LabourUK	LibDemUK	ConsUK
Age	0.14*	−0.24**	0.05	0.11*
Female	−0.03	0.03	0.01	−0.01
Education	0.02	−0.20**	0.19**	−0.06
Income	−0.16**	−0.03	−0.03	0.28**
Left-right	0.08	−0.43**	−0.10	0.42**
Moral liberalism	−0.08*	0.04	0.12**	−0.08*
Cynicism	−0.21**	0.00	0.03	0.11**
Identity	0.32**	0.08	−0.12*	−0.19**
AttachSC	0.32**	0.00	0.01	−0.14**
AttachUK	−0.25**	0.27**	−0.01	0.04
N	1,021	1,021	1,021	1,021

$**p \leq 0.01$; $*p \leq 0.05$ (two-tailed tests).

ing more extreme views on these issues. For the model as a whole, we would expect the national question to be less salient than it is for devolved elections (third hypothesis). What we do find fits, partially, with these expectations.

With respect to long-term factors, we see in table 5.13 that education operates in a similar way as in Scottish parliamentary elections, with less educated voters backing Labour and university-educated respondents being more supportive of the LibDems. Similarly as for devolved elections, less affluent respondents tend to support the SNP, and wealthier individuals tend to back the Conservative Party. When we look at political views, we see that there is a significant and strong relationship between being right-wing and voting Conservative, with Labour as the inheritor of this mantle on the opposite side of the spectrum. Scots with morally liberal views are more likely to vote for the LibDems, whereas those with more conservative views appear more likely to vote SNP or Conservative.

Results for the models including the national identity variables are displayed in tables 5.14 and D9. A look at these estimates suggests that in state-level elections those who prioritize their Scottish identity support the SNP whereas those who prioritize a British identity vote for either the LibDems or the Conservatives. The two attachment variables are less important here than they were for vote choice in devolved elections, but we still see that SNP support is stronger among those who

Table 5.15
Change in probabilities for voting models of general election in Scotland:
Cost-benefit variables

	SNPUK	LabourUK	LibDemUK	ConsUK
Age	0.13*	−0.22**	0.05	0.11*
Female	−0.03	0.03	0.01	−0.01
Education	0.01	−0.19**	0.19**	−0.06
Income	−0.16**	−0.02	−0.03	0.28**
Left-right	0.08	−0.43**	−0.10	0.42**
Moral liberalism	−0.08*	0.04	0.12**	−0.08*
Cynicism	−0.20**	−0.01	0.03	0.11**
Identity	0.31**	0.09	−0.12*	−0.19**
AttachSC	0.31**	0.01	0.01	−0.13**
AttachUK	−0.23**	0.23**	−0.01	0.05
Values	0.05	−0.10*	−0.00	0.02
Market	0.09	−0.14*	−0.00	−0.01
N	1,021	1,021	1,021	1,021

$**p \leq 0.01$; $*p \leq 0.05$ (two-tailed tests).

feel more attached to Scotland and weaker among those who feel more attached to the UK (the opposite is true for Labour support).

Finally, as was the case with Scottish parliamentary elections, cost-benefit calculus related to constitutional options, preferences about the future of Scotland (more powers, independence), and the importance attached to the Scottish question are all linked to Scots' vote choice in UK general elections, but to a lesser degree than for devolved elections (see tables 5.15 to 5.17 and D10 to D12). These results underline the fact that the national question plays a different role in state-level and sub-state elections, which in turn brings up the question of establishing whether the national question represents a key issue structuring partisan preferences in the latter case and a niche issue in the former case.

A look at the explanatory power of variables tapping various dimensions of the national question for both types of elections is useful to address this question. For devolved elections, the increase in the value of the pseudo-R^2 when measures of identity, cost-benefit considerations, and constitutional preferences are added to the different vote models is larger for all four parties than it is for UK general elections. The respective values of this increase for the different parties are +0.26 (substate) and +0.23 (state) for the SNP, +0.12 (substate) and +0.11 (state) for the Conservatives, +0.11 (substate) and +0.05 (state) for Labour, and

Table 5.16
Change in probabilities for voting models of general election in Scotland:
Constitutional options

	SNPUK	LabourUK	LibDemUK	ConsUK
Age	0.17**	−0.24**	0.00	0.09
Female	−0.01	0.02	0.00	−0.02
Education	0.02	−0.19*	0.19**	−0.09
Income	−0.12*	−0.03	−0.04	0.25**
Left-right	0.09	−0.38**	−0.13	0.41**
Moral liberalism	−0.08	0.01	0.12**	−0.06
Cynicism	−0.09*	−0.03	0.01	0.07
Identity	0.23**	0.09	−0.10	−0.16**
AttachSC	0.28**	0.06	0.01	−0.12*
AttachUK	−0.09	0.12	−0.07	0.03
Values	0.03	−0.08	−0.00	0.04
Market	0.03	−0.08	−0.03	0.06
Independence	0.19**	−0.20**	−0.07*	−0.07*
More powers	0.10**	0.06	0.01	−0.08**
N	852	852	852	852

$**p \leq 0.01$; $*p \leq 0.05$ (two-tailed tests).

+0.08 (substate) and +0.02 (state) for the LibDems. On average, the increase in the proportion of explained variance that is observed with the inclusion of the national question variables is about 1.5 times greater for devolved elections compared with UK ones, a figure similar to what was observed for Quebec in the previous chapter.

Four conclusions stand out from this section's findings. First, as was just discussed and in accordance with our third hypothesis, it clearly appears that the national question plays a larger role in Scots' voting decision in substate elections than in state-level contests. Second, in accordance with our fourth and fifth hypotheses, the SNP appears as the main beneficiary of this issue at both the substate and state levels. Third, the Scottish national question presents the main characteristics of a niche issue in UK general elections. The contribution of this issue in explaining support for statewide parties remains strong in the case of the SNP and moderate for the Conservatives, while becoming marginal for both Labour and the LibDems. Finally, the contribution of the national question to an explanation of the vote in Scotland is the weakest for the LibDems, for both devolved and UK general elections.

Table 5.17
Change in probabilities for voting models of general election in Scotland:
Salience of the national question

	SNPUK	LabourUK	LibDemUK	ConsUK
Age	0.17**	−0.23**	0.00	0.09
Female	−0.01	0.10	−0.01	−0.01
Education	0.02	−0.16*	0.15*	−0.10
Income	−0.12*	−0.04	−0.05	0.24**
Left-right	0.08	−0.40**	−0.13	0.44**
Moral liberalism	−0.09*	0.03	0.13**	−0.07
Cynicism	−0.09*	−0.02	0.01	0.06
Identity	0.22**	0.09	−0.10	−0.15**
AttachSC	0.22*	0.04	0.02	−0.10
AttachUK	−0.09	0.11	−0.07	0.05
Values	0.02	−0.08	0.00	0.02
Market	0.03	−0.08	−0.01	0.04
Independence	0.19**	−0.21**	−0.07	−0.05
More powers	0.11**	0.07	−0.00	−0.08**
IMPCONST	0.12*	0.09	−0.06	−0.12*
N	812	812	812	812

**$p \leq 0.01$; *$p \leq 0.05$ (two-tailed tests).

These conclusions about the role of the national question in the decision-making calculus of Scottish voters in substate and state-level elections need to be nuanced in order to account for the relative importance of this issue in explaining Conservative support in devolved and
UK general elections. The results for the SNP, Labour, and the LibDems
neatly confirm the niche hypothesis. The stability in the influence of
the national question variables for both types of elections for the SNP
was expected since, as seen in chapter 3, this party primes this issue on
both occasions. Similarly, the decrease in the explanatory power of these
variables for Labour and the LibDems was also expected since both parties tend to downplay the Scottish question in state-level elections, urg-
ing individuals to cast their vote based on other issues. For a long time,
including in the 2010 election, this strategy was successful as it led a
certain number of Scottish nationalists to cast their vote not for the
SNP but for Labour or the LibDems. Consequently, the relationship between constitutional preferences and vote preferences in Scotland has
been weaker in UK general elections.

Table 5.18
Change in probabilities for regression models of support for Scotland's independence

	(1)	(2)	(3)	(4)
Age	−0.16**	−0.08	−0.10	−0.13*
Female	−0.09**	−0.07**	−0.07**	−0.07**
Education	−0.06	−0.02	−0.04	−0.06
Income	−0.24**	−0.17**	−0.18**	−0.14**
Left-right	−0.43**	−0.16*	−0.15*	−0.20**
Moral liberalism	−0.14**	−0.11**	−0.10**	−0.10*
Cynicism	−0.44**	−0.26**	−0.23**	−0.21**
Identity	−	0.20**	0.17**	0.16**
AttachSC	−	0.26**	0.24**	0.23**
AttachUK	−	−0.52**	−0.46**	−0.45**
Values	−	−	0.12**	0.13**
Market	−	−	0.20**	0.21**
IMPCONST	−	−	−	0.17**
N	1,212	1,168	1,168	1,093

**$p ≤ 0.01$; *$p ≤ 0.05$ (two-tailed tests).

But how can we explain the diverging pattern observed for the Conservative vote? It appears that voting for the Tories in Scotland during UK elections has not only been a way for voters to express their conservatism but also a way to voice their Britishness. This dual meaning of the Conservative vote in Scotland during UK elections may explain why the contribution of the national question in explaining the vote for this party is roughly similar for both devolved and state-level elections.

SUPPORT FOR CONSTITUTIONAL OPTIONS

Up to this point, we have examined the determinants of voting behaviour in Scotland by focusing on factors associated with the national question. Constitutional preferences, which represent the positional dimension of this issue, occupy a central role within these factors. For this reason, it is useful to extend the analysis of the impact of the national question on Scots' political choices by establishing which factors best explain voters' support in this region for the two constitutional options on the political agenda, namely, more powers for Scotland or its independence from the UK.

Tables 5.18 and 5.19 (and appendix tables D13 and D14) present regression results that look at support for the two options of independence and greater constitutional autonomy within the UK. In each case, the dependent variable takes the value of 1 if the respondents stated their intention (in 2012) to support these options in hypothetical referendums on these issues, and 0 otherwise (nonresponses were excluded from the analysis; see tables 5.4 and 5.5 for the distribution of these variables). As was done for the voting models above, the independent variables are treated as part of blocs that "locate" themselves along a funnel of causality, with longer- and shorter-term factors entered successively in the estimation.

Results for the model on Scotland independence are presented in tables 5.18 and D13. Regarding the socioeconomic determinants of support for this option, the results highlight the impact of age, gender, and income, showing that older respondents, those with higher incomes, and women are less likely to support independence. This finding is consistent with what we know both of the structure of constitutional preferences in Scotland (Curtice 2013; Carman, Johns, and Mitchell 2014) and of predictors of support for independence in the 2014 Scottish referendum (Henderson and Liñeira 2014; Henderson, Delaney, and Liñeira 2014; Henderson, Jeffery, and Liñeira 2015). Perhaps of particular note is the negative impact of age on independence support, which conforms to the pattern long observed in Quebec, except in very recent years (see chapter 4).

When we turn to our political variables, we see that respondents who are located towards the right of the left-right spectrum and those who hold morally liberal views are less likely to support independence. On the left-right dimension this is consistent with what we know of the relationship between party competition in Scotland and support for independence, namely, that parties on the left, and their supporters, are more favourable to independence than those on the right. With respect to moral liberalism, which is measured here as support for same-sex marriage and opposition to the death penalty, however, we might have predicted that it would be linked to greater support for independence given the stated position of the SNP government, particularly with respect to the legalization of same-sex marriage. This result might well reinforce the idea of two axes of competition and highlight where they do not necessarily align. The cynicism scale works in the expected direction. Those with higher scores, in other words those who are least satisfied with the way democracy works in Scotland, are more likely to support independence.

We find predictable results for national identity, with those prioritizing their Scottishness more likely to support independence while the reverse is true for those prioritizing Britishness. However, the size of the effect is greater for the variable of attachment to the UK, which is also consistent with what we know: not everyone who describes themselves as Scottish supports independence, but the balance of opposition to independence among those who prioritize their Britishness is much greater. In addition to national identity, we see independent effects of perceived distinct values, a priority for sovereignty over market size, and the salience of the constitutional issue – all producing positive and significant coefficients in support of Scotland's independence.

These findings do not contradict the received wisdom on the structure of support for independence, but we take particular heart that they are consistent not only with what we knew of such support when our survey was conducted but also with what we have come to know about more recent constitutional preferences in the post-referendum period. The fully specified model accounts for approximately 33 per cent of the variation in the dependent variable, although the significant improvement in model fit occurs once we start to include different measures of national identity.

Where the findings are particularly useful is in their comparison with support for more constitutional powers to the Scottish Parliament. These are, of course, two different formulations of change. They differ both with respect to their extreme nature – with more powers being closer to the status quo than independence – and, arguably, with respect to their precision. Our survey was conducted during the long campaign for a Scottish referendum when there was considerable debate about what independence would mean. While independence itself was not a unified proposal – indeed the Scottish government's white paper differed slightly from the proposals of the Yes Scotland campaign team – it was considerably more precise than "more powers," which in the eyes of voters could mean anything from additional authority over existing areas of jurisdiction to full fiscal autonomy for Scotland within a United Kingdom.

The results pertaining to the more powers option (see tables 5.19 and D14) differ in important ways from those obtained for the independence option. First, the sociodemographic variables are less important, with only income determining support for more powers, in this case with wealthier respondents less favourable. Given the expectation that an increase in fiscal autonomy would be accompanied by an increase in taxes for wealthier members of the electorate (see, for example, SNP 2015) this is perhaps not surprising. Although the effect disappears

Table 5.19
Change in probabilities for regression models of support for more powers for
Scotland

	(1)	(2)	(3)	(4)
Age	−0.07	−0.02	0.05	−0.05
Female	0.00	0.01	0.01	0.01
Education	0.01	0.08	0.05	0.03
Income	−0.22**	−0.19**	−0.20**	−0.19**
Left–right	−0.25**	−0.07	−0.06	−0.09
Moral liberalism	0.01	0.01	0.02	0.02
Cynicism	−0.45**	−0.31**	−0.29**	−0.29**
Identity	–	0.29**	0.26**	0.26**
AttachSC	–	0.23**	0.21**	0.18**
AttachUK	–	−0.27**	−0.20**	−0.20**
Values	–	–	0.18**	0.18**
Market	–	–	0.19**	0.20**
IMPCONST	–	–	–	0.14**
N	1,136	1,101	1,101	1,025

$**p \leq 0.01$; $*p \leq 0.05$ (two-tailed tests).

when additional variables are included, it is also important to note that
left-oriented respondents also support the option of greater autonomy
for Scotland within the UK. The results for income and ideology, for
both the independence and more powers options, thus seem to confirm our second hypothesis about the existence of a priming effect
pushing parties, particularly on the left, to adopt a more nationalist
stance on the political status of Scotland.

Identity works in the intended direction, but the asymmetry of the
effects of Scottish and British attachment disappears. Scottish identifiers are more supportive than British identifiers, but the size of
these effects is roughly equal. The measures of ideology and moral
liberalism, which were negatively associated with support for independence, are not significant here. The remaining variables – a belief
in the existence of distinct Scottish values, a preference for sovereignty over market size, and the salience of the constitutional issue
– are all positively related to support for more powers. In short, many
of the same variables work in the same direction, but we see fewer
significant variables, and the level of opposition among British identifiers is weaker.[11]

The main message, overall, is that strict devolutionists (i.e., voters favourable to more autonomy for Scotland but opposed to its independence) represent a pivotal group of moderate voters in the debate on the constitutional future of Scotland. It seems safe to conclude that the battle to attract these soft nationalists, particularly intense between the SNP and Labour in recent years, will remain at the forefront of Scotland's electoral politics for the foreseeable future. That being said, the fact that about 35 per cent of Scottish voters favour the status quo for their region (i.e., voters opposed both to more powers and to independence for Scotland) gives some hope for the Conservatives. After years of political turmoil, two referendums (including Brexit), and the prospect of a third one, the Tories' strong calling for political stability will perhaps resonate more deeply with Scottish voters in the years to come.

CONCLUSION

The models' fit statistics suggest that the variables we have assembled here do a fair job of accounting for voting behaviour in Scotland, with the full model explaining around 40 per cent of the variation in support for the Conservatives and the SNP. If there are two axes to party competition in Scotland, the constitutional axis plays a greater role for the two parties at the poles of the spectrum. If we look at the Labour Party and the Liberal Democrats, by contrast, we see slight variations. First, their models' fit statistics are not as good. Our set of variables account for around 20 per cent of the variation in Labour and LibDem support. We might well argue that we have identified useful predictors of SNP and Conservative support but not of Labour and LibDem support. This conclusion is further clarified when we look at the individual predictors. Education remains the most important predictor of LibDem support, while for Labour the left-right spectrum plays this role.

Although the Labour Party and the Liberal Democrats have occupied something of a middle ground – sharing constitutional preferences with the SNP before devolution and with the SCUP afterwards – both national identity and constitutional preferences play a role in structuring their support. Those attached to the UK and who do not think that Scotland has distinct values are more likely to vote for Labour, while support for independence tends to propel voters to other parties. Likewise, for the Liberal Democrats, attachment to the UK makes one significantly more likely to vote for the party, while support for independence makes one significantly less likely. The fact that constitutional preferences and identity structure support for two parties that are not at the poles of the national question – that are not perceived to be the best defenders of the nation's interests and that are not advocates of polar opposite constitutional preferences – speaks to the salience of the national question in Scottish voting and highlights the ways in which it operates as both a positional and a valence issue.

In terms of our hypotheses, the findings indicate that the most nationalist party, the SNP, is perceived as being more adept at defending Scotland's interests and culture (fourth hypothesis). Furthermore, the SNP seems to have been gaining ground on the valence dimensions of the national question in Scotland, mostly at the expense of the Labour Party. Our fifth hypothesis about the dominance of the SNP over the national question also seems to be confirmed. The increase in the proportion of explained variance due to the variables tapping this issue is clearly higher for the SNP than for its opponents, for both devolved and UK general elections. The idea that support for parties with more radical views (the SNP and the Conservatives) is more linked to the national question is globally borne out by the data, but with some nuances. This sixth hypothesis receives stronger confirmation for statewide elections than for substate ones. For devolved elections, support for the SNP is the most tightly linked to the national question (this is also true for UK elections during which this question presents the characteristics of a niche issue), followed by the Conservatives, Labour, and the LibDems. Two political dynamics seem to operate in Scotland with regard to the national question: the struggle over identity, between the SNP and the Conservatives; and the debate over Scotland's promotion of its more egalitarian values within the UK, which opposes the SNP to Labour. The only political party that seems totally absent from the debate about the national question in Scotland thus appears to be the Liberal Democrats. The dominance of the national question over the other cleavages (first hypothesis) is also confirmed – although, contrary to Quebec, other issues also significantly contribute to structure party choice in Scotland. The notion that there might be a priming effect pushing left-oriented parties to adopt more affirmed nationalist positions (second hypothesis) seems to fit with the stance adopted by Labour – as well as the Greens and the Scottish Socialist Party, whose support we did not examine in this chapter. Finally, the national question does seem to have more influence on Scots' vote decision in devolved elections than in UK general elections (third hypothesis), a finding that provides evidence in favour of the idea of Scottish parliamentary elections being first-order elections.

In the end, the results in this chapter give strong support to the idea that the national question is multidimensional, composed of both positional and valence elements. On the question of national interests, the SNP is clearly perceived to be the party best able to defend the interests of Scotland, with the Conservatives viewed as the least able to defend them, particularly among Scottish identifiers. When it comes to Labour and the Liberal Democrats, support for them depends in part on the other (socioeconomic) axis animating partisan competition, with Lib-Dem supporters distinguishing themselves on both their British identity and their moral liberalism. In terms of structuring partisan support, the national question is important, and we see improvements in model fit once we examine identity and constitutional preferences, but this is most obviously the case for the parties standing at the poles – the SNP and the Conservatives. For the other parties in the analysis, the left-right axis remains important, and here Labour appears most rooted in this "old politics" landscape, but having lost a strong relationship with the income variable that once served to structure its support.

These findings help to put into context the results of the 2015 and 2017 UK general elections and the 2016 Scottish Parliament election, for they herald the decline in Labour's image as defender of Scotland's interests. What these results are less able to capture, however, is the extent to which more powers has become a valence issue in Scottish politics which, when coupled with identity, presents obvious challenges to the unionist parties. On the one hand, one could well argue that the Conservatives, who were least supportive of more powers, are in a particularly precarious position; but the extent to which they have capitalized on their position as one of the national poles, and so clearly dominate in terms of support among British identifiers, suggest that they may in fact be less vulnerable to electoral abandonment than Labour and the LibDems. If once the "Scottish question" was a niche issue, there is evidence that even before the 2014 independence referendum it was nonetheless serving to structure party competition in Scotland, in both devolved and UK elections.

6

Electoral Politics in Two Substate Nations

The objective of this book was to analyze the impact of the national question on electoral dynamics in Quebec and Scotland. A comparative look at these two specific cases justifies itself easily. Quebec and Scotland can both be characterized as nations with distinct institutions and traditions within the framework of a larger, multilevel state. Since the 1960s they have experienced the rise of modern nationalist movements and have held referendums on proposals for self-government. Nationalist movements in both places also emphasize their civic and democratic credentials. Yet, we can also find significant differences between these regions. For instance, the Quebec and Scottish parliaments do not enjoy the same degree of legislative autonomy vis-à-vis their respective central governments. Another clear difference relates to the centrality of the Scottish and Quebec issue in their respective states. Due in part to the significant demographic weight of Quebec within Canada, the debate over its political status has been at the forefront of Canadian politics for decades. The same has not been true for the Scottish question in UK politics.

Our interest in studying Quebec and Scotland in a comparative perspective relies on these similarities and differences. We believe that a more detailed and considered analysis can produce broad-ranging conclusions about the role of the national question in the political life of substate nations (Henderson and Coates 2005). While Quebec and Scotland have been frequently compared, notably with regard to the emergence of their nationalist movements (Keating 1996, 2009), their party systems' origins (Chhibber and Kollman 2004; Hepburn 2010a), and the role of nationalism in the development of their welfare states (McEwen 2006; Béland and Lecours 2008), few studies have examined the way in which the debate on the political and constitutional future of Quebec and Scotland influences electoral dynamics in these two sub-state nations. The purpose of this book was precisely to analyze the consequences of this debate on the electoral politics of Quebec and Scotland in a comparative and systematic fashion.

Our examination of the national question in Quebec and Scotland was based on two general assumptions. First, we argued that the national question is more of a "niche" issue at the state level, whereas it typically operates as a "mainstream" issue at the regional level. By "mainstream," we mean that the national question dominates – or is of equal prime importance to – other cleavages in substate politics, including the traditional divide between left-right ideologies, and can act as a kind of "super issue" that structures electoral dynamics. Second, we argued that the national question is better understood as a multifaceted electoral issue, with both valence and positional dimensions. On one hand, all parties in a substate party system seem bound to agree on the general need to strengthen and promote substate powers and identity, more or less leading to a relative partisan consensus on these two dimensions of the national question. On the other hand, there is disagreement among parties when it comes to the constitutional dimension of the national question, particularly on the question of whether the substate nation should secede or not. Our analyses were based on the notion that parties position themselves on these dimensions in order to attract voter support. Therefore, party strategies rest on the belief that voters' decisions in substate politics are largely driven by the various dimensions of the national question.

These questions were examined in chapters 2 through 5. We first focused our attention on studying the impact of the national question on party strategies (chapters 2 and 3) before turning our attention to voter behaviour (chapters 4 and 5). In the preceding chapters, these questions were examined separately for Quebec and Scotland, and we will now compare more systematically our findings between the two regions. We will first address the question of how political parties in both regions position themselves strategically on the national question. Next, we consider to what extent voters' decisions in Quebec and Scotland are influenced by this issue.

PARTY BEHAVIOUR IN QUEBEC AND SCOTLAND COMPARED

In chapters 2 and 3 we identified a number of hypotheses about the way the national question might structure party behaviour in Quebec and Scotland. Most notable among these was that the national question is a central component of political parties' positioning; that nationalist parties "own" the national question; and that these dynamics are stronger at the substate level than at the state level. To what extent have these hypotheses been confirmed in the case studies? Here, we can offer a simple answer, and then a more nuanced one. The simple answer is that these hypotheses have been confirmed in general terms. The national question is a central component of party competition, with all parties adopting a stance on it and promoting it with varying degrees of intensity. Also, nationalist parties have succeeded in pushing the national question onto the political scene, particularly at the substate level. However, while we can say that our expectations have been met in a general sense, this answer does not address the multidimensional nature of the national question.

On this point, the manifesto content analysis and elite interview data from the empirical case chapters clearly revealed that some aspects of the national question have a much stronger resonance among parties than others. Thus, nationalist parties may "own" some dimensions of the national question, but they may fail to lead on other dimensions. Likewise, while parties at the substate level may act as a territorial bloc on some issues relating to the national question, they may experience some levels of inter-party division over other issues. To understand fully the nature of party positioning on these issues, we must explore parties' attention to the different dimensions of the national question.

The Constitutional Dimension

The first dimension of the national question that we examined pertained to the constitutional issue. In the empirical case studies, we separated out two aspects of this issue: (a) support for/opposition to secession, and (b) support for/opposition to more powers and autonomy. The Parti Québécois/Bloc Québécois and the Scottish National Party have pursued similar constitutional positions, in that they have sought independence for their territories, while retaining some functional or economic ties with the remainder of the state. However, the extent to which nationalist parties were the sole proponents of different issues varies by dimension and party. We must distinguish between the constitutional issue understood as a general desire for constitutional change, and specific proposals for change such as independence or more powers. Within Quebec, the Coalition Avenir Québec, much like its predecessor the Action Démocratique du Québec, emphasizes constitutional change more than does the Parti Québécois. It appears that the PQ's strategic preference is to emphasize other themes such as good governance, as well as other dimensions of the national question such as identity and regional interests. At the statewide level, the Bloc Québécois is obviously the only federal party advocating constitutional change for Quebec, in large part because it is the only federal party that contests seats in only one province. In this sense, there are some similarities between the BQ and the SNP: neither party faces a challenger on the issue of constitutional change in their respective statewide party systems.

Second, we can contrast this situation with the relative isolation of parties on specific forms of constitutional change, namely, independence and a desire for more powers. On the issue of independence, it appears that the main nationalist parties have been joined by only smaller niche parties in both Quebec and Scotland. In Quebec these parties include Québec Solidaire and Option Nationale, while in Scotland these include the Scottish Greens and Scottish Socialists. Unsurprisingly, the Bloc Québécois has found no support for Quebec secession among other federal parties. In short, all of the major parties in both cases and at both territorial levels have remained resistant to secession. Furthermore, in both cases we find one substate party occupying the opposing position (being firmly against independence and making a big deal about it) – the Parti Libéral du Québec and the Scottish Conservative and Unionist Party – and each of these parties actually avoided mentioning this specific issue in their manifestos (2014 and 2011, respectively). As a result, we can surmise that when it comes down to the issue of independence, the constitutional dimension of the national question remains very much a polarized, positional issue in both cases.

Third, and in contrast to the secession issue, there seems to be more convergence between nationalist and non-nationalist parties when it comes to the question of "more powers." Other large political parties in Quebec and Scotland operating at the substate level – including Scottish Labour, the LibDems, and Conservatives, and the Coalition Avenir Québec and Québec Solidaire – have at times favoured enhancing the autonomy and policy competences of the substate nation within the wider state. The Parti Libéral du Québec appears the most resistant to advocating "more powers" in Quebec, although it typically shies away from advocating *against* more powers. The call for "more powers" in Quebec and Scotland therefore reflects more consensus than the call for independence, with those opposed to further devolution – at times the Conservatives in Scotland and the PLQ in Quebec – isolated from other parties.

The comparative picture is rather different at the state level. While Scottish and UK parties have adopted calls for more powers across the board, there has been significant resistance to more powers for Quebec among certain Canadian statewide parties. In particular, while the NDP is open to further decentralization to Quebec in some policy areas, and in the election campaign of 2015 offered the prospect of full compensation opt outs from federally funded programs, the Canadian Liberal and Conservative parties remain opposed to extending what they perceive to be special favours to Quebec. So while "more powers" for Scotland has been endorsed by all UK parties and has therefore become a consensus issue in UK statewide politics, in Canadian federal politics there is significant opposition to more powers for Quebec, and thus partisan polarization on this issue. The result of these dynamics is a relative consensus across substate and state parties in Scotland on the issue of more powers. In Canada these same dynamics ensure a centre-region frame featuring pan-Canadian parties at the federal level (the Bloc Québécois being the exception) and territorial-based parties in Quebec that have developed their own identities or severed their ties with federal parties either due to their nationalist orientation or for fear of not appearing committed enough to defending the province's interests (Dion 1975; Lemieux 2008).

This greater cross-level discrepancy found across statewide and substate elections in Quebec highlights the role played by the structure of statewide political parties. In Quebec, all of the parties have full organizational and policy autonomy and compete as Quebec-based parties. As noted in chapter 1, the Parti Libéral du Québec broke off all links to the federal Liberal Party in the 1960s, the Coalition Avenir Québec emerged as a home-grown Quebec nationalist party, and Québec Solidaire has evolved as a thoroughly provincial leftist party.[1] This means that all parties in Quebec can freely position themselves on the national question without having to "toe the federal line" or obtain endorsement of statewide parties before taking a position on an issue. In contrast, the Scottish branches of the Labour Party, Conservatives, and Liberal Democrats are all fully integrated into the UK party structures (exercising various degrees of autonomy within them), which has prevented them from being able to freely position themselves on the national question. For instance, a significant number of Labour voters supported independence in the 2014 referendum, but despite this Labour has sometimes been portrayed as a unionist party controlled by London. Clearly, this makes it difficult for Labour – and others – to take stronger positions on some aspects of the national question. It also means that the Scottish National Party has had an easier time in owning the national question, as it does not face the same competition as the PQ does in Quebec – for instance from a strong pro-Quebec CAQ.

Regarding the constitutional dimension, we can finally note that both the Scottish National Party and the Parti Québécois have in many respects moderated their stances during the period under analysis. The SNP supported the prospect of "devo-max" at various points before and after the September 2014 independence referendum, a concept that, although ill-defined and contested, appeared to involve decentralizing all power short of defence and foreign policy to Scotland. Similarly, the PQ supported the concept of *gouvernance souverainiste*, which was viewed as either an intermediary stepping-stone to independence or an end-game method of achieving as much independence as possible within Canada.[2] It is worth noting that in both cases such stances were consistent with majority preferences among the electorate, as seen in chapters 4 and 5. That said, it is clear that "more powers" cannot really be understood as a constitutional option per se for these parties. At best, such a positioning allows them to vigorously defend regional interests (in relation to our third dimension of the national question); at worst, it may be viewed as a counterproductive approach by their independentist supporters.

Identity

National identity is the second dimension of the national question, and here we have explored two aspects: (a) cosmopolitanism (diversity), and (b) language. On the first issue, we found that both the SNP and the PQ/BQ have strongly emphasized immigration and integration in their party manifestos, but with different stances that no doubt reflect the demographic composition of their electorates. While the SNP emphasized the need to recognize and accommodate the cultural and religious diversity that migrants bring to Scotland, the PQ has, during the period we examined, placed more emphasis on the need for migrants to assimilate into a secular culture, adopt "Quebec values," and learn French in order to be seen as full members of the national community. This PQ discourse marks a significant departure from the party's past efforts to emphasize the civic nature of Quebec society, notwithstanding long-standing preferences for immigrants to acquire French as an additional language of use.

To what extent does the SNP or PQ vision reflect a consensus across parties? While in Scotland the SNP's position on multiculturalism reflects majority views across political parties if not across the electorate, in Quebec the PQ position – and in particular the Charter of Quebec Values – was divisive within provincial politics. In particular, while the Coalition Avenir Québec supported this model of integration, the Parti Libéral du Québec and Québec Solidaire vigorously opposed it as being overly restrictive and assimilationist, and instead insisted that Quebec should embrace the values of multiculturalism. Clearly, the PQ/BQ stance was much more difficult to accommodate than the SNP one. As a result, the issues of cosmopolitanism, multiculturalism, and immigration have strongly divided Quebec's political parties, while in Scotland there is relative consensus among political parties, if not the population, on creating an open, plural society that celebrates diversity and welcomes increased numbers of newcomers. As intimated by Kymlicka (2011), this consensus may have been facilitated by the relatively small non-UK-born population in Scotland. In Quebec, on the other hand, linguistic minorities (anglophones or allophones) form around 20 per cent of the population, and their support of the PLQ as well as federalism have allowed them in the past to play an important role in Quebec politics. Furthermore, the perceived attractiveness of the English language among the growing immigrant population in Quebec has often been at the forefront of political debates in this province.

The second aspect of the identity dimension that was analyzed in the empirical chapters – language – proved to be less divisive. Nationalist parties have sought stronger protection for the French language and Scottish Gaelic; and the SNP, PQ, and BQ have each emphasized this issue more than any other parties in their manifestos. However, the SNP and PQ/BQ are not alone: we also see support (but one of varied commitment) from all parties in both cases for protecting the substate language, including the CAQ, PLQ, and QS in Quebec, and Scottish Labour, LibDems, and Conservatives in Scotland. Therefore, language is clearly an issue on which there is consensus if unequal attention, with no party seeking to come out against protecting the language or reducing its place in Quebec/Scottish society. Language protection is not the preserve of niche or pro-independence parties at the substate level in either Quebec or Scotland. The cross-case difference is in salience, with far greater attention to the protection of French in Quebec than the protection of Gaelic in Scotland, as well as in the intensity (or zeal) with which parties defend the language issue. The salience of the language issue is further reflected across the territorial scales, where the lower level of attention in Scotland (relative to Quebec) is smaller still at the UK level, whereas statewide Canadian parties devote attention in their manifestos to the protection of French. This situation reflects the different demographic weight of French- and Gaelic-speaking populations not just in Quebec and Scotland but also within Canada and the UK respectively.

On the national identity dimension of the national question, the empirical analysis thus revealed a key difference between the two cases of Quebec and Scotland, which relates to structural differences in the language communities. While Scotland's indigenous language – Gaelic – is spoken by less than 1 per cent of the population and is a peripheral political issue in Scotland (with all parties supporting protection of the language to varying extents), in Quebec the French language is the cornerstone of Quebec identity. The differing sizes of the language communities in Scotland and Quebec do not only influence party positions on this issue. The existence of a strong minority language in Quebec – English – has also shaped the PQ/BQ position on cosmopolitanism. There has been a fear in Quebec that migrants have been integrating into the anglophone community (for opinion survey evidence on this question, see Bilodeau and Turgeon 2014; Bilodeau 2016). The continuing socialization of migrants into the anglophone community of Quebec was at the heart of the 1970s' PQ language legislation that required newcomers to send their children to French-speaking elementary and secondary schools. This fear of French-speakers becoming a minority in their own province has also partly driven the more assimilationist (intercultural) approach propounded by the PQ/BQ (and supported by the CAQ). These parties' opposition to the Canadian multiculturalist approach is grounded in the view that the latter is perceived to trivialize Québécois culture, which has been a core grievance of the nationalist movement in Quebec. In contrast, given the low number of migrants to Scotland and the shared majority language with England, the SNP does not seem compelled to promote assimilation of migrants into a particular language community or culture. In other words, there are perceived to be fewer obstacles to becoming Scottish than to becoming Québécois, notably due to the strength and importance of the French language in Quebec.

Regional Interests

We separate the third dimension of the national question, "regional interests," into three areas: social interests, economic interests, and supranational interests. On the first of these areas, we found that nationalist parties in both cases argued for the existence of a substate "model of governance" and regionally specific social values, and for the preservation of these social interests. In Quebec, the PQ and BQ both emphasize a Quebec social model and distinct brand of social values, and they do so more than any other party, although Québec Solidaire portrays a similar vision of Quebec. In Scotland, a similar social model is portrayed by all parties except the Scottish Conservatives. The prevalence of such views is a direct reflection of the left-right structure of party competition. With fewer parties on the right, the discourse around social spending is stronger in Scotland than elsewhere in the UK.

In both cases the progressive attitudes and social welfare preferences are juxtaposed against what are perceived to be more market-driven principles in the rest of the state. During the period of study, however, we see strengthened arguments from the Parti Libéral du Québec and Coalition Avenir Québec, as well as from within the Parti Québécois, that the statist Quebec social model warrants careful scrutiny. In general there is more robust criticism of a regional social model in Quebec than in Scotland. In Scotland, however, using such distinctiveness as an argument for constitutional change has found more traction since it was invoked in calls for devolution before 1997. The argument is a familiar one in Quebec but of late seems less of a valence issue. Instead, these parties have suggested that there is a need to revise the Quebec social model in light of the economic downturn and constraints on public spending, where they believe there are other more important priorities than providing extensive universal benefits. There is an interesting counterpoint with public opinion data, however. In practice the attitudes of Quebecers on social interests are arguably more distinct within Canada than are the views of Scots within the UK, particularly with respect to support of welfare redistribution.

On the second aspect of regional interests – the economic area – we see slightly different dynamics. In Quebec and in Scotland, all parties attempt to portray themselves as the best guardians of the nation's economic interests. Certainly the Parti Libéral du Québec and Coalition Avenir Québec have emphasized its salience, although we can note that the PLQ's emphasis is less nationalistic in orientation than the CAQ's since the Liberals tend to explicitly present the economy as being a policy priority that is much more important, and worthy of more attention, than is independence. In Scotland, SNP and Labour claims to manage the economy better were helped by the presence of a Conservative-LibDem coalition at the UK level, which these parties portrayed as being neither effective in the face of global recession nor very attuned to Scotland's economic interests. We note that the SNP has moved to the centre-right on some elements of economic policy in the past (for example, by supporting low corporation taxes[3]) but occupies the left/centre-left on others, most notably with policies on free university tuition, free care for the elderly, free prescriptions, free bus passes and, in the manifestos we examined, proposed increased taxes for middle- and high-income earners. Finally, one common element to both cases is the emphasis put by most substate parties on the need to broaden the fiscal autonomy of their region within the larger Canadian/UK framework.

Third, we explored how political parties link supranational integration to the national question. In both cases, we found that nationalist parties were most likely to portray the region as more supportive of the EU and NAFTA, with the SNP, PQ, and BQ emphasizing this issue more than any other substate party in their manifestos. Furthermore, nationalists in both cases have sought to show how the EU/NAFTA could provide larger economic structures within which to bed the self-determination of their state, thereby strongly linking supranational issues to economic health and to constitutional arrangements. Other parties make similar arguments, but make them less often. This is not to say that all parties share the same view. In Scotland, the LibDems are the most pro-EU party and the Conservatives are the least pro-EU party, with the SNP and Labour somewhere in between – although they all list benefits of EU membership for Scotland. In Quebec one can trace a similar story, with all of the substate political parties endorsing NAFTA to varying extents (with PQ/CAQ/PLQ very enthused and QS less so) and viewing it as an important trading framework for regional autonomy. So while there are differences between parties on integration – such as the extent of political integration, or whether Quebec/Scotland should be full member(-states) of these organizations – there is agreement on the general direction of maintaining substate influence within these larger structures.

To what extent are regional interests important in the discourse and positioning of nationalist political parties in Quebec and Scotland?

Not surprisingly, the theme of regional interests is emphasized the most in nationalist parties' manifestos in both substate nations. That said, we can nonetheless note that regional interests are emphasized more in Scotland than in Quebec. Indeed, in the latter region the theme of national identity is emphasized almost as much as regional interests, and clearly much more so than it is in Scotland where identity is the dimension of the national question that occupies less space in the SNP's manifestos. Interestingly, the constitutional dimension is similarly emphasized by nationalist parties in the two regions, but it is not emphasized as much as the other two dimensions, which are more valence in nature.

A comparison between nationalist parties (PQ/BQ and SNP) and all other political parties is also telling. First, nationalist parties, on the whole, tend to emphasize the national question the most in their manifesto content. This is true in both regions and in both state and substate elections, and for each of the three dimensions of the national question (constitution, identity, and interests). Second, and bringing nuance to that first conclusion, it appears that the national question can be perceived as a niche issue at the state level, where the issue attentiveness gap between nationalist parties and the other parties is more pronounced than at the substate level. In the latter case, non-nationalist parties also engage with the national question in their campaign manifestos, making it less of a niche issue that would be emphasized by a single niche party.

We explored not just salience but also the direction or degree of support that each party devoted to the national question in their election manifestos. We found that the overall direction of mentions is slightly more positive across substate political parties than across statewide ones, particularly in the case of Quebec. The directional polarization on the national question at the substate level materializes to some degree between the most nationalist parties on one side (PQ and SNP) and the most federalist/unionist parties on the other side (PLQ and Scottish Conservatives), whose issue mentions are less positive in tone.

Our analysis of party positioning on the national question thus shows the extent to which the strategic behaviour of parties is motivated by the need to take into account other competitors' stances and their own past positions on the issue, but even more importantly by the desire to respond to the Quebec and Scottish electorates' nationalist inclinations. How these parties' behaviour dynamics mirror citizens' voting choices in both substate regions is taken up in the next section.

VOTER BEHAVIOUR
IN QUEBEC AND SCOTLAND COMPARED

The results based on public opinion data presented in chapters 4 and 5 showed that the national question as an electoral issue plays an important role in Quebec and Scotland. These same results have also allowed us to highlight some similarities, but also significant differences, between these two regions in terms of how this issue influences vote choice. We will now review these points with an eye towards assessing the extent to which this comparison between voting behaviour in Scotland and Quebec can lead to more general conclusions about the role of the national question on the electoral dynamics of substate nations.

Public Opinion and the National Question
in Quebec and Scotland

To understand the similarities and differences in how the national question affects vote choice in Quebec and Scotland, it is necessary to draw a comparative picture of public opinion in these two regions on this issue. One point is immediately clear: Quebecers and Scots have nationalist sensibilities that are expressed via a greater attachment to their region than to their state. In both cases, approximately three out of five respondents (59 per cent in Quebec and 60 per cent in Scotland) are very attached to their region, whereas only about a third of respondents (30 per cent in Quebec and 36 per cent in Scotland) feel the same way about their state (Canada or the United Kingdom).

These feelings of attachment are unique to Scots and Quebecers within their respective statewide contexts. Citizens of other regions within Canada and the United Kingdom tend to report a greater, or at the very least an equal, attachment to both their region and their state (Mendelsohn 2002; Henderson 2007). Without a doubt, this strong attachment to the region explains the centrality of the national question in Quebec and Scotland. In both regions, between eight and nine out of every ten voters say that party positioning and performance on the various dimensions of the national question (be it defined as how well the parties understand the region's history and culture, their commitment to defending the region's interests, or party positions about the region's political future) have a significant influence on their voting decision.[4] However, these feelings of attachment do not necessarily translate into majority support for secession. Indeed, in our survey data we found that only 34 per cent of people in Quebec and 37 per cent in Scotland would support independence (at the time of data collection). This is 15 percentage points less than self-determination polled in Quebec in 1995 and 8 percentage points less than independence polled in Scotland in 2014 (although consistent with pre-referendum polls). While Quebecers and Scots may not largely support secession, they do however want more autonomy for their region. About 64 per cent of Quebecers and 67 per cent of Scots are in favour of transferring more powers from the central government to their region. Thus, voters in both regions appear to have the common characteristic of being more autonomist than independentist.[5]

It is interesting to see where the electoral clienteles of each party stand on these issues. Disaggregating our survey data by party identification gives us some interesting points of comparison regarding how differently voters for each of the parties are attached to their state and region. We find two parties, the Parti Québécois and the Scottish National Party, whose identifiers are much more attached to their region than their state. We also find two other parties, the Parti Libéral du Québec and the Scottish Conservative Party, where the opposite is true. In between these two extremes lie the other parties. Labour partisans in Scotland, along with QS and CAQ partisans in Quebec, are generally more attached to their region than their state, while the Scottish Liberal Democrats are the only group of partisans who are strongly attached to both the region and the state.[6] Nonetheless, significant differences can be noted. In Quebec, the two partisan groups that are the most distinctive in terms of their attachments to their region and state support the parties (the PQ and the PLQ) that have the most entrenched positions on the constitutional question and have dominated Quebec politics for decades. By contrast, in Scotland these positions are occupied by a dominant party (the SNP) and a political party that was long thought to be a third party (the Conservatives). In Quebec, autonomist rather than pro-independence sentiment is particularly strong among partisans of a centre-right party (the CAQ), while in Scotland this sentiment is typically found among supporters of a centre-left party (Labour). Finally, those few who support the most leftist party in Quebec (QS) are more attached to Quebec than Canada, while partisans of the smallest major party in Scotland (the LibDems) are equally attached to Scotland and the United Kingdom.

The distribution of constitutional preferences among different partisan groups in Quebec and Scotland overlaps with their feelings of attachment. Support for independence is very high among supporters of nationalist parties in both regions (75 per cent and 71 per cent for PQ and SNP supporters, respectively) and very low among supporters of parties opposed to this option (PLQ and Conservatives). That said, the political orientations of those who support parties occupying an intermediate position on the national question (Labour and CAQ) are no less interesting. These two parties have different orientations on socioeconomic issues, with Labour occupying the centre-left of the political spectrum in Scotland and the CAQ being a centre-right party in Quebec. Both political parties are supported by autonomist voters, as a clear majority of their supporters are in favour of transferring more powers from the central government to their region. Moreover, there is a significant bloc of voters within each of these two parties who are favourable to the political independence of their region (17 per cent for Labour and 18 per cent for the CAQ). It is noteworthy that the autonomist option is supported by two major political parties in Quebec and Scotland, one of which has already been in power (Labour) and the other aspiring to be (CAQ).

It is a different story for the smaller parties. Québec Solidaire is a leftist party that won 8 per cent of the vote in the 2014 election, the highest score in its short history. This party's clientele appears divided over the question of Quebec independence (with 52 per cent being in favour), with a large majority of them (80 per cent) favouring a transfer of powers to the province. Support for the latter option is also prevalent among Liberal Democrat supporters (55 per cent). But unlike the supporters of QS (and to a lesser extent those of the CAQ and Labour), those in the LibDem camp support the autonomist option, while also massively rejecting Scottish independence. In fact, Liberal Democrat voters' level of support for independence is similar to that found among Conservative voters.

In order to understand the impact of the national question on voting behaviour, it is necessary to look at where the voters perceive the parties to be on each dimension of the national question. In both regions, the most nationalist parties (PQ and SNP) are overwhelmingly seen as best able to defend the identity and culture of their region. They are also viewed as best able to defend the region's interests, although not by as large of a margin. In the Scottish case, this was clearly seen when respondents were asked which party would be best at dealing with the

Westminster Parliament. While 28 per cent of respondents chose the SNP, 19 per cent named Scottish Labour and 13 per cent the SCUP. These results reiterate that nationalist parties have a strategic interest in addressing the national question by presenting themselves as the best defenders of both the identity and the interests of their region, although their advantage appears less pronounced in the latter case. This is probably why federalist/unionist parties sometimes try to counter the issue-ownership advantage that nationalist parties have by focusing the debate on this second dimension, that of regional interests. In this way, they can argue that their party would be better able than the secessionist party to get the most out of their region remaining within the larger state, particularly in terms of economic and financial benefits.

A comparison of parties' electoral support and the popularity of their constitutional option is also revealing. Pro-independence parties in Quebec and Scotland are perceived to dominate the issues of defence of identity and regional interests, whereas federalist/unionist parties have a clear advantage on the constitutional dimension of the national question. This means that, in order to succeed, pro-independence parties in both regions must either get the support of voters who have an unfavourable view of their constitutional option or benefit from the division of the unionist/federalist vote among their opponents. This is the case of the SNP, which not only receives a higher vote share than its preferred constitutional option does, but also takes advantage of unionist vote-splitting between Labour, the Conservatives, and the Liberal Democrats.

The situation in Quebec appears somewhat different. In this case, support for the pro-independence parties (PQ and QS) matches quite closely with support for that constitutional option (32 per cent vs. 34 per cent). Moreover, the anti-independence vote is not distributed across three political parties as in Scotland, but rather between two (the PLQ and the CAQ). The PLQ reaps the lion's share of these votes, which could help explain why that party has almost continuously held on to power since 2003 and why it has done so while winning more votes than its opponents during the last five out of six provincial elections (recall table 1.1).

The above discussion shows how the distribution of supporters and opponents of independence across political parties plays a key role in the electoral dynamics of substate politics. This distribution of supporters tends to favour the SNP in Scotland and the PLQ in Quebec. It also indicates that political dynamics largely depend not on the choices made by supporters at either end of the constitutional spectrum (pro-independence versus federalist/unionist) but rather on those of moderate autonomists found in the middle. These autonomists first supported Labour after devolution and then turned, if perhaps temporarily, to the SNP. In Quebec, they have long supported the PQ (and the Bloc Québécois at the federal level), contributing to the polarization of electoral competition between the PQ and the PLQ. The rise of an autonomist party – the CAQ – now divides the nationalist vote in two, between the PQ independentists and the CAQ autonomists, a division that overall favours the PLQ. In Scotland, a return of autonomist voters to Labour could recreate a dynamic similar to that which prevailed during the first few post-devolution substate elections.

Determinants of Vote Choice in Quebec and Scotland

We now turn our attention to the determinants of vote choice in Quebec and Scotland in order to assess how much impact the national question has in shaping voters' decisions in these two regions. We first discuss state-level elections. How similar or different Quebecers and Scots appear to be in their voting behaviour at statewide elections seems to depend on the time period under analysis. We can first note the differences in the trajectories of Quebec and Scottish nationalist parties at the state level. Because Scotland did not have a regional Parliament before 1999, Scottish nationalists used UK general elections to advance their cause well before Quebec sovereignists did so in federal elections. In addition, due to the demographic weight of Quebec within the Canadian federation, questions over the province's constitutional status have long been at the heart of political debate in Canada (Johnston et al. 1992). Far from being a marginal issue, the question of the place of Quebec within Canada has played a central role in Canadian politics, and massive support from Quebec voters over time has enabled the Liberal Party of Canada to become the natural governing party in that state (Dion 1975). Until the end of the 1980s, it is probably fair to say that the national question was a niche issue supported by the Scottish National Party in the UK and a mainstream issue in Canada that has long benefited the federal Liberal Party.

The arrival of the Bloc Québécois on the political scene in 1993 transformed the dynamics of federal elections in Quebec. Over the next two decades, the national question became a niche issue exploited by the BQ and gradually abandoned by the other statewide political parties.

During this more recent period, we can say that there has been some convergence between Quebec and Scotland over the role of the national question in statewide and substate elections. In state-level elections, this issue has clearly been a niche one supported by the Bloc Québécois and the Scottish National Party. But beyond this overall similarity, some differences can nonetheless be noted. For fifteen years, the Bloc Québécois has received greater support than the SNP on the state level, thanks to the joint support of sovereignists and those attracted to the BQ's rhetoric of defending Quebec's interests. In the 2011 and 2015 federal elections, these nationalist, but not sovereignist, voters largely deserted the Bloc, whose support fell below the 20 per cent mark. In Scotland, the opposite trend has been unfolding. For years, the Scottish National Party had been unable to win the support of many separatists in Westminster elections. However, the broad coalition of voters who supported it in the 2015 general election suggests that the SNP was finally able to mobilize not only the pro-independence vote but also a significant proportion of autonomist voters. Its drop in 2017 to 37 per cent is still a level of support that, pre-2015, would have been considered an historic high. The SNP's recent performance is reminiscent of the BQ's own during the federal elections held between 1993 and 2008. It remains to be seen if the Bloc will continue to decline and if the SNP will remain popular among voters. The result of upcoming elections in both Quebec and Scotland will of course help determine whether the distinction that the national question is a niche issue in statewide elections and a "super issue" in regional ones remains relevant.

Substate elections are even more interesting to examine, if only because they can lead to independence referendums. Therefore, we will pay particular attention here to the impact of the national question in Quebec and Scottish substate elections. We first focus on the long-term variables (that is, variables other than those related to the national question) that structure vote choice in Quebec and Scotland. In comparing the two regions, one difference emerges. Quebec has a significant nonfrancophone population (about 20 per cent of its total population) that is strongly attached to Canada and overwhelmingly opposed to Quebec independence. Furthermore, the language variable is not a significant determinant of vote choice in Scotland. However, we find groups of "unionist" voters, notably along Scotland's southern border with England, whose feelings of attachment towards the UK are reminiscent of the strong support for Canadian federalism found among Quebec's nonfrancophone minorities.

A frequently asked question is whether pro-independence parties can win support from newer cohorts of voters, as was the case for the Parti Québécois when it first competed in the 1970s (Blais and Nadeau 1984a; Lemieux 2011; Mahéo and Bélanger, forthcoming). Our analysis indicates that this may no longer be the case. In Quebec, older voters currently support the PQ, while the youngest are now turning to Québec Solidaire. Even in Scotland, the youngest voters support Labour while older ones are more supportive of the LibDems.

Another interesting question is whether support for parties offering a project as radical as independence is greater among left-wing voters, while support for parties advocating the status quo is greater among those on the right. The reality is more complex than this depiction suggests. It is true that the two most right-wing parties in both regions, the Parti Libéral in Quebec[7] and the Conservative Party in Scotland, are also the strongest supporters of the constitutional status quo. It is also true that the centre-right voters of the CAQ in Quebec and the LibDems in Scotland are also unfavourable to independence. However, the picture is more nuanced when looking at the left of the ideological spectrum. In both regions, the main parties with left-leaning clienteles are either generally opposed to independence (like Labour in Scotland) or divided on the issue (like QS in Quebec). Finally, it appears that those who vote for pro-independence parties are mostly centre-left voters. Two reasons can explain this phenomenon. First, staunchly leftist voters will privilege social issues over the national question, leading them to support QS in Quebec and Labour in Scotland. Second, the independence project must be based on a broad coalition in order to succeed, including both left-leaning and right-leaning nationalists.[8]

We hypothesized in chapters 4 and 5 that the national question in substate elections is a "super issue" in Quebec and Scotland that structures political choices and dominates all other issues, including the difference between ideological left and right. It seems that this characterization is particularly apt for describing Quebec provincial elections. Including variables related to identification and attachment to Quebec and Canada makes the influence of left-right ideology on vote choice completely disappear, with the only exception being for the small leftist party Québec Solidaire. However, the situation is different in Scotland. Including these variables helps eliminate the effect of ideology where it was already weak, most notably in explanatory models of SNP and LibDem vote choice. But adding these variables, as well as those corresponding to the other dimensions of the national question (i.e., cost-benefit, constitutional options, salience), has virtually no impact on the strength of the relationship between respondents' ideological orientation and their likelihood to support either Labour or the Conservatives.[9]

The conclusion is clear. While the national question almost entirely structures electoral dynamics in Quebec, this issue in itself is not sufficient to account for vote choice in Scotland.[10] It seems that in the latter case, the traditional left-right divide also plays an important role in voting decisions. That said, all parties in Quebec and Scotland need to position themselves on both the national question and the left-right axis. In search of this balance, the pro-independence parties, who are bearers of a radical project but anxious to expand their support base, tend to locate themselves on the centre-left (PQ and SNP). Parties most fervently supporting the constitutional status quo in both regions are the most right-leaning (Conservatives and PLQ). The two leftist parties focus on social issues while adopting an autonomist stance (Labour and QS).[11] With regard to the Liberal Democrats, their positions on social policy and on the constitutional issue (i.e., federalism) have not yet been electorally successful. The Coalition Avenir Québec, the only party that has explicitly sought to extricate itself from the debate over the national question and focus instead on economic and fiscal issues, decided in 2015 to adopt a more affirmed nationalist position (in favour of more devolved powers) in an attempt to increase its support.

The impact of the different dimensions of the national question on voting behaviour in Quebec and Scotland displays interesting similarities and differences. First, we see that prioritizing identification with either one's region or one's state has a significant impact on supporting a party situated on one end of the spectrum regarding the region's political status. In Quebec, these voters support either the PQ or the PLQ, and in Scotland, the SNP or the SCUP. We also see that the degree of attachment to one's state over one's region is the driving variable behind vote choice in Quebec and Scotland. Voters for pro-independence parties in both regions (SNP, PQ, and QS) express little attachment to the state they want to leave, while supporters of federalist or unionist political parties (PLQ and CAQ in Quebec; Labour, LibDems, and Conservatives in Scotland) display stronger attachment to the state that they hope to remain part of.

Significant differences between the two regions appear with regard to the effect of variables measuring the costs and benefits of various constitutional options. First, believing that citizens in other regions of their state have fundamentally different values from theirs has a significant impact on the vote decision of Scots, but not Quebecers. This point of divergence between the Quebec and Scottish cases is interesting. It appears that the discourse contrasting Quebec values with those of the rest of Canada does not have the same mobilizing power that it may have had in the past. Its effectiveness in Scotland may be due to two factors. First is the fact that this argument is central to the SNP's platform. Second, Scotland's relatively small demographic weight can help reinforce the idea that the people of this region have little influence over state-level decisions that affect them.

When deciding whether or not to support a project of national emancipation like independence, individuals weigh the benefits of increased political sovereignty against the benefits of continuing to be part of a larger economic market. Not surprisingly, the preference for increased political sovereignty over remaining part of a larger unit is related to support for the two most resolutely sovereignist parties in this study, the Parti Québécois and the Scottish National Party. By contrast, preferring continued integration within a larger market is positively related to support for the two federalist parties in Quebec (PLQ and CAQ) and Labour in Scotland. As further evidence of the ambivalence of Québec Solidaire voters, this trade-off between political sovereignty and economic integration exerts no effect on the likelihood of supporting that party. The limited effect of cost-benefit considerations for Scottish Conservative and Unionist Party support is more surprising and suggests that the motivations of this party's supporters related to the national question are based more on feelings of identity than on a cost-benefit calculus.

In looking at the relationship between constitutional preferences and vote choice, we see noteworthy similarities between Quebec and Scotland. First, the way respondents feel about the transfer of more powers (defined as autonomism in Quebec and devolution in Scotland) appears much less important to their voting decision than how they feel about their region's political independence. Interestingly, this "more powers" variable is significant for the pro-independence parties (PQ and SNP), which suggests that some autonomist individuals support these parties strategically in seeking more powers for their regional parliament. Nonetheless, it is obviously respondents' position on the issue of independence that has the most influence on their vote choice. In Quebec as in Scotland, support for independence is positively related to support for parties promoting this option (PQ and SNP) and negatively associated with the likelihood of voting for a party that rejects it (PLQ and CAQ in Quebec; Labour, LibDems, and Conservatives in Scotland). The only exception to this trend is the case of Québec Solidaire, an officially sovereignist party but whose support is negatively related to support for Quebec independence.

The last aspect that was examined in our vote choice models relates to the actual importance given to the constitutional question by individual voters. Here the results differ between Quebec and Scotland. In the first case, voters concerned about this issue support parties that have long embodied the polarization between sovereignist and federalist options: Parti Québécois and the Parti Libéral du Québec. By contrast, voters less interested in the constitutional question lean towards parties whose discourse and positions adhere more to a left-right logic (QS and CAQ). The effect of the salience variable is much smaller in Scotland. It is significant (and negative) in the case of the Liberal Democrats, a party that seems to have had difficulty winning voters, even though its constitutional proposals are rather close to the preferences of the median voter. These across-case differences may be explained by the longevity of the debate over Quebec independence, which has lasted several decades, resulting in a certain amount of weariness among the population and a desire to support parties offering a new perspective on Quebec politics. This political fatigue has not yet manifested itself so clearly in Scotland, but it is not inconceivable that it could happen there too as time goes by.

A final question has to do with the overall contribution of the national question to explaining voting behaviour in Quebec and Scotland. In Quebec, our hypothesis that support for parties representing opposite ends in the constitutional debate is most consistently linked to the national question was unequivocally confirmed. It is clear that the Parti Québécois and the Parti Libéral du Québec both benefit greatly from this issue, to the detriment of Québec Solidaire and the Coalition Avenir Québec. In Scotland, this opposition is less clear-cut. The main beneficiary of the debate over the national question is clearly the Scottish National Party. As expected, the second party that benefits most from this issue is the Conservative Party. But the gap between them and their other competitors, who are also opposed to Scottish independence (Labour and LibDems), is not as pronounced as it is between the PQ/PLQ, the CAQ, and QS in Quebec. That said, it appears that the 2016 Scottish election and subsequent 2017 UK general election may have been a turning point and that the constitutional issue may have now become a more important determinant of the Conservative vote in Scotland.

Support for Constitutional Options in Quebec and Scotland

Looking at the determinants of constitutional preferences in Quebec and Scotland reveals some interesting similarities, but also strong contrasts. Age has long been an important determinant of support for Quebec sovereignty, with younger voters more favourable to the independence project (Blais and Nadeau 1984b; Martin and Nadeau 2002). However, this is no longer the case today (see also Mahéo and Bélanger, forthcoming). In Scotland, the pro-independence option has seen more support among younger voters. The large amount of support for the autonomist option found among older voters in Quebec is not surprising; it is an option that is less radical than independence and that corresponds to a traditional nationalist discourse in Quebec.

Unlike in Quebec, support for both independence and further devolution in Scotland remains tied to an individual's socioeconomic status and ideological orientation, even after controlling for other factors. In general, those in Scotland who ideologically locate themselves most to the right and who have the highest incomes are the least favourable to constitutional change (and especially independence), all things being equal. Another important difference between the two regions relates to the political cynicism variable. The impression of not being heard by politicians and by existing political institutions is strongly linked to support for constitutional change in Scotland, but not in Quebec. The impact of perceived value differences between one's region and the rest of the state is also different in the two regions. While this variable contributes significantly to explaining support for independence in Scotland, this is not the case in Quebec. However, deciding between political sovereignty and having access to a larger market plays a greater role in Quebec than in Scotland. Those who support Scottish independence often argue that an independent Scotland would continue to be part of a larger economic ensemble – the European Union – which is an argument that supporters of Quebec independence cannot so readily make.

Our findings thus highlight a number of differences between Quebec and Scotland that are attributable to their different contexts. With less demographic weight and long without their own parliamentary institutions, Scots seem to be more driven in their voting decisions by a sense of alienation from the central government than Quebecers are. However, Scotland's membership in the European Union mitigates an argument that is often used by federalists in Quebec against independence: the economic benefits of remaining part of the larger unit that is the Canadian federation. That said, some of these differences can be explained by a common motivation: the need for recognition and autonomy. In the case of Quebec, support for independence is more related to feelings of identity, such as attachment to the nation (Quebec) and state (Canada), than it is in Scotland.[12] This is understandable for two reasons. The first is that in Quebec the independence project is largely the domain of francophones, a minority group within Canada and North America that is concerned about the survival of their language and culture. The second is that unlike the Scottish nation, which was recognized without having its own parliamentary institutions, the Quebec nation has almost always had significant political autonomy without its existence being explicitly recognized.

The Scottish case is clearly different. It seems that while Scotland had recognition, it was lacking in democratic autonomy. Without their own political institutions and representing less than 10 per cent of the total UK population, Scots seem to be driven more by a desire to implement their own societal project, with more egalitarian values than those prevalent in the rest of the UK. Therefore, it is perhaps not surprising that when compared with Quebec, the independence movement in Scotland is currently more to the left ideologically, more animated by a sense of alienation from the centre, and more committed to creating a societal project that is different from the rest of the UK.

CONCLUSION

We have seen in this comparative analysis that many aspects of the national question present the character of valence issues in Quebec and Scottish politics, with political parties agreeing on the general direction that policies relating to the national question should take (i.e., more constitutional powers, more protection of the substate culture and language, a stronger defence of regional interests), rather than taking opposing sides. The exception to this phenomenon, of course, is the constitutional question, which is more positional in nature, particularly when it comes to the more clear-cut issue of independence. The fact that all parties in both cases have accepted the importance of identity-related issues and regional interests to the future of the substate territory demonstrates that the national question is no longer (and arguably, never has been) a niche issue in the substate politics of multinational and multilevel states. Instead, in Quebec and Scotland, the national question is best viewed as a political issue whose multiple-ordering nature structures party and voter behaviour. Furthermore, in both cases analyzed, we have seen that the territorial dimension of party competition has often taken precedence over the left-right cleavage in determining party positions and voting choices, although more so in Quebec than in Scotland.

We have also witnessed the importance of issue salience and ownership. Here, we have seen that the leading nationalist party in Quebec and Scotland – the Parti Québécois and the Scottish National Party – have sought to "own" the national question. However, in response to nationalist party claims to ownership, rather than witnessing other parties that perform relatively worse on the issue seeking to downplay it – a common assumption in the literature on issue ownership – what we have seen is that the Parti Québécois and the Scottish National Party have been regularly challenged in their ownership of various aspects of the national question. Other parties in the Quebec and Scottish political systems – including regional branches of statewide parties – have taken up the banner of the national question and sought to portray themselves as the party standing up for national identity, constitutional change, or regional interests. This has, for example, been evident in the Scottish Labour Party's claim to be the "father" of devolution, the Coalition Avenir Québec's support for stronger language protection policies and for more powers devolved to Quebec, the Scottish Conservative's U-turn on seeking to grant the Scottish Parliament additional devolved powers, and Québec Solidaire's staunch defence of Quebec's distinct socioeconomic model of governance.

While the national question influences the behaviour of political parties and voters in these two regions, effectively making substate Quebec and Scottish elections first order, some differences between the two cases have been noted. For one, national identity is more of a concern for parties and voters in Quebec than Scotland – although it leads to more disagreement in Quebec, especially when it comes to cosmopolitanism as the recent episode surrounding the PQ's Charter of Quebec Values showed. For another, regional interests have more of an impact on the electoral politics of Scotland than Quebec. These differences seem mostly driven by these regions' respective demographic weight within the state (greater in the Quebec case than in the Scottish case), their particular linguistic makeup (the prominence of a distinct language in Quebec that is the majority language within the province but a minority language within the state and the larger North American continent), their differing degrees of constitutional autonomy (lower in Scotland than Quebec), or the organizational structure of statewide parties (more vertically integrated in Scotland than Quebec). Thus, the national question's general influence over the electoral politics of Quebec and Scotland is modulated to some extent by these case-specific characteristics.

There are a number of ways in which our study could be expanded. Regarding a comparison of Quebec and Scottish electoral politics, the analysis presented in this book is but a snapshot since it restrained itself to the 2010–14 period. To be sure, the historical overview provided in chapter 1 hinted at the usefulness of adopting a longitudinal perspective when comparing these two cases. But the recent period that forms the backbone of our empirical analysis finds Quebec and Scotland to be at very different places in their respective political life. While in Scotland the debate over the national question has been in full swing and has led to a relative convergence of substate parties' positions vis-à-vis the issue of Scotland's political autonomy, the national question in Quebec has experienced a setback that seems to have facilitated the fragmentation of the substate party system and Quebecers' voting choices. However, we suspect that this current divergence between these two cases may be contextual (or temporary) since it seems mostly tied to the mobilization effect that surrounded the lead up to the 2014 Scottish referendum on independence. For this reason, the national question currently plays more in favour of nationalist parties (essentially the SNP) in Scotland and more in favour of federalist parties (particularly the PLQ) in Quebec.

There is thus a need, we believe, to put the systematic comparison of Quebec and Scottish electoral dynamics into a broader temporal perspective in order to better assess the degree of similarity in the evolution of their respective party and voter behaviours as they pertain to the national question. What such a longitudinal study may bring to light is the notion that Quebec and Scotland may be going through the same cycles of high and low intensity in their national debate (and of high and low support for the idea of secession), with the difference simply being that these two territories did not start their cycles at the same moment and may be going through them at a different speed. While the exact nature of the national question may be different from one case to the other – for example, with more emphasis on language protection in Quebec and on the acquisition of additional powers for the government at Holyrood in Scotland – the overall trends in the intensity of the debate may be following the same cyclical shape and may be responding to a similar set of exogenous factors.[13]

We think that another interesting avenue of future research could be to try to establish more firmly the extent to which the strategic decisions on the national question made by Quebec party elites might influence those of Scottish party elites, and vice versa. In other words, do the elites of one territory "learn" from the strategies and arguments adopted by the elites of another territory, and does this learning help explain in part the cyclical nature of support for nationalist parties and their preferred constitutional option? For example, recent work has confirmed the existence of a "diffusion effect" of strategies and arguments from one state to another within the context of the 2005 referendum campaigns on the Constitution of the European Union (Atikcan 2015; see also Böhmelt et al. 2016 for a more general view on this phenomenon). Although such reciprocal influence between Quebec and Scottish parties – regardless of their positions on the national question – is certainly plausible, until now only a couple of studies have explicitly referred to this phenomenon (Lynch 2005; Brie 2016).[14]

Finally, it is also our belief that the analytical approach proposed in this book could be fruitfully applied beyond Quebec or Scotland, to other cases of regions nested in multilevel states. The cases of Spain (Catalonia, Galicia, Basque Country), Belgium (Flanders), and Italy (Sardinia, Veneto) certainly come to mind, in no small part due to the relative strength of their substate nationalist movements. Extant studies having examined these cases – and other interesting ones like Germany, Austria, and France – confirm that the national question plays an important role in their substate politics (e.g., Hooghe 1991; Meadwell 1991; Cento Bull and Gilbert 2001; Balfour and Quiroga 2007; Lecours 2007; Libbrecht et al. 2009; Dandoy, Matagne, and Van Wynsberghe 2013; Demuro, Mola, and Ruggiu 2013; Deschouwer 2013; Henderson, Jeffery, and Wincott 2013; Lublin 2014). However, in most cases the analysis has arguably not paid sufficient attention to the multidimensional character of the national question conceived of as an *electoral issue*. As seen in our study of the Quebec and Scotland cases, nationalist parties do not necessarily "own" all dimensions of the national question. In addition, the constitutional dimension leads to greater party and voter polarization than the other two dimensions – the defence and promotion of national identity and regional interests – which, in our cases at least, have tended to be more consensual in nature. Furthermore, our distinction between the state level, where the national question has more the character of a niche issue in determining the configuration of party competition, and the substate level, where it acts more as a "super issue" that structures the behaviour of parties and voters, offers opportunities for further study. Extending the universe of cases beyond those of Quebec and Scotland and applying our framework to an examination of the extent to which political parties in these other multinational states are successful at maximizing their electoral support by exploiting the multidimensionality of the national question would allow others to test the robustness of the conclusions presented in the current study.

What Next for Quebec and Scotland?

For this book, we draw on theory and empirics to develop an analytical framework that we hope allows us to account for political events that happen beyond the period under study. Our analysis is mainly based on a number of elections that took place between 2010 and 2014. In the years since, Scotland has gone through a referendum on independence in 2014, two general elections in 2015 and 2017, and both a devolved election and a UK-wide referendum on continued EU membership in 2016. Meanwhile, there was a federal election in Canada in 2015 during which support for the Bloc Québécois dropped below 20 per cent. Furthermore, a resolutely sovereignist Parti Québécois leader stepped down after leading his party for less than a year, the Coalition Avenir Québec has significantly shifted its constitutional position towards a more nationalist stance, and Québec Solidaire and the small independentist Option Nationale have taken steps towards merging their respective parties. The question then is whether the conceptual tools developed and used in this book can account for some of these more recent events, and whether these events make a comparison of Quebec and Scotland even more relevant.

We believe that we can provide positive answers to the aforementioned questions. To be sure, the course of events in the two regions presents some striking similarities. The enthusiasm within the pro-independence camp in Scotland following their better-than-expected result in the 2014 referendum is reminiscent of what happened with the Quebec sovereignists after their narrow defeat in 1995. Amplified by the electoral system, the SNP's landslide in the 2015 UK general election is not unlike the Bloc Québécois' victories in the 1993 and 2004 federal elections, when the national question was central to the political debate in Canada. The shift of moderate nationalist voters in both regions thus contributed to important electoral change. The BQ, once dominant in federal politics in Quebec from 1993 to 2008, saw a significant drop in its support when these moderately nationalist voters chose to support the NDP in 2011 and to split their votes in 2015. In Scotland, the opposite happened: the moderately nationalist voters seem to have moved from Labour to the SNP. Once dominant in Scotland during both statewide and substate elections, Labour found itself outmanoeuvred by the SNP during the 2015 UK election and beaten by the Conservatives in both the 2016 Scottish election and the 2017 UK general election.

The concepts presented in this book help us to understand these events. At the state level, the SNP success in the 2015 general election occurred at a high point of nationalist sentiment in Scotland primed by the previous referendum. The decline of the Bloc Québécois, not surprisingly, took place in an entirely different context. To recall, the main, if not the sole, purpose of that party when it emerged in the early 1990s was to facilitate the advent of Quebec's independence, which was expected to happen in the following years. Although its founders had made clear that the BQ would have a short-lived existence, as time went by, and with no new referendum in sight, the party changed its raison d'être to eventually portray itself as the guardian of Quebec's interests in the Canadian Parliament. After fifteen years of electoral successes, this message became less attractive to Quebec voters. In recent years, with the Parti Québécois in the opposition and with support for sovereignty at its lowest levels in decades, the Bloc Québécois failed to convince Quebecers of its continued relevance and eventually experienced a sharp drop of its vote.

In Scotland, Labour's recent troubles seem to illustrate to a certain extent the dangers of not having a distinct position on the national question. Interestingly, certain party spokespeople reacted to the disastrous results of the 2016 Scottish election by putting forward the idea that there were now three clear constitutional positions in Scotland – independence, unionism, and devolution – and that their party must position itself accordingly. Labour's reaction is not unlike how the Coalition Avenir Québec recently changed its stance on the national question. This relatively young party contested its first two provincial elections by advocating for a truce on any debate over the national question. However, after being accused of not having a position on such a central issue in Quebec politics, and not wanting to be disadvantaged in the future by the PQ-PLQ polarization, the party took a nationalist turn, demanding new powers from the central government and advocating for the vigorous defence of the French language and Quebec identity. The goal of this strategy is clear: it aims to draw a number of nationalist, if not quite sovereignist, voters away from the PQ and towards the CAQ. It also highlights a plausible third option in Quebec electoral politics, one between the pro-independence Parti Québécois and the staunchly federalist Parti Libéral.[15] As for the proposed plan to merge Québec Solidaire with the more radical Option Nationale, it seems aimed at positioning QS more clearly on the independence issue, possibly as an attempt to take advantage of the Parti Québécois's decision not to push for separation in the next election.

Other parallels between the Quebec and Scottish political contexts emerge. The Conservatives, for instance, claimed that the issue of holding a second referendum on independence was central to the 2016 Scottish election campaign and repeated this claim in 2017. Their improved electoral fortunes in 2017 can be attributed to a healthy degree of tactical voting from those who supported other parties but wished to stop a second independence referendum. This seems to signal that the idea of further referendums could, as in Quebec, play a more central role in future Holyrood and Westminster elections in Scotland. It is also interesting to note that the two Scottish parties that have benefited the most from the heightened salience of the national question have the most entrenched positions on the issue, namely, the SNP and the Conservatives. It is obviously too early to predict whether the national question will become as dominant in Scotland as it is in Quebec. It is also too early to say whether the competition between ideological left and right will play a less important role in Scotland in the future.[16] It nonetheless seems fair to say that the national question has now become a central issue in Scotland as it has in Quebec, something unavoidable on the political scene; and that parties that do not have a clear position on this issue may have to pay a high political price for it.

One final similarity is perhaps even more striking. Quebecers,[17] like Scots, have adopted a posture towards their political future that some have described as "ambivalent," referring to the dominant but not exclusive attachment to their region and their nationalist if not quite sovereignist position. This state of public opinion has helped keep the national question on the agenda without settling the question of Quebec's political status and future (Pinard 2005; Létourneau 2006). During an election campaign, these dynamics compel the Parti Québécois to concentrate on protecting Quebec identity and interests while leading the Parti Libéral du Québec to focus on the threat of another independence referendum. This situation then forces sovereignist party leaders to dodge these attacks, arguing that any new referendum would be held only under favourable conditions and if the pro-sovereignty side has the moral assurance of winning the consultation. The resignation in 2016 of a PQ leader, Pierre Karl Péladeau, who was outspoken on independence is no doubt a sign that support for Quebec sovereignty, while still significant, is far from enough to allow for this constitutional option to prevail in the short to medium term. Péladeau's successor, Jean-François Lisée, has already adopted a more moderate position on the issue of sovereignty by pledging that there will be no referendum on this issue if the Parti Québécois is elected at the next provincial election in Quebec.

It is not inconceivable that this kind of rhetoric between the Scottish National Party and its opponents may become central to Scottish politics in the near future. SNP leaders find themselves using more and more of the same vocabulary as the Parti Québécois (state of public opinion, winning conditions, moral assurance of a victory before calling a referendum, etc.) to talk about holding a new referendum if their party returns again to power. It is also reasonable to believe that, like in Quebec, no party can now afford to have an ambiguous position on the national question in Scotland. It remains to be seen how moderate nationalist (autonomist) and hardcore nationalist (separatist) voters in both regions distribute themselves in the coming years. The merging or splitting of nationalist support will play an important role in determining the political future of both Quebec and Scotland.

In the end, while it is difficult to predict the future – particularly in the wake of the Brexit referendum's outcome – it seems rather certain, given the ambivalence of Quebecers and Scots towards the nation and the state they belong to, that the dynamics surrounding the national question explored in this book will remain at the centre of Quebec and Scottish political life for the foreseeable future. It is also not inconceivable that similar dynamics will be at the heart of politics in other substate nations, especially Catalonia. Ultimately, the cases of Quebec and Scotland, while displaying their respective specificities, seem useful to understanding the role of the national question in substate politics. If this conclusion is correct, this may mean that the analysis of the national question proposed in this book not only contributes to a better knowledge of a particular type of issue voting but could also help to explain why the path to independence is so arduous for substate nations belonging to well-developed, modern states.

APPENDICES

Appendix A

PARTY MANIFESTO CODING SCHEMES

Table A1
Salience coding scheme

THEME 1: The Constitutional Issue

---

11. CONSTITUTIONAL ARRANGEMENTS

    111 Political union

    112 Sovereignty, partnership, sovereignty association (includes referendums)

    113 Subsidiarity

    114 Constitutional preferences

12. ECONOMIC POWERS

    121 Distribution of fiscal resources

    122 Regional fiscal autonomy

    123 Fiscal equalisation – distribution of resources (fair/unfair)

    124 Ability to borrow

    125 Allocation of funds for regions for economic development

13. SELF-RULE

    131 Transfer of competences to regional level

    132 Support for existing regional competences

14. SHARED RULE

    141 Regional influence in central government decisions or institutions

    142 Cooperation and coordination within state

    143 Cooperation across regions

    144 Regional representation in central institutions, including courts, upper houses

    145 Shared competences at regional/state level

Table A1 (*continued*)

15. CENTRALIZATION
  151 Transfer of competences to central level
  152 State control (or excessive control) over policy areas

THEME 2: Identity/Cosmopolitanism

---

21. IDENTITY/PRIDE/ATTACHMENT
  211 Single substate identity (Scottish/Québécois)
  212 Single state identity (British/Canadian)
  213 Plural/dual identity
  214 Multicultural identity
  215 Transnational identity (attachments to different nation-states)
  216 Pride (substate)

22. CULTURAL HERITAGE
  221 References to region as nation
  222 Cultural heritage of region, state as a whole
  223 Symbols of identity (e.g., flag, religion, ceremonies, holidays)
  224 Way(s) of life
  225 Culture and the arts
  226 References to existence of Scottish/Québécois people, Scottish/Québécois voice (includes diaspora populations)
  227 Historical struggles, triumphs, losses

23. COSMOPOLITANISM
  231 Cultural and religious diversity
  232 Scotland/Quebec or Canada/UK as plurinational state
  233 Scotland/Quebec or Canada/UK as a multicultural/intercultural state
  234 Treatment of national minorities and immigrants (including Aboriginal peoples, Catholic minority in Scotland)
  235 Threats to identity (immigration, dilution of language)
  236 Discrimination on basis of identity, language, cultural heritage

24. NATIONALISM
  241 Civic and ethnic nationalism
  242 History of nationalism/nationalist movement in Quebec/Canada, Scotland/UK (including the teaching of history in schools)

THEME 3: Identity/Language

---

  311 Language as symbol of identity or cultural heritage
  312 Bilingualism
  313 Linguistic minorities and minority languages
  314 Language as a tool for integration
  315 Status of language

Table A1 (*continued*)

---

316 Teaching foreign languages
317 Language training in schools
318 Language in public life and workplace

THEME 4: Regional Interests/Supranationalism

---

41. EU/NAFTA

411 General continental integration
412 Influence in EU/NAFTA
413 Differential support across state/region for EU/NAFTA
414 Benefits/risks of EU/NAFTA
415 Political representation in EU/NAFTA (including party success in EU elections)
416 Policy areas governed by EU/NAFTA

42. OTHER SUPRANATIONAL

421 References to other supranational institutions (NATO, UN, etc.)
422 Peacekeeping
423 Foreign policy (includes development aid and cooperation)

THEME 5: Regional Interests/Social Model

---

51. VALUES/POLITICAL CULTURE

511 References to distinct voice, preferences, values
512 Diversity within state on values of governing ("we do things one way; others do things another way")
513 Shared solidarity
514 Shared understandings across state re preferences, priorities
515 Discrimination against regional preferences, values
516 References to region as distinct (including distinct society)
517 Nation/region possesses distinct destiny
518 Own interests

52. MODE OF GOVERNING

521 Quebec/Scottish model
522 New politics after devolution
523 Shared vision of best way to govern
524 Central parties (e.g., London, Ottawa parties) all same; we in region (and/or this particular regional party) are different
525 Different/higher standards (e.g., of ethics)

Table A1 (*continued*)

THEME 6: *Regional Interests/Economy*

611 Build strong regional economy
612 Infrastructure and investment for economic growth
613 State planning
614 Natural resources (including control of resources for economic regeneration)
615 Laissez-faire approach to economy
616 Interventionist approach to economy
617 Budget cuts
618 Regional debt and unemployment (includes job creation)
619 Have not/have distinctions within state

Table A2
Directional coding scheme

THEME 1: *The Constitutional Issue*

-2 Centralist direction
- Negative feelings towards the transfer of competences in the past
- Need for transfer of some competences back to the central government
- Need for a stronger political union
- Need for further centralization of fiscal resources
- Need for less regional influence in central government decisions or institutions
- Need for less regional representation in central institutions, including courts, upper houses

-1 Status quo centralist
- Importance of continuing to be part of the joint state, of maintaining partnership (future)
- Importance of relationship with other regions (promoted and accomplished by the central state)
- Interterritorial solidarity and general statements about a strong country
- Importance of coordination and cooperation between the central state and the regions
- Allocation of means to the regions to develop more, but keeping the competence/control/task central
- Institutional dimension of partnership/policy coordination with central government
- Constitutional dimension of partnership/policy coordination with central government
- Opposition to further decentralization: general statements

Table A2 (*continued*)

- Opposition to further decentralization: reference to specific competences
- Statements on danger of separatism and against break-up of the nation
- Statements on danger of unequal treatment of different communities
- Negative feelings about the nationalism/regionalist politics of other parties
- Positive mention of centralized powers, emphasizing the importance of keeping this specific power centralized
- Unhappy with regional influence on the centre
- Negative position towards fiscal autonomy, including borrowing powers
- Negative statements about regional influence on central government's decisions or institutions
- Negative statements about regional representation in central institutions, including courts, upper houses
- Need for more intergovernmental cooperation/coordination led by central authorities

o Status quo
- Neutral statements of fact and collaboration between different levels of government, if all act within their own competences and if both region and centre are equally involved and benefit from it
- Other statements that can be interpreted ambiguously in the context of regionalism (e.g., decentralization to strengthen the union)

+1 Status quo autonomist
- Positive statements about decentralization in the past or present: general
- Criticizing previous governments that did not take responsibility and criticizing decisions or policy of current governments in the past without implicitly/explicitly asking for more powers
- Positive statements about decentralization in the past or present, with regard to specific policy domains
- Statements about the opportunities that decentralization will offer in the future: general
- Statements about the opportunities that decentralization will offer in the future: specific policy domains
- Cooperation with(in) central government in favour of the region
- Criticizing/influencing central government in its decisions related to the region
- Opposition to further decentralization in the short run
- Dangers of re-centralization, derogatory statements about parties under the influence of central government
- Statements on the specificity of the region that require a different policy
- Cooperation with central government and other regions to strengthen the region or to allow the region to fulfil its competences better
- Criticizing other governments that did not take responsibility
- Positive statements on the transfer of competences to the regions, but making very clear they do not want to go any further
- Positive statements about existing fiscal autonomy or allocation of means, including borrowing powers

Table A2 (*continued*)

- Criticizing previous systems and improving the existing system without asking for more autonomy
- Positive statements about regional influence in central government's decisions or institutions
- Positive statements about regional representation in central institutions, including courts, upper houses
- Positive statements about regional influence over cooperation/coordination within state

+2 Autonomist

- Proposals for institutional reform strengthening the position of the regions on the federal level, stance in favour of full-fledged federal system, or even independence
- Claims for additional powers to be given to the regional parliament: general
- Claims for additional powers to be given to the regional parliament/the region with regard to specific policy domains
- Disadvantages/dangers stemming from absence of further decentralization, negative evaluation of continuing to be part of the union
- Need to defend regional autonomy and powers
- Support for subsidiarity as an argument in favour of more autonomy
- Cooperation with other regions in order to give more powers to the regions and with other areas considered to be part of the region and currently not the case
- Demand for additional fiscal autonomy or additional resources to the region, including borrowing powers
- Need for more regional influence in central government's decisions or institutions
- Need for more regional representation in central institutions, including courts, upper houses
- Need for more intergovernmental cooperation/coordination led by regional authorities

---

THEME 2: Identity/Cosmopolitanism

-2 Centralist direction

- Scale down some accomplishments in cultural matters

-1 Status quo centralist

- Positive mention of common statewide historical/cultural heritage (past and present)
- Warnings against excessive ethno-nationalism and/or further decentralization as a possible threat to national identity
- Dual identity: positive
- Pride in the common historical or cultural heritage, importance of common identity

Table A2 (*continued*)

- Supporting a regional culture, more embedded in the national culture
- Cohesion with other regional identities
- Cultural cooperation between the regions and the central state
- Interregional cooperation (with central impulse)
- Cooperation to improve mutual knowledge as positive from a more centralist perspective
- Warnings against further threat to harmony between the inhabitants of the region because of cultural differences
- Positive mention of state immigration policy and statewide integration of immigrants
- Positive mention of state minorities policy and statewide treatment of minorities
- Negative feelings about the nationalism of other parties (culturally), if they threaten national/regional unity

0 Status quo
- Neutral statements of fact
- Statements that can be interpreted ambiguously in the context of regionalism

+1 Status quo autonomist
- Positive statements about (the promotion of) regional identity/regional heritage/regional conscience in the past and present
- Diversity, dual/plural identity/reality positive, if meant positive for the regions/the regional culture, etc.
- Opposing threats to regional identity (immigration, dilution of language)
- Positive statements about immigrants bolstering population and economic growth of region
- Positive statements about multiculturalism/interculturalism of the region
- Immigrants forming a key part of a cosmopolitan region
- Positive towards the historical/cultural patrimony of the region
- Positive feelings towards regional identity but making a clear difference between the identity they are proposing and the identity other parties propose
- Positive mention of regional immigration policy and regional integration of immigrants
- Positive mention of regional minorities policy and regional treatment of minorities (i.e., ethnic and religious groups, national minorities, First Nations)
- Reference to cultural politics in the future
- Promoting cultural collaboration between the regions to get to know different regional cultures

+2 Autonomist direction
- Strengthening regional identity if positive towards the regional cultures/ identities

Table A2 (*continued*)

- Establishing (new institutions to preserve) the region's cultural heritage
- Seeking more control over regional immigration policy, including immigrant integration
- Seeking more regional control over national and ethnic minorities policy (e.g., First Nations)
- Suggestions for new regionalist ceremonies
- Need to defend the regional identity and the regional patrimony
- Stimulating more regionalist attitude of government and population

---

THEME 3: *Identity/Language*

-2 Centralist direction
- Scale down some accomplishments in linguistic matters

-1 Status quo centralist
- Positive statements about promotion of state language in the past and present
- Importance of bilingualism, against discrimination of people not speaking the regional language; collaboration between two languages and people speaking these languages, stressing harmony
- Importance of the national/shared language
- Positive towards the promotion of the national language (as an element that binds the country)
- Negative feelings about the promotion of the regional language (by the other parties) or being hesitant about the current language policy

o Status quo
- Neutral statements of fact
- Statements that can be interpreted ambiguously in the context of regionalism

+1 Status quo autonomist
- Positive statements about promotion of regional language in the past and the present; revival of regional language
- Discrimination of the regional language by other parties/governments in daily life
- Talking about the national language as the "regional language," so the national language as a binding element of the region
- Reference to language policy in the future
- Positive attitude towards the regional language, but opposing what they see as divisive/extremist language policy

+2 Autonomist direction
- Strengthening the positions of the regional language(s)
- Negative statements about perceived discrimination against regional language

Table A2 (*continued*)

• Reduce usage of the state language

THEME 4: *Regional Interests/Supranationalism*

-2 Centralist direction
- • Reduce powers/representation of the region in supranational forums, including the EU/NAFTA

-1 Status quo centralist
- • Defence of a strong union, for this reason promoting cooperation/dialogue with the regions concerning relevant EU or NAFTA issues
- • Promoting the union to strengthen the state's influence in supranational affairs (i.e., EU/NAFTA) and international affairs (i.e., UN peacekeeping, other foreign affairs)
- • Cooperation between the regions and the state to perform better on European and North American levels and stressing the loyalty of the regions to the state in EU/NAFTA
- • General promotion of the state abroad

0 Status quo
- • Neutral statements of fact on supranational impact and opportunities to represent the region in supranational forums
- • Statements that can be interpreted ambiguously on EU/NAFTA matters

+1 Status quo autonomist
- • Positive impact of decentralization on the region's presence in international and supranational forums in the past and present: general
- • Positive impact of decentralization on the region's presence in international and supranational forums in the past and present with regard to the EU/NAFTA
- • Positive impact of decentralization on the region's presence in international and supranational forums in the past and present: specific examples other than EU and NAFTA (e.g., UN bodies)
- • Decentralization as an instrument to promote the region's presence in international forums in the future: general
- • Decentralization as an instrument to promote the region's presence in international forums in the future with regard to the EU/NAFTA
- • Decentralization as an instrument to promote the region's presence in international forums in the future: specific examples other than EU and NAFTA (e.g., UN bodies)
- • Better representation of the region through the joint state's foreign policy instruments
- • General promotion of the region abroad
- • General promotion of paradiplomatic activities and the external relations of the region

Table A2 (*continued*)

___

+2 Autonomist direction
- Strengthening the position of the region in international forums: general
- Strengthening the position of the region in international forums with regard to the EU/NAFTA
- Strengthening the position of the region in international forums, specific examples other than EU and NAFTA
- Strengthening the paradiplomatic activities and external relations of the region

___

THEME 5: *Regional Interests/Social Model*

___

-2 Centralist direction
- Negative feelings towards existence of regional political culture
- Need for a stronger statewide political culture
- Negative feeling towards regional mode of governance

-1 Status quo centralist
- Positive mention of statewide political culture and mode of governance (past and present)
- Positive mention of common statewide political/economic heritage (past and present)
- Positive mention of statewide solidarity
- Positive mention of shared understandings across state regarding preferences, priorities
- Importance of continuing to share in statewide political culture (future)
- Importance of the national/shared political culture
- Positive towards the promotion of a national political culture (as an element that binds the country)
- Negative feelings about the promotion of a regional political culture (by the other parties)

0 Status quo
- Neutral statements of fact
- Statements that can be interpreted ambiguously on regional and national political culture

+1 Status quo autonomist
- Positive mention of regional political/economic heritage (past or present and even future)
- Positive mentions of regional diversity within state on values of governing ("we do things one way; others do things another way")
- Positive references to region as distinct (including distinct society)
- Positive statements about promotion of regional political culture in the past and the present; revival of regional "ways of doing things"
- Discrimination of the regional political culture/mode of governance by other parties/governments in daily life

Table A2 (*continued*)

- Statements on the specificity of the region that require a different mode of governance

+2 Autonomist direction
- Strengthening the regional political culture and mode of governance
- Strengthening distinctiveness of region (including distinct society)
- Promotion of regional solidarity, as opposed to statewide solidarity
- Negative statements on the impact of national political culture on the region
- Negative statements on the impact of national modes of governance on the region

---

THEME 6: Regional Interests/Economy

-2 Centralist direction
- Need for stronger statewide economic planning and development
- Need for reduced regional powers in economic planning and development

-1 Status quo centralist
- Positive mention of statewide economic model and state planning (past and present)
- Importance of continuing to share in statewide economic model (future)
- Negative feeling towards regional modes of economic development and the promotion of a separate regional economy

o Status quo
- Neutral statements of fact
- Statements that can be interpreted ambiguously on regional and national political culture

+1 Status quo autonomist
- Positive statements about promotion of regional economic model and regional development and planning (past and present)
- Positive statements about a regional economic approach or "way of doing things"

+2 Autonomist direction
- Strengthening the regional economic approach
- Strengthening powers over regional development and planning
- Criticizing harmful effects of statewide economic approach on regional economic development
- Criticizing harmful effects of statewide economic approach on regional natural resources

Appendix B

Table B1
Variables for Quebec

		Dependent variables[a]
PQ	Dummy	1 = Vote for Parti Québécois in Quebec provincial election 2014 0 = Vote for another party
QS	Dummy	1 = Vote for Québec Solidaire in Quebec provincial election 2014 0 = Vote for another party
CAQ	Dummy	1 = Vote for Coalition Avenir Québec in Quebec provincial election 2014 0 = Vote for another party
PLQ	Dummy	1 = Vote for Parti Libéral du Québec in Quebec provincial election 2014 0 = Vote for another party
CPC	Dummy	1 = Vote for Conservative Party of Canada in Canadian federal election 2011 0 = Vote for another party
NDP	Dummy	1 = Vote for New Democratic Party in Canadian federal election 2011 0 = Vote for another party

BQ	Dummy	1 = Vote for Bloc Québécois in Canadian federal election 2011
		0 = Vote for another party
LPC	Dummy	1 = Vote for the Liberal Party of Canada in Canadian federal election 2011
		0 = Vote for another party

Sociodemographic variables

Age	Scale	Age of respondents, rescaled from (0) to (1)
Female	Dummy	1 = Female; 0 = Male
Language	Dummy	1 = Respondents who speak French at home
		0 = Non-French

Socioeconomic variables[b]

| Education | 11-point scale | Highest level of education that has been completed by the respondents. Scores are rescaled from 0 (no education) to 1 (masters or doctorate). |
| Income | 9-point scale | Respondents' household income on a 9-point scale, rescaled from 0 (less than $8,000) to 1 ($104,000 and more). |

Political attitudes[c]

Left-right	11-point scale	Respondents' ideology on an 11-point level scale, rescaled from 0 (left) to 1 (right).
Moral liberalism	Scale	Scores are means of two variables: Are you for or against marriage between people of the same sex? 0 (against); 0.5 (missing); 1 (for) Are you for or against the death penalty? 0 (for); 0.5 (missing); 1 (against)
Cynicism	Scale	Scores are means of three variables: The National Assembly of Quebec does not care much about what people think: 0 (disagree); 0.5 (missing); 1 (agree) People like me have no say in what the provincial government in Quebec does: 0 (disagree); 0.5 (missing); 1 (agree) Overall, are you satisfied with the way democracy works in Quebec? 0 (satisfied); 0.5 (missing); 1 (unsatisfied)

Table B1 (*continued*)

		Identity[c]
Identity	5-point scale	Respondents' opinion on their identity, varying from 1 (only Canadian, not Quebecer) to 5 (only Quebecer, not Canadian). Scores are rescaled from 0 to 1.
AttachQC	4-point scale	Respondents' level of attachment to Quebec, varying from 1 (not at all attached) to 4 (very attached), rescaled from 0 to 1.
AttachCAN	4-point scale	Respondents' level of attachment to Canada, varying from 1 (not at all attached) to 4 (very attached), rescaled from 0 to 1.

		Values[c]
Values	11-point scale	Respondents' opinion on their distinct values, varying from 0 (same values) to 10 (distinct values). Scores are rescaled from 0 to 1.
Market	11-point scale	Respondents' opinion on the importance of market, varying from 0 (larger market with less sovereignty) to 10 (more sovereignty with smaller market). Scores are rescaled from 0 to 1.

		Political issues
Independence	Dummy	0 = Otherwise 1 = Opinion in favour of Quebec independence Missing observations are coded as missing.
More powers	Dummy	0 = Otherwise 1 = Opinion in favour of more powers for the National Assembly of Quebec Missing observations are coded as missing.
IMPCONST	4-point scale	Respondents' opinion on the constitutional preferences of the party varying from 1 (not at all important) to 4 (very important). Scores are rescaled from 0 to 1. Missing observations are coded as 0.5.
IMPCONSTIND	Scale	Interactive variable IMPCONST*Independence
IMPCONSTPWRS	Scale	Interactive variable IMPCONST*Powers

Table B1 (*continued*)

		Instrumental variables (IVs)
IVPLQ	Dummy	1 = Parti Libéral du Québec best stands up for the interests of Quebec 0 = Otherwise
IVPQ	Dummy	1 = Parti Québécois best stands up for the interests of Quebec 0 = Otherwise
IVCAQ	Dummy	1 = Coalition Avenir Québec best stands up for the interests of Quebec 0 = Otherwise
IVQS	Dummy	1 = Québec Solidaire best stands up for the interests of Quebec 0 = Otherwise

Technical note: To expunge partisan projection effect in the instrumental variables, we isolate the unexplained component by partisan identification (PID), considering the prediction errors of regression models concerning the PID effect on the instrumental variables. The approach consists of running the appropriate regression model (IVPARTY = f(PIDPARTY) and creating a new variable (IVPARTY_RESID), whose scores correspond to residuals of the regression.

IVPLQ_RESID = scores are the residuals of the model: IVPLQ = f(PIDPLQ).
IVPQ_RESID = scores are the residuals of the model: IVPQ = f(PIDPQ).
IVCAQ_RESID = scores are the residuals of the model: IVCAQ = f(PIDCAQ).
IVQS_RESID = scores are the residuals of the model: IVQS = f(PIDQS).

Notes:
[a] Abstentions, blank votes, or missing observations are coded as missing.
[b] Missing observations are coded as missing.
[c] Missing observations are coded as 0.5.

Table B2
Variables for Scotland

	Dependent variables[a]	
SNP	Dummy	1 = Vote for Scottish National Party in devolved Scottish election 2011 0 = Vote for another party
Labour	Dummy	1 = Vote for Labour Party in devolved Scottish election 2011 0 = Vote for another party
LibDem	Dummy	1 = Vote for Liberal Democrats in devolved Scottish election 2011 0 = Vote for another party
Cons	Dummy	1 = Vote for Conservative Party in devolved Scottish election 2011 0 = Vote for another party
SNPUK	Dummy	1 = Vote for Scottish National Party in UK general election 2010 0 = Vote for another party
LabourUK	Dummy	1 = Vote for Labour Party in UK general election 2010 0 = Vote for another party
LibDemUK	Dummy	1 = Vote for Liberal Democrats in UK general election 2010 0 = Vote for another party
ConsUK	Dummy	1 = Vote for Conservative Party in UK general election 2010 0 = Vote for another party
	Sociodemographic variables	
Age	Scale	Age of respondents, rescaled from (0) to (1)
Female	Dummy	1 = Female; 0 = Male
	Socioeconomic variables[b]	
Education	11-point scale	Highest level of education that has been completed by respondents. Scores are rescaled from 0 (no education) to 1 (masters or doctorate).

Table B2 (*continued*)

Income	9-point scale	Respondents' household income on a 9-point scale, rescaled from 0 (less than £5,000) to 1 (£65,000 and more).

Political attitudes[c]

Left-right	11-point scale	Respondents' ideology on an 11-point scale, rescaled from 0 (left) to 1 (right).
Moral liberalism	Scale	Scores are means of two variables: Are you for or against marriage between people of the same sex? 0 (against); 0.5 (missing); 1 (for) Are you for or against the death penalty? 0 (for); 0.5 (missing); 1 (against)
Cynicism	Scale	Scores are means of three variables: The Scottish Parliament does not care much about what people think: 0 (disagree); 0.5 (missing); 1 (agree) People like me have no say in what the Scottish Parliament does: 0 (disagree); 0.5 (missing); 1 (agree) Overall, are you satisfied with the way democracy works in Scotland? 0 (satisfied); 0.5 (missing); 1 (unsatisfied)

Identity[c]

Identity	5-point scale	Respondents' opinion on their identity, varying from 1 (only British, not Scottish) to 5 (only Scottish, not British). Scores are rescaled from 0 to 1.
AttachSC	4-point scale	Respondents' level of attachment to Scotland, varying from 1 (not at all attached) to 4 (very attached), rescaled from 0 to 1.
AttachUK	4-point scale	Respondents' level of attachment to the UK, varying from 1 (not at all attached) to 4 (very attached), rescaled from 0 to 1.

Table B2 (*continued*)

		Values[c]
Values	11-point scale	Respondents' opinion on their distinct values, varying from 0 (same values) to 10 (distinct values). Scores are rescaled from 0 to 1.
Market	11-point scale	Respondents' opinion on the importance of market, varying from 1 (larger market with less sovereignty) to 10 (more sovereignty with smaller market). Scores are rescaled from 0 to 1.

		Political issues
Independence	Dummy	0 = Otherwise 1 = Opinion in favour of Scotland's independence Missing observations are coded as missing.
More powers	Dummy	0 = Otherwise 1 = Opinion in favour of more powers for the Scottish Parliament Missing observations are coded as missing.
IMPCONST	4-point scale	Respondents' opinion on the constitutional preferences of the party, varying from 1 (not at all important) to 4 (very important). Scores are rescaled from 0 to 1. Missing observations are coded as 0.5.
IMPCONSTIND	Scale	Interactive variable IMPCONST*Independence
IMPCONSTPWRS	Scale	Interactive variable IMPCONST*Powers

		Instrumental variables (IVs)
IVSNP	Dummy	1 = Scottish National Party best stands up for the interests of Scotland 0 = Otherwise
IVLABOUR	Dummy	1 = Labour Party best stands up for the interests of Scotland 0 = Otherwise

Table B2 (*continued*)

| IVLIBDEM | Dummy | 1 = Liberals Democrats best stand up for the interests of Scotland
0 = Otherwise |
| IVCONS | Dummy | 1 = Conservative Party best stands up for the interests of Scotland
0 = Otherwise |

Technical note: To expunge partisan projection effect in the instrumental variables, we isolate the unexplained component by partisan identification (PID), considering the prediction errors of regression models concerning the PID effect on instrumental variables. The approach consists of running the appropriate regression model (IVPARTY = f(PIDPARTY) and creating a new variable (IVPARTY_RESID) which scores correspond to residuals of the regression.

IVSNP_RESID = scores are the residuals of the model: IVSNP = f(PIDSNP).
IVLABOUR_RESID = scores are the residuals of the model: IVLABOUR= f(PIDLABOUR).
IVLIBDEM_RESID = scores are the residuals of the model: IVLIBDEM = f(PIDLIBDEM).
IVCONS_RESID = scores are the residuals of the model: IVCONS = f(PIDCONS).

Notes:
[a] Abstentions, blank votes, or missing observations are coded as missing.
[b] Missing observations are coded as missing.
[c] Missing observations are coded as 0.5.

Appendix C

REGRESSION RESULTS, QUEBEC

Table C1
Logistic regression voting models for provincial election in Quebec:
Sociodemographic and attitudinal variables

	PQ	QS	CAQ	PLQ
Age	1.38**	−2.65**	−0.47	0.47
	(0.31)	(0.55)	(0.32)	(0.33)
Female	−0.14	0.06	−0.31*	0.45**
	(0.15)	(0.24)	(0.15)	(0.16)
Language	2.40**	1.69**	2.24**	−3.08**
	(0.40)	(0.55)	(0.36)	(0.25)
Education	−0.86**	1.88**	−0.48	0.50
	(0.33)	(0.57)	(0.34)	(0.34)
Income	−0.75**	−0.15	0.62*	0.30
	(0.29)	(0.45)	(0.30)	(0.30)
Left-right	−1.89**	−3.16**	0.90*	2.22**
	(0.36)	(0.63)	(0.36)	(0.38)
Moral liberalism	0.83**	2.12**	−0.81**	−0.67**
	(0.25)	(0.52)	(0.25)	(0.25)
Cynicism	−0.59*	1.01*	0.91**	−0.83**
	(0.25)	(0.43)	(0.26)	(0.26)
Constant	−1.93**	−4.85**	−3.37**	0.65
	(0.57)	(0.93)	(0.57)	(0.50)
Nagelkerke pseudo-R^2	0.21	0.29	0.14	0.37
% correctly predicted	72.1%	92.7%	76.7%	77.1%
N	1,127	1,127	1,127	1,127

**$p \leq 0.01$; *$p \leq 0.05$ (two-tailed tests). Entries represent unstandardized logistic regression coefficients (with standard deviations in parentheses).

Table C2
Logistic regression voting models for provincial election in Quebec:
Attachment and identification variables

	PQ	QS	CAQ	PLQ
Age	1.49**	−2.47**	−0.26	0.50
	(0.38)	(0.57)	(0.33)	(0.40)
Female	0.03	0.11	−0.36*	0.41*
	(0.17)	(0.25)	(0.16)	(0.18)
Language	0.81	1.47*	2.50**	−2.02**
	(0.45)	(0.62)	(0.37)	(0.28)
Education	−1.39**	1.64**	−0.48	0.72
	(0.38)	(0.58)	(0.35)	(0.42)
Income	−0.50	−0.12	0.54	0.01
	(0.33)	(0.46)	(0.31)	(0.36)
Left right	−0.25	−2.81**	0.46	0.89
	(0.42)	(0.67)	(0.39)	(0.47)
Moral liberalism	0.38	2.00**	−0.69**	−0.26
	(0.29)	(0.53)	(0.25)	(0.30)
Cynicism	−0.80**	0.82	0.87**	−0.80**
	(0.29)	(0.44)	(0.26)	−(0.30)
Identity	3.19**	−0.84	0.32	−1.65**
	(0.63)	(0.90)	(0.49)	(0.53)
AttachQC	1.90**	−0.72	−1.16**	−0.67
	(0.56)	(0.75)	(0.41)	(0.48)
AttachCAN	−2.21**	−1.72**	0.77*	4.18**
	(0.35)	(0.55)	(0.32)	(0.44)
Constant	−3.52**	−2.54*	−3.15**	−1.28
	(0.87)	(1.15)	(0.69)	(0.72)
Nagelkerke pseudo-R^2	0.46	0.31	0.16	0.59
% correctly predicted	79.9%	92.6%	76.4%	83.6%
N	1,127	1,127	1,127	1,127

**$p \leq 0.01$; *$p \leq 0.05$ (two-tailed tests). Entries represent unstandardized logistic regression coefficients (with standard deviations in parentheses).

Table C3
Logistic regression voting models for provincial election in Quebec:
Cost-benefit variables

	PQ	*QS*	*CAQ*	*PLQ*
Age	1.62**	−2.46**	−0.33	0.42
	(0.38)	(0.57)	(0.34)	(0.41)
Female	0.03	0.10	−0.36*	0.38*
	(0.17)	(0.25)	(0.16)	(0.19)
Language	0.81	1.45*	2.51**	−2.01**
	(0.47)	(0.63)	(0.37)	(0.29)
Education	−1.45**	1.60**	−0.47	0.82
	(0.38)	(0.58)	(0.35)	(0.42)
Income	−0.43	−0.12	0.52	−0.10
	(0.35)	(0.46)	(0.31)	(0.36)
Left-right	−0.11	−2.82**	0.41	0.71
	(0.43)	(0.70)	(0.39)	(0.48)
Moral liberalism	0.31	1.97**	−0.66**	−0.21
	(0.29)	(0.53)	(0.26)	(0.30)
Cynicism	−0.82**	0.78	0.91**	−0.78**
	(0.30)	(0.44)	(0.26)	(0.30)
Identity	2.83**	−1.04	0.50	−1.22*
	(0.66)	(0.92)	(0.50)	(0.55)
AttachQC	1.49**	−0.93	−1.02*	−0.45
	(0.57)	(0.77)	(0.42)	(0.48)
AttachCAN	−1.53**	−1.49*	0.49	3.59**
	(0.39)	(0.60)	(0.36)	(0.47)
Values	0.32	0.08	−0.11	−0.46
	(0.34)	(0.57)	(0.30)	(0.32)
Market	1.70**	0.75	−0.71*	−1.27**
	(0.40)	(0.59)	(0.36)	(0.41)
Constant	−4.35**	−2.68*	−2.84**	−0.51
	(0.91)	(1.19)	(0.72)	(0.76)
Nagelkerke pseudo-R^2	0.48	0.32	0.17	0.60
% correctly predicted	81.5%	92.6%	76.1%	83.0%
N	1,127	1,127	1,127	1,127

**$p \leq 0.01$; *$p \leq 0.05$ (two-tailed tests). Entries represent unstandardized logistic regression coefficients (with standard deviations in parentheses).

Table C4
Logistic regression voting models for provincial election in Quebec:
Constitutional preferences

	PQ	QS	CAQ	PLQ
Age	1.58**	−2.56**	−0.38	0.75
	(0.39)	(0.58)	(0.35)	(0.43)
Female	0.14	0.02	−0.45**	0.36
	(0.18)	(0.25)	(0.16)	(0.19)
Language	0.88	1.20	2.31**	−2.04**
	(0.48)	(0.64)	(0.37)	(0.30)
Education	−1.27**	1.56**	−0.63	0.70
	(0.40)	(0.59)	(0.36)	(0.43)
Income	−0.35	−0.20	0.45	−0.29
	(0.35)	(0.46)	(0.31)	(0.37)
Left-right	−0.03	−3.13**	0.32	0.65
	(0.44)	(0.73)	(0.40)	(0.49)
Moral liberalism	0.14	1.94**	−0.68**	−0.18
	(0.31)	(0.53)	(0.26)	(0.31)
Cynicism	−0.82**	0.77	0.88**	−0.77*
	(0.31)	(0.44)	(0.27)	(0.31)
Identity	1.94**	−1.07	0.73	−0.58
	(0.69)	(0.95)	(0.53)	(0.58)
AttachQC	0.93	−0.62	−0.73	−0.33
	(0.58)	(0.80)	(0.42)	(0.49)
AttachCAN	−0.87*	−1.76**	−0.07	3.00**
	(0.42)	(0.63)	(0.38)	(0.49)
Values	0.04	0.03	−0.01	−0.14
	(0.36)	(0.58)	(0.31)	(0.34)
Market	1.01*	1.01	−0.34	−0.87*
	(0.43)	(0.62)	(0.38)	(0.43)
Independence	1.36**	−0.86*	−1.33**	−1.20**
	(0.23)	(0.36)	(0.24)	(0.37)
More powers	0.55*	0.64	0.28	−0.75**
	(0.23)	(0.35)	(0.19)	(0.21)
Constant	−4.31**	−2.42*	−2.40**	−0.18
	(0.91)	(1.20)	(0.73)	(0.78)
Nagelkerke pseudo-R^2	0.52	0.33	0.21	0.62
% correctly predicted	83.4%	92.4%	77.8%	83.7%
N	1,127	1,127	1,127	1,127

$**p \leq 0.01$; $*p \leq 0.05$ (two-tailed tests). Entries represent unstandardized logistic regression coefficients
(with standard deviations in parentheses).

Table C5

Logistic regression voting models for provincial election in Quebec:
Salience of the national question

	PQ	QS	CAQ	PLQ
Age	1.57**	−2.52**	−0.45	0.92*
	(0.39)	(0.59)	(0.36)	(0.43)
Female	0.14	0.03	−0.41*	0.32
	(0.18)	(0.25)	(0.16)	(0.19)
Language	0.99*	0.95	2.10**	−1.86**
	(0.48)	(0.65)	(0.37)	(0.31)
Education	−1.31**	1.58**	−0.71	0.81
	(0.40)	(0.60)	(0.36)	(0.43)
Income	−0.26	−0.29	0.36	−0.15
	(0.35)	(0.47)	(0.32)	(0.38)
Left-right	−0.02	−3.27**	0.35	0.47
	(0.44)	(0.75)	(0.42)	(0.49)
Moral liberalism	0.20	1.90**	−0.81**	−0.10
	(0.31)	(0.53)	(0.27)	(0.32)
Cynicism	−0.78*	0.67	0.81**	−0.70*
	(0.31)	(0.44)	(0.27)	(0.32)
Identity	1.99*	−1.24	0.48	−0.32
	(0.67)	(0.96)	(0.54)	(0.59)
AttachQC	0.75	−0.48	−0.53	−0.53
	(0.58)	(0.81)	(0.43)	(0.50)
AttachCAN	−0.92*	−1.80**	0.09	2.84**
	(0.42)	(0.64)	(0.39)	(0.49)
Values	0.02	0.06	0.02	−0.17
	(0.36)	(0.59)	(0.31)	(0.34)
Market	0.95*	1.16	−0.29	−0.92*
	(0.43)	(0.64)	(0.39)	(0.43)
Independence	1.30**	−0.69	−1.13**	−1.42**
	(0.24)	(0.37)	(0.25)	(0.37)
More powers	0.60**	0.53	0.25	−0.76**
	(0.23)	(0.35)	(0.19)	(0.21)
IMPCONST	0.78*	−1.25**	−1.45**	1.65**
	(0.32)	(0.43)	(0.27)	(0.33)
Constant	−4.82**	−1.31	−1.24	−1.43
	(0.94)	(1.27)	(0.77)	(0.83)
Nagelkerke pseudo-R^2	0.52	0.35	0.24	0.64
% correctly predicted	83.5%	93.0%	77.0%	85.0%
N	1,127	1,127	1,127	1,127

$**p \leq 0.01$; $*p \leq 0.05$ (two-tailed tests). Entries represent unstandardized logistic regression coefficients (with standard deviations in parentheses).

Table C6
Logistic regression voting models for provincial election in Quebec:
Interactive variables

	PQ	QS	CAQ	PLQ
Age	1.51**	−2.46**	−0.46	0.98*
	(0.40)	(0.59)	(0.36)	(0.44)
Female	0.15	0.01	−0.41*	0.32
	(0.19)	(0.25)	(0.16)	(0.20)
Language	0.87	1.03	2.10**	−1.86**
	(0.51)	(0.66)	(0.37)	(0.31)
Education	1.47**	1.61**	−0.68	0.83
	(0.42)	(0.60)	(0.37)	(0.44)
Income	−0.26	−0.28	0.40	−0.18
	(0.36)	(0.47)	(0.32)	(0.38)
Left-right	0.21	−3.35**	0.25	0.44
	(0.47)	(0.76)	(0.42)	(0.50)
Moral liberalism	0.18	1.85**	−0.79**	−0.09
	(0.31)	(0.53)	(0.27)	(0.32)
Cynicism	−0.79*	0.65	0.81**	−0.69*
	(0.32)	(0.45)	(0.27)	(0.32)
Identity	1.61*	−1.11	0.56	−0.25
	(0.70)	(0.96)	(0.54)	(0.60)
AttachQC	0.88	−0.51	−0.56	−0.54
	(0.59)	(0.81)	(0.43)	(0.50)
AttachCAN	−0.99*	−1.82**	0.07	2.87**
	(0.43)	(0.64)	(0.39)	(0.50)
Values	−0.13	0.05	0.11	−0.15
	(0.38)	(0.59)	(0.32)	(0.35)
Market	0.94*	1.20	−0.27	−0.90*
	(0.45)	(0.65)	(0.39)	(0.44)
Independence	−0.98*	−0.19	0.05	0.18
	(0.48)	(0.63)	(0.46)	(0.91)
More powers	0.66	0.62	−0.41	−0.54
	(0.51)	(0.68)	(0.39)	(0.52)
IMPCONST	−0.93	−0.72	−1.54**	1.93**
	(0.59)	(0.79)	(0.39)	(0.40)
IMPCONSTIND	3.68**	−0.90	−2.09**	−2.18
	(0.68)	(0.94)	(0.71)	(1.25)
IMPCONSTPWRS	−0.05	−0.19	1.07	−0.37
	(0.71)	(0.98)	(0.57)	(0.70)
Constant	−3.44**	−1.67	−1.21	−1.68*
	(1.02)	(1.36)	(0.80)	(0.85)
Nagelkerke pseudo-R^2	0.55	0.35	0.25	0.64
% correctly predicted	84.6%	92.6%	77.1%	85.1%
N	1,127	1,127	1,127	1,127

**$p \leq 0.01$; *$p \leq 0.05$ (two-tailed tests). Entries represent unstandardized logistic regression coefficients (with standard deviations in parentheses).

Table C7
Logistic regression voting models for provincial election in Quebec:
Party image models

	PQ	QS	CAQ	PLQ
Age	1.53**	−2.50**	−0.45	0.80
	(0.41)	(0.59)	(0.37)	(0.45)
Female	0.15	−0.01	−0.41*	0.34
	(0.19)	(0.26)	(0.17)	(0.20)
Language	0.73	1.06	2.05**	−1.98**
	(0.52)	(0.67)	(0.38)	(0.31)
Education	−1.61**	1.52*	−0.67	0.95*
	(0.43)	(0.60)	(0.38)	(0.45)
Income	−0.28	−0.31	0.44	−0.13
	(0.36)	(0.47)	(0.33)	(0.39)
Left-right	0.17	−3.08**	−0.07	0.54
	(0.48)	(0.77)	(0.45)	(0.51)
Moral liberalism	0.11	1.83**	−0.79**	0.15
	(0.32)	(0.53)	(0.28)	(0.32)
Cynicism	−0.76*	0.61	0.62*	−0.53
	(0.32)	(0.45)	(0.28)	(0.33)
Identity	1.60*	−1.15	0.47	−0.27
	(0.71)	(0.97)	(0.56)	(0.61)
AttachQC	0.93	−0.36	−0.48	−0.75
	(0.60)	(0.81)	(0.45)	(0.51)
AttachCAN	−0.95*	−1.97**	0.09	2.71**
	(0.44)	(0.65)	(0.41)	(0.50)
Values	−0.21	0.05	0.14	−0.12
	(0.39)	(0.60)	(0.32)	(0.35)
Market	0.88	1.08	−0.25	−0.86
	(0.46)	(0.65)	(0.40)	(0.45)
Independence	−0.87	−0.28	0.01	0.39
	(0.49)	(0.64)	(0.49)	(0.92)
More powers	0.58	0.75	−0.48	−0.50
	(0.51)	(0.68)	(0.41)	(0.54)
IMPCONST	−0.96	−0.58	−1.68**	2.03**
	(0.60)	(0.80)	(0.40)	(0.42)
IMPCONSTIND	3.59**	−0.80	−2.04**	−2.33
	(0.70)	(0.96)	(0.74)	(1.26)
IMPCONSTPWRS	−0.04	−0.37	1.31*	−0.34
	(0.72)	(0.99)	(0.59)	(0.72)
IVPQ_RESID	1.20**	–	–	–
	(0.23)			
IVQS_RESID	–	1.16**	–	–
		(0.40)		
IVCAQ_RESID	–	–	1.77**	–
			(0.25)	

Table C7 (*continued*)

	PQ	QS	CAQ	PLQ
IV<small>PLQ</small>_RESID	–	–	–	1.33**
				(0.25)
Constant	−3.13**	−1.77	−0.99	−1.59
	(1.04)	(1.36)	(0.83)	(0.87)
Nagelkerke pseudo-R^2	0.57	0.36	0.31	0.66
% correctly predicted	84.6%	92.9%	82.0%	86.4%
N	1,127	1,127	1,127	1,127

$**p \leq 0.01$; $*p \leq 0.05$ (two-tailed tests). Entries represent unstandardized logistic regression coefficients (with standard deviations in parentheses).

Table C8

Logistic regression voting models for federal election in Quebec: Sociodemographic and attitudinal variables

	BQ	NDP	LPC	CPC
Age	0.38	−0.77**	1.19**	0.07
	(0.32)	(0.26)	(0.40)	(0.42)
Female	−0.37*	0.45**	0.09	−0.31
	(0.15)	(0.13)	(0.19)	(0.21)
Language	4.32**	0.21	−1.68**	−0.41
	(0.95)	(0.19)	(0.21)	(0.27)
Education	0.66	−0.61*	1.26**	−1.31**
	(0.34)	(0.29)	(0.45)	(0.45)
Income	0.07*	−0.11	−0.24	0.30
	(0.29)	(0.24)	(0.38)	(0.38)
Left-right	−2.79**	−0.10	2.05**	3.44**
	(0.39)	(0.31)	(0.49)	(0.52)
Moral liberalism	0.73**	0.04	0.49	−1.60**
	(0.26)	(0.21)	(0.32)	(0.30)
Cynicism	0.79**	0.49**	−0.52*	−1.60**
	(0.23)	(0.18)	(0.27)	(0.27)
Constant	−5.19**	−0.07	−3.12**	−1.04
	(1.05)	(0.40)	(0.62)	(0.63)
Nagelkerke pseudo-R^2	0.24	0.05	0.19	0.27
% correctly predicted	75.1%	58.8%	86.9%	87.1%
N	1,091	1,091	1,091	1,091

$**p \leq 0.01$; $*p \leq 0.05$ (two-tailed tests). Entries represent unstandardized logistic regression coefficients (with standard deviations in parentheses).

Table C9
Logistic regressions voting models for federal election in Quebec:
Identity and attachment

	BQ	NDP	LPC	CPC
Age	0.69	−0.91**	0.89*	0.28
	(0.37)	(0.27)	(0.42)	(0.45)
Female	−0.32	0.42**	0.03	−0.28
	(0.17)	(0.13)	(0.20)	(0.21)
Language	2.23*	0.55*	−0.74**	0.34
	(0.97)	(0.22)	(0.25)	(0.30)
Education	0.80*	−0.61*	1.34**	−1.28**
	(0.39)	(0.29)	(0.47)	(0.47)
Income	0.26	−0.18	−0.49	0.23
	(0.33)	(0.24)	(0.39)	(0.40)
Left-right	−0.99*	−0.51	0.91	2.83**
	(0.46)	(0.34)	(0.53)	(0.56)
Moral liberalism	0.13	0.15	0.80*	−1.31**
	(0.30)	(0.21)	(0.33)	(0.32)
Cynicism	0.40	0.59**	−0.27	−1.45**
	(0.27)	(0.19)	(0.27)	(0.28)
Identity	5.58**	−0.47	−1.40*	−0.94
	(0.72)	(0.40)	(0.57)	(0.59)
AttachQC	0.71	0.31	0.22	−1.93**
	(0.52)	(0.33)	(0.47)	(0.47)
AttachCAN	−1.05**	0.63*	2.22**	0.85
	(0.37)	(0.28)	(0.50)	(0.50)
Constant	−7.99**	−0.50	−4.31**	−0.24
	(1.26)	(0.50)	(0.76)	−(0.77)
Nagelkerke pseudo-R^2	0.46	0.06	0.28	0.34
% correctly predicted	81.1%	59.0%	87.7%	88.8%
N	1,091	1,091	1,091	1,091

$**p \leq 0.01$; $*p \leq 0.05$ (two-tailed tests). Entries represent unstandardized logistic regression coefficients (with standard deviations in parentheses).

Table C10
Logistic regressions for voting models for federal election in Quebec:
Cost-benefit variables

	BQ	NDP	LPC	CPC
Age	0.67	−0.90**	0.91*	0.16
	(0.37)	(0.27)	(0.42)	(0.45)
Female	−0.27	0.42**	−0.04	−0.48*
	(0.17)	(0.13)	(0.21)	(0.22)
Language	2.15*	0.54*	−0.70**	0.34
	(0.97)	(0.22)	(0.25)	(0.30)
Education	0.84*	−0.61*	1.42**	−1.23*
	(0.39)	(0.29)	(0.48)	(0.49)
Income	0.29	−0.17	−0.59	0.04
	(0.34)	(0.24)	(0.40)	(0.40)
Left-right	−0.61	−0.49	0.73	2.41**
	(0.48)	(0.34)	(0.54)	(0.57)
Moral liberalism	0.11	0.14	0.84*	−1.31**
	(0.30)	(0.21)	(0.33)	(0.32)
Cynicism	0.42	0.60**	−0.28	−1.52**
	(0.27)	(0.19)	(0.27)	(0.29)
Identity	5.24**	−0.49	−1.22*	−0.36
	(0.73)	(0.40)	(0.58)	(0.61)
AttachQC	0.36	0.30	0.30	−1.79**
	(0.53)	(0.34)	(0.48)	(0.48)
AttachCAN	−0.57	0.67*	1.87**	−0.13
	(0.39)	(0.31)	(0.54)	(0.55)
Values	0.64	−0.08	−0.24	−1.19**
	(0.36)	(0.25)	(0.36)	(0.38)
Market	0.89*	0.17	−0.79	−1.75**
	(0.38)	(0.28)	(0.43)	(0.50)
Constant	−8.73**	−0.54	−3.76**	1.63
	(1.28)	(0.54)	(0.82)	(0.87)
Nagelkerke pseudo-R^2	0.47	0.07	0.28	0.38
% correctly predicted	81.1%	59.6%	86.9%	89.0%
N	1,091	1,091	1,091	1,091

** $p \leq 0.01$; * $p \leq 0.05$ (two-tailed tests). Entries represent unstandardized logistic regression coefficients (with standard deviations in parentheses).

Table C11
Logistic regressions for voting models for federal election in Quebec:
Constitutional options

	BQ	NDP	LPC	CPC
Age	0.65	−0.98**	1.04*	0.35
	(0.37)	(0.27)	(0.42)	(0.46)
Female	−0.19	0.41**	−0.12	−0.53*
	(0.18)	(0.13)	(0.21)	(0.22)
Language	2.02*	0.33	−0.66**	0.49
	(0.97)	(0.22)	(0.25)	(0.31)
Education	0.83*	−0.59*	1.37**	−1.37**
	(0.39)	(0.29)	(0.48)	(0.50)
Income	0.31	−0.18	−0.64	0.06
	(0.34)	(0.25)	(0.40)	(0.41)
Left-right	−0.56	−0.53	0.61	2.37**
	(0.48)	(0.35)	(0.54)	(0.57)
Moral liberalism	0.08	0.14	0.86**	−1.27**
	(0.30)	(0.22)	(0.33)	(0.33)
Cynicism	0.38	0.55**	−0.23	−1.43**
	(0.28)	(0.19)	(0.27)	(0.29)
Identity	4.98**	−0.52	−1.01	−0.09
	(0.74)	(0.42)	(0.58)	(0.62)
AttachQC	0.16	0.30	0.52	−1.56**
	(0.55)	(0.35)	(0.49)	(0.49)
AttachCAN	−0.21	0.45	1.22*	−0.51
	(0.42)	(0.33)	(0.58)	(0.59)
Values	0.45	−0.09	−0.01	−0.98*
	(0.37)	(0.26)	(0.37)	(0.40)
Market	0.53	0.33	−0.48	−1.51**
	(0.40)	(0.29)	(0.45)	(0.52)
Independence	0.61*	−0.77**	−1.17**	−0.15
	(0.25)	(0.21)	(0.43)	(0.41)
More powers	0.29	0.72**	−0.27	−0.85**
	(0.27)	(0.18)	(0.26)	(0.27)
Constant	−8.69**	−0.34	−3.39**	1.68
	(1.29)	(0.55)	(0.83)	(0.89)
Nagelkerke pseudo-R^2	0.47	0.10	0.29	0.39
% correctly predicted	81.6%	61.9%	87.4%	89.4%
N	1,091	1,091	1,091	1,091

**$p \leq 0.01$; *$p \leq 0.05$ (two-tailed tests). Entries represent unstandardized logistic regression coefficients (with standard deviations in parentheses).

Table C12
Logistic regressions for voting models for federal election in Quebec:
Salience of the national question

	BQ	NDP	LPC	CPC
Age	0.57	−0.89**	1.00*	0.35
	(0.37)	(0.28)	(0.42)	(0.46)
Female	−0.19	0.44**	−0.17	−0.54*
	(0.18)	(0.13)	(0.21)	(0.23)
Language	1.97*	0.37	−0.69**	0.49
	(0.97)	(0.23)	(0.26)	(0.31)
Education	0.89*	−0.69*	1.42**	−1.37**
	(0.39)	(0.30)	(0.48)	(0.50)
Income	0.31	−0.18	−0.60	0.06
	(0.34)	(0.25)	(0.40)	(0.41)
Left-right	−0.51	−0.54	0.53	2.37**
	(0.48)	(0.35)	(0.54)	(0.57)
Moral liberalism	0.07	0.17	0.84*	−1.27**
	(0.30)	(0.22)	(0.34)	(0.33)
Cynicism	0.37	0.54**	−0.20	−1.43**
	(0.28)	(0.19)	(0.27)	(0.29)
Identity	4.99**	−0.64	−0.95	−0.09
	(0.74)	(0.42)	(0.59)	(0.63)
AttachQC	−0.01	0.47	0.50	−1.56**
	(0.56)	(0.35)	(0.49)	(0.49)
AttachCAN	−0.23	0.53	1.08	−0.51
	(0.42)	(0.34)	(0.59)	(0.59)
Values	0.39	−0.00	−0.04	−0.98*
	(0.37)	(0.26)	(0.37)	(0.40)
Market	0.45	0.41	−0.49	−1.51**
	(0.41)	(0.30)	(0.45)	(0.52)
Independence	0.62*	−0.68**	−1.28**	−0.16
	(0.25)	(0.21)	(0.44)	(0.41)
More powers	0.31	0.66**	−0.27	−0.85**
	(0.27)	(0.18)	(0.27)	(0.27)
IMPCONST	0.50	−0.95**	0.62	0.02
	(0.30)	(0.22)	(0.34)	(0.35)
Constant	−8.78**	0.06	−3.63**	1.67
	(1.29)	(0.56)	(0.85)	(0.90)
Nagelkerke pseudo-R^2	0.48	0.12	0.30	0.39
% correctly predicted	82.0%	63.1%	87.1%	89.3%
N	1,091	1,091	1,091	1,091

**$p \leq .01$; *$p \leq 0.05$ (two-tailed tests). Entries represent unstandardized logistic regression coefficients (with standard deviations in parentheses).

Table C13
Logistic regression models of support for Quebec independence

	(1)	(2)	(3)	(4)
Age	0.42	−0.08	−0.02	−0.04
	(0.28)	(0.41)	(0.43)	(0.43)
Female	−0.49**	−0.41*	−0.37	−0.39*
	(0.13)	(0.18)	(0.19)	(0.20)
Language	2.38**	−0.23	−0.59	−0.55
	(0.31)	(0.42)	(0.45)	(0.45)
Education	−0.37	−1.48**	−1.60**	−1.52**
	(0.30)	(0.43)	(0.45)	(0.46)
Income	−0.50	−0.14	−0.04	0.03
	(0.25)	(0.36)	(0.38)	(0.38)
Left-right	−2.83**	−1.01*	−0.76	−0.77
	(0.35)	(0.48)	(0.55)	(0.55)
Moral liberalism	0.84**	0.49	0.39	0.44
	(0.23)	(0.31)	(0.33)	(0.33)
Cynicism	−0.03	−0.21	−0.31	−0.27
	(0.22)	(0.32)	(0.34)	(0.35)
Identity	–	4.82**	4.55**	4.84**
		(0.77)	(0.84)	(0.86)
AttachQC	–	4.03**	3.24**	2.92**
		(0.59)	(0.62)	(0.62)
AttachCAN	–	−4.60**	−3.53**	−3.60**
		(0.41)	(0.45)	(0.46)
Values	–	–	0.68	0.60
			(0.38)	(0.39)
Market	–	–	4.27**	4.13**
			(0.54)	(0.54)
IMPCONST	–	–	–	1.16**
				(0.37)
Constant	−1.41**	−3.37**	−5.33**	−5.96**
	(0.48)	(0.90)	(0.99)	(1.02)
Nagelkerke pseudo-R^2	0.24	0.67	0.720	0.722
% correctly predicted	76.4%	87.0%	89.0%	89.7%
N	1,323	1,323	1,323	1,323

**$p \leq 0.01$; *$p \leq 0.05$ (two-tailed tests). Entries represent unstandardized logistic regression coefficients (with standard deviations in parentheses).

Appendix C

Table C14
Regression logistic models of support for more powers for Quebec

	(1)	(2)	(3)	(4)
Age	1.51**	1.66**	1.69**	1.69**
	(0.27)	(0.31)	(0.31)	(0.31)
Female	−0.28	−0.20	−0.14	−0.14
	(0.12)	(0.14)	(0.14)	(0.14)
Education	0.24	0.16	0.03	0.03
	(0.29)	(0.32)	(0.33)	(0.33)
Income	−0.47	−0.30	−0.23	−0.24
	(0.24)	(0.26)	(0.27)	(0.27)
Left-right	−1.69**	−0.53	−0.28	−0.28
	(0.31)	(0.36)	(0.37)	(0.37)
Moral liberalism	0.95**	0.74**	0.69**	0.69**
	(0.21)	(0.23)	(0.24)	(0.24)
Cynicism	0.24	0.32	0.30	0.30
	(0.21)	(0.23)	(0.24)	(0.24)
Identity	–	2.52**	2.18**	2.16**
		(0.44)	(0.46)	(0.45)
AttachQC	–	1.34**	1.02**	1.04**
		(0.37)	(0.37)	(0.38)
AttachCAN	–	−1.95**	−1.26**	−1.26**
		(0.30)	(0.33)	(0.33)
Values	–	–	1.05**	1.05**
			(0.25)	(0.25)
Market	–	–	0.88**	0.89**
			(0.32)	(0.32)
IMPCONST	–	–	–	−0.08
				(0.25)
Constant	−1.58**	−2.52**	−3.45**	−3.39**
	(0.39)	(0.57)	(0.62)	(0.64)
Nagelkerke pseudo-R^2	0.23	0.43	0.45	0.45
% correctly predicted	67.4%	77.6%	77.7%	77.8%
N	1,323	1,323	1,323	1,323

**$p \leq 0.01$; *$p \leq 0.05$ (two-tailed tests). Entries represent unstandardized logistic regression coefficients (with standard deviations in parentheses).

Table C15
Change in probabilities for regression models of support for more powers for Quebec, excluding supporters of independence

	(1)	(2)	(3)	(4)
Age	0.44**	0.38**	0.36**	0.36**
Female	0.06	0.06	0.07	0.06
Language	0.37**	0.21**	0.20**	0.20**
Education	0.18*	0.17*	0.14	0.14
Income	−0.10	−0.09	−0.08	−0.08
Left-right	−0.24*	−0.15	−0.15	−0.15
Moral liberalism	0.08	0.03	0.02	0.03
Cynicism	0.07	0.11	0.10	0.11
Identity	–	0.38**	0.36**	0.36**
AttachQC	–	0.27**	0.25**	0.25**
AttachCAN	–	−0.28**	−0.19*	−0.20*
Values	–	–	0.23**	0.23**
Market	–	–	0.04	0.04
IMPCONST	–	–	–	0.03
N	617	617	617	617

$**p \leq 0.01$; $*p \leq 0.05$ (two-tailed tests). Entries are change in probabilities.

Appendix D

REGRESSION RESULTS, SCOTLAND

Table D1

Logistic regression voting models for devolved election in Scotland: Sociodemographic and attitudinal variables

	SNP	*Labour*	*LibDem*	*Cons*
Age	0.09	−1.17**	1.40**	0.51
	(0.34)	(0.38)	(0.53)	(0.51)
Female	−0.41**	0.30	0.65**	−0.04
	(0.15)	(0.16)	(0.24)	(0.23)
Education	−0.18	−1.18**	2.09**	0.55
	(0.38)	(0.42)	(0.65)	(0.56)
Income	−1.14**	0.16	−0.37	2.71**
	(0.33)	(0.36)	(0.51)	(0.52)
Left-right	−0.89*	−1.94**	1.17	4.39**
	(0.38)	(0.42)	(0.61)	(0.62)
Moral liberalism	−0.49*	0.79**	0.90*	−1.07**
	(0.25)	(0.27)	(0.40)	(0.39)
Cynicism	−2.22**	1.39**	0.98**	1.57**
	(0.23)	(0.25)	(0.35)	(0.34)
Constant	2.51**	−0.02	−6.19**	−6.81**
	(0.44)	(0.47)	(0.78)	(0.75)
Nagelkerke pseudo-R²	0.11	0.08	0.07	0.25
N	893	893	893	893

**$p \leq 0.01$; *$p \leq 0.05$ (two-tailed tests). Entries represent unstandardized logistic regression coefficients (with standard deviations in parentheses).

Table D2

Logistic regression voting models for devolved election in Scotland: Attachment and identification variables

	SNP	Labour	LibDem	Cons
Age	0.54	−1.47**	1.01	0.56
	(0.38)	(0.40)	(0.57)	(0.56)
Female	−0.45**	0.24	0.72**	0.00
	(0.16)	(0.17)	(0.25)	(0.25)
Education	−0.14	−1.21**	2.27**	0.19
	(0.41)	(0.43)	(0.66)	(0.58)
Income	−1.09**	0.01	−0.55	3.00**
	(0.35)	(0.36)	(0.52)	(0.56)
Left-right	−0.07	−2.31**	0.50	3.80**
	(0.41)	(0.44)	(0.63)	(0.65)
Moral liberalism	−0.42	0.82**	0.74	−1.23**
	(0.27)	(0.28)	(0.41)	(0.41)
Cynicism	−1.70**	1.13**	0.57	0.95*
	(0.25)	(0.26)	(0.38)	(0.37)
Identity	1.33**	−0.09	−0.32	−1.68**
	(0.35)	(0.35)	(0.50)	(0.49)
AttachSC	0.60	0.06	0.18	−1.00
	(0.51)	(0.47)	(0.68)	(0.58)
AttachUK	−1.95**	1.33**	2.32**	1.39*
	(0.34)	(0.35)	(0.67)	(0.64)
Constant	1.59*	−0.45	−7.26**	−5.36**
	(0.63)	(0.62)	(1.08)	(0.94)
Nagelkerke pseudo-R^2	0.20	0.10	0.11	0.32
N	883	883	883	883

**$p \leq 0.01$; *$p \leq 0.05$ (two-tailed tests). Entries represent unstandardized logistic regression coefficients (with standard deviations in parentheses).

Table D3
Logistic regression voting models for devolved election in Scotland:
Cost-benefit variables

	SNP	Labour	LibDem	Cons
Age	0.36	−1.32**	1.06	0.55
	(0.38)	(0.41)	(0.57)	(0.57)
Female	−0.45**	0.24	0.73**	0.00
	(0.16)	(0.17)	(0.25)	(0.25)
Education	−0.27	−1.08*	2.27**	0.19
	(0.41)	(0.43)	(0.66)	(0.58)
Income	−1.18**	0.11	−0.54	2.99**
	(0.36)	(0.37)	(0.52)	(0.57)
Left-right	−0.02	−2.41**	0.54	3.81**
	(0.42)	(0.45)	(0.63)	(0.65)
Moral liberalism	0.38	0.77**	0.70	−1.23**
	(0.27)	(0.28)	(0.42)	(0.41)
Cynicism	−1.62**	1.05**	0.52	0.96*
	(0.26)	(0.27)	(0.38)	(0.37)
Identity	1.20**	0.07	−0.31	−1.70**
	(0.36)	(0.36)	(0.51)	(0.50)
AttachSC	0.59	0.08	0.15	−0.99
	(0.52)	(0.49)	(0.68)	(0.58)
AttachUK	−1.70**	1.03**	2.26**	1.41*
	(0.34)	(0.36)	(0.68)	(0.65)
Values	0.75**	−0.87**	−0.07	0.06
	(0.29)	(0.30)	(0.42)	(0.43)
Market	1.19**	−1.06**	−0.61	0.02
	(0.33)	(0.34)	(0.47)	(0.45)
Constant	0.68	0.50	−6.87**	−5.41**
	(0.66)	(0.67)	(1.13)	(1.01)
Nagelkerke pseudo-R^2	0.22	0.12	0.12	0.32
N	883	883	883	883

$**p \leq 0.01$; $*p \leq 0.05$ (two-tailed tests). Entries represent unstandardized logistic regression coefficients (with standard deviations in parentheses).

Appendix D

Table D4
Logistic regression voting models for devolved election in Scotland:
Constitutional preferences

	SNP	Labour	LibDem	Cons
Age	0.57	−1.48**	1.03	0.48
	(0.47)	(0.47)	(0.62)	(0.63)
Female	−0.33	0.04	0.69*	−0.02
	(0.20)	(0.20)	(0.28)	(0.27)
Education	0.15	−1.36**	2.03**	0.05
	(0.51)	(0.50)	(0.72)	(0.64)
Income	−1.02*	0.06	−0.97	2.59**
	(0.45)	(0.43)	(0.58)	(0.63)
Left-right	0.15	−2.89**	0.40	4.01**
	(0.54)	(0.55)	(0.75)	(0.76)
Moral liberalism	−0.72*	0.84*	0.66	−1.06*
	(0.33)	(0.33)	(0.46)	(0.46)
Cynicism	−1.02**	0.55	0.19	0.61
	(0.33)	(0.32)	(0.44)	(0.43)
Identity	0.84	0.31	−0.03	−1.20*
	(0.44)	(0.44)	(0.59)	(0.57)
AttachSC	−0.28	0.77	−0.21	−0.57
	(0.61)	(0.58)	(0.72)	(0.65)
AttachUK	−0.65	−0.16	1.51	1.36
	(0.44)	(0.46)	(0.79)	(0.83)
Values	0.48	−0.86*	0.40	0.24
	(0.37)	(0.36)	(0.49)	(0.49)
Market	0.34	−0.46	−0.62	0.45
	(0.41)	(0.40)	(0.54)	(0.51)
Independence	2.03**	−1.85**	−1.59**	−1.72**
	(0.24)	(0.29)	(0.45)	(0.52)
More powers	0.88**	−0.35	0.15	−0.38
	(0.25)	(0.24)	(0.32)	(0.31)
Constant	−0.61	1.90*	−5.34**	−5.40**
	(0.84)	(0.81)	(1.26)	(1.20)
Nagelkerke pseudo-R^2	0.37	0.19	0.15	0.37
N	752	752	752	752

**$p \leq 0.01$; *$p \leq 0.05$ (two-tailed tests). Entries represent unstandardized logistic regression coefficients (with standard deviations in parentheses).

Table D5
Logistic regression voting models for devolved election in Scotland:
Salience of the national question

	SNP	*Labour*	*LibDem*	*Cons*
Age	0.81	−1.60**	1.14	0.41
	(0.49)	(0.48)	(0.64)	(0.65)
Female	−0.22	−0.07	0.69*	0.02
	(0.21)	(0.20)	(0.28)	(0.29)
Education	0.18	−1.22*	2.04**	−0.18
	(0.52)	(0.50)	(0.74)	(0.67)
Income	−0.99*	0.03	−1.01	2.68**
	(0.46)	(0.43)	(0.60)	(0.66)
Left-right	−0.22	−2.61**	0.59	4.23**
	(0.56)	(0.56)	(0.79)	(0.80)
Moral liberalism	−0.83*	0.93**	0.79	−1.19*
	(0.34)	(0.34)	(0.47)	(0.48)
Cynicism	−0.99**	0.53	0.32	0.58
	(0.33)	(0.33)	(0.46)	(0.45)
Identity	0.86	0.29	0.09	−1.31*
	(0.46)	(0.44)	(0.62)	(0.60)
AttachSC	−0.26	0.74	−0.14	−0.56
	(0.63)	(0.58)	(0.75)	(0.66)
AttachUK	−0.62	−0.30	1.79*	1.52
	(0.45)	(0.47)	(0.83)	(0.87)
Values	0.47	−0.88*	0.27	0.38
	(0.38)	(0.36)	(0.51)	(0.52)
Market	0.55	−0.60	−0.67	0.28
	(0.43)	(0.41)	(0.57)	(0.54)
Independence	2.05**	−1.97**	−1.61**	−1.47**
	(0.25)	(0.31)	(0.48)	(0.53)
More powers	0.84**	−0.25	0.14	−0.50
	(0.26)	(0.25)	(0.33)	(0.33)
IMPCONST	0.27	0.46	−1.53**	−0.46
	(0.43)	(0.41)	(0.55)	(0.57)
Constant	−0.90	1.59	−4.80**	−5.08**
	(0.90)	(0.86)	(1.30)	(1.27)
Nagelkerke pseudo-R²	0.38	0.19	0.17	0.38
N	718	718	718	718

**$p \leq 0.01$; *$p \leq 0.05$ (two-tailed tests). Entries represent unstandardized logistic regression coefficients
(with standard deviations in parentheses).

Table D6
Logistic regression voting models for devolved election in Scotland:
Interactive variables

	SNP	Labour	LibDem	Cons
Age	0.81	−1.59**	1.11	0.30
	(0.49)	(0.49)	(0.65)	(0.66)
Female	−0.22	−0.04	0.68*	0.04
	(0.21)	(0.20)	(0.29)	(0.29)
Education	0.18	−1.17*	1.99**	−0.41
	(0.52)	(0.51)	(0.75)	(0.68)
Income	−0.99*	0.06	−1.02	2.76**
	(0.46)	(0.44)	(0.60)	(0.68)
Left-right	−0.22	−2.72**	0.56	4.55**
	(0.56)	(0.57)	(0.79)	(0.83)
Moral liberalism	−0.83*	0.85*	0.76	−1.15*
	(0.35)	(0.34)	(0.47)	(0.49)
Cynicism	−0.99**	0.49	0.33	0.68
	(0.33)	(0.33)	(0.46)	(0.46)
Identity	0.85	0.26	0.07	−1.33*
	(0.46)	(0.44)	(0.62)	(0.61)
AttachSC	−0.25	0.81	−0.13	−0.66
	(0.63)	(0.59)	(0.75)	(0.68)
AttachUK	−0.62	−0.36	1.77*	1.40
	(0.45)	(0.47)	(0.84)	(0.86)
Values	0.47	−0.91*	0.28	0.36
	(0.38)	(0.37)	(0.51)	(0.53)
Market	0.54	−0.69	−0.67	0.42
	(0.43)	(0.41)	(0.57)	(0.55)
Independence	2.16**	−0.72	−0.65	−8.81*
	(0.72)	(0.79)	(1.14)	(3.81)
More powers	0.80	−1.34*	0.09	1.82*
	(0.72)	(0.67)	(0.81)	(0.92)
IMPCONST	0.29	0.05	−1.38	0.23
	(0.76)	(0.60)	(0.78)	(0.70)
IMPCONSTIND	−0.05	−0.60	−0.50	2.98*
	(0.31)	(0.34)	(0.56)	(1.35)
IMPCONSTPWRS	0.02	0.53	0.03	−1.16**
	(0.32)	(0.30)	(0.38)	(0.43)
Constant	−0.90	1.99*	−4.82**	−5.56**
	(1.00)	(0.92)	(1.34)	(1.32)
Nagelkerke pseudo-R^2	0.38	0.20	0.17	0.41
N	718	718	718	718

**$p \leq 0.01$; *$p \leq 0.05$ (two-tailed tests). Entries represent unstandardized logistic regression coefficients (with standard deviations in parentheses).

Table D7
Logistic regression voting models for devolved election in Scotland:
Party image models

	SNP	Labour	LibDem	Cons
Age	1.01*	−1.90**	1.01	0.11
	(0.51)	(0.55)	(0.70)	(0.73)
Female	−0.08	−0.14	0.63*	0.01
	(0.22)	(0.23)	(0.31)	(0.33)
Education	0.32	−1.78**	1.48	−0.03
	(0.54)	(0.57)	(0.79)	(0.75)
Income	−1.02*	0.34	−0.96	2.80**
	(0.47)	(0.49)	(0.67)	(0.75)
Left-right	−0.25	−1.77**	0.36	3.32**
	(0.58)	(0.62)	(0.85)	(0.89)
Moral liberalism	−0.71*	1.11**	0.57	−1.41**
	(0.36)	(0.38)	(0.50)	(0.55)
Cynicism	−0.91**	0.44	0.75	0.83
	(0.35)	(0.36)	(0.51)	(0.51)
Identity	0.67	0.29	−0.19	−1.31
	(0.47)	(0.49)	(0.68)	(0.68)
AttachSC	−0.26	0.69	0.09	−0.76
	(0.65)	(0.64)	(0.82)	(0.71)
AttachUK	−0.45	−0.31	1.43	1.30
	(0.47)	(0.52)	(0.91)	(0.97)
Values	0.51	−0.60	0.18	−0.07
	(0.39)	(0.41)	(0.56)	(0.58)
Market	0.57	−0.66	−0.90	0.48
	(0.45)	(0.46)	(0.63)	(0.59)
Independence	2.10**	−0.82	−0.37	−7.10
	(0.73)	(0.87)	(1.24)	(3.84)
More powers	0.88	−1.52*	−0.07	1.06
	(0.72)	(0.73)	(0.90)	(1.04)
IMPCONST	0.07	0.06	−1.45	0.14
	(0.77)	(0.64)	(0.85)	(0.74)
IMPCONSTIND	−0.10	−0.53	−0.52	2.47
	(0.32)	(0.37)	(0.61)	(1.37)
IMPCONSTPWRS	−0.00	0.56	0.21	−0.81
	(0.33)	(0.33)	(0.42)	(0.48)
IVSNP_RESID	1.73**	–	–	–
	(0.33)			
IVLABOUR_RESID	–	3.45**	–	–
		(0.41)		
IVLIBDEM_RESID	–	–	3.19**	–
			(0.48)	

Table D7 (*continued*)

	SNP	Labour	LibDem	Cons
IV$_{CONS}$_RESID	–	–	–	2.70**
				(0.42)
Constant	−1.08	1.60	−4.35**	−5.00**
	(1.03)	(0.99)	(1.41)	(1.44)
Nagelkerke pseudo-R^2	0.41	0.32	0.29	0.49
N	718	718	718	718

**$p ≤ 0.01$; *$p ≤ 0.05$ (two-tailed tests). Entries represent unstandardized logistic regression coefficients (with standard deviations in parentheses).

Table D8
Logistic regression voting models for general election in Scotland:
Sociodemographic and attitudinal variables

	SNPUK	LabourUK	LibDemUK	ConsUK
Age	0.70*	−1.00**	0.42	0.74
	(0.35)	(0.34)	(0.42)	(0.44)
Female	−0.26	0.25	0.01	−0.12
	(0.15)	(0.15)	(0.18)	(0.19)
Education	−0.15	−1.07**	1.61**	0.00
	(0.37)	(0.37)	(0.51)	(0.46)
Income	−1.13**	0.02	−0.25	2.26**
	(0.33)	(0.31)	(0.38)	(0.43)
Left-right	−0.27	−2.05**	−0.61	4.31**
	(0.39)	(0.39)	(0.50)	(0.54)
Moral liberalism	−0.50*	0.14	1.16**	−0.77*
	(0.24)	(0.24)	(0.31)	(0.31)
Cynicism	−2.09**	0.19	0.40	1.50**
	(0.24)	(0.22)	(0.28)	(0.28)
Constant	0.73	0.98*	−3.60**	−5.91**
	(0.44)	(0.43)	(0.59)	(0.63)
Nagelkerke pseudo-R^2	0.09	0.04	0.05	0.23
N	1,047	1,047	1,047	1,047

**$p ≤ 0.01$; *$p ≤ 0.05$ (two-tailed tests). Entries represent unstandardized logistic regression coefficients (with standard deviations in parentheses).

Table D9
Logistic regressions voting models for general election in Scotland:
Identity and attachment

	SNPUK	*LabourUK*	*LibDemUK*	*ConsUK*
Age	0.93*	−1.28**	0.45	1.09*
	(0.40)	(0.36)	(0.43)	(0.48)
Female	−0.21	0.17	0.08	−0.12
	(0.17)	(0.15)	(0.19)	(0.21)
Education	0.13	−1.09**	1.61**	−0.59
	(0.42)	(0.38)	(0.52)	(0.49)
Income	−1.06**	−0.15	−0.29	2.70**
	(0.37)	(0.32)	(0.39)	(0.47)
Left-right	0.52	−2.30**	−0.86	4.09**
	(0.45)	(0.41)	(0.51)	(0.57)
Moral liberalism	−0.55*	0.23	1.05**	−0.78*
	(0.27)	(0.25)	(0.32)	(0.34)
Cynicism	−1.35**	0.01	0.28	1.06**
	(0.26)	(0.23)	(0.30)	(0.31)
Identity	2.08**	0.41	−0.99*	−1.84**
	(0.41)	(0.32)	(0.39)	(0.42)
AttachSC	2.10**	0.02	0.07	−1.31**
	(0.67)	(0.43)	(0.50)	(0.49)
AttachUK	−1.63**	1.45**	−0.10	0.43
	(0.32)	(0.32)	(0.38)	(0.50)
Constant	−2.50**	0.08	−2.80**	−3.77**
	(0.75)	(0.57)	(0.71)	(0.76)
Nagelkerke pseudo-R^2	0.22	0.06	0.06	0.31
N	1,021	1,021	1,021	1,021

**$p \leq 0.01$; *$p \leq 0.05$ (two-tailed tests). Entries represent unstandardized logistic regression coefficients (with standard deviations in parentheses).

Table D10
Logistic regressions voting models for general election in Scotland:
Cost-benefit variables

	SNPUK	LabourUK	LibDemUK	ConsUK
Age	0.85*	−1.20**	0.45	1.07*
	(0.40)	(0.36)	(0.44)	(0.48)
Female	−0.20	0.16	0.07	−0.11
	(0.17)	(0.15)	(0.19)	(0.21)
Education	0.06	−1.01**	1.61**	−0.60
	(0.42)	(0.38)	(0.52)	(0.49)
Income	−1.08**	−0.12	−0.29	2.70**
	(0.37)	(0.32)	(0.39)	(0.47)
Left-right	0.56	−2.33**	−0.86	4.12**
	(0.45)	(0.41)	(0.51)	(0.57)
Moral liberalism	−0.55*	0.22	1.05**	−0.80*
	(0.27)	(0.25)	(0.33)	(0.34)
Cynicism	−1.32**	−0.05	0.28	1.08**
	(0.26)	(0.23)	(0.30)	(0.32)
Identity	2.02**	0.48	−0.99*	−1.89**
	(0.41)	(0.33)	(0.39)	(0.43)
AttachSC	2.06**	0.05	0.07	−1.31**
	(0.67)	(0.44)	(0.50)	(0.49)
AttachUK	−1.51**	1.25**	−0.11	0.49
	(0.33)	(0.33)	(0.39)	(0.51)
Values	0.31	−0.54*	−0.01	0.22
	(0.29)	(0.26)	(0.34)	(0.36)
Market	0.57	−0.74*	−0.01	−0.04
	(0.34)	(0.30)	(0.38)	(0.40)
Constant	−2.88**	0.72	−2.79**	−3.88**
	(0.78)	(0.60)	(0.77)	(0.83)
Nagelkerke pseudo-R^2	0.22	0.07	0.06	0.31
N	1,021	1,021	1,021	1,021

**$p \leq 0.01$; *$p \leq 0.05$ (two-tailed tests). Entries represent unstandardized logistic regression coefficients (with standard deviations in parentheses).

Table D11
Logistic regressions voting models for general election in Scotland:
Constitutional options

	SNPUK	LabourUK	LibDemUK	ConsUK
Age	1.31**	−1.38**	0.00	0.86
	(0.48)	(0.41)	(0.49)	(0.53)
Female	−0.05	0.10	0.00	−0.23
	(0.20)	(0.17)	(0.21)	(0.23)
Education	0.15	−1.09*	1.63**	−0.90
	(0.49)	(0.43)	(0.59)	(0.55)
Income	−0.92*	−0.18	−0.36	2.36**
	(0.43)	(0.36)	(0.43)	(0.51)
Left-right	0.68	−2.19**	−1.14	3.91**
	(0.52)	(0.47)	(0.59)	(0.63)
Moral liberalism	−0.59	0.07	0.99**	−0.56
	(0.32)	(0.28)	(0.36)	(0.37)
Cynicism	−0.71*	−0.16	0.07	0.67
	(0.32)	(0.28)	(0.35)	(0.36)
Identity	1.72**	0.50	−0.86	−1.52**
	(0.49)	(0.38)	(0.45)	(0.48)
AttachSC	2.08**	0.34	0.05	−1.16*
	(0.80)	(0.51)	(0.58)	(0.56)
AttachUK	−0.70	0.67	−0.61	0.24
	(0.39)	(0.39)	(0.46)	(0.58)
Values	0.21	−0.47	−0.03	0.34
	(0.34)	(0.30)	(0.38)	(0.40)
Market	0.22	−0.44	−0.25	0.53
	(0.39)	(0.34)	(0.43)	(0.43)
Independence	1.43**	−1.12**	−0.59*	−0.71*
	(0.23)	(0.23)	(0.29)	(0.33)
More powers	0.77**	0.32	0.07	−0.72**
	(0.29)	(0.21)	(0.27)	(0.26)
Constant	−5.05**	1.09	−1.68	−2.90**
	(0.97)	(0.71)	(0.88)	(0.91)
Nagelkerke pseudo-R^2	0.32	0.09	0.07	0.34
N	852	852	852	852

**$p \leq 0.01$; *$p \leq 0.05$ (two-tailed tests). Entries represent unstandardized logistic regression coefficients (with standard deviations in parentheses).

Table D12

Logistic regressions voting models for general election in Scotland: Salience of the national question

	SNPUK	LabourUK	LibDemUK	ConsUK
Age	1.28**	−1.29**	−0.04	0.83
	(0.49)	(0.42)	(0.51)	(0.55)
Female	−0.06	0.06	−0.07	−0.06
	(0.20)	(0.17)	(0.22)	(0.23)
Education	0.14	−0.92*	1.32*	−0.99
	(0.51)	(0.44)	(0.61)	(0.56)
Income	−0.92*	−0.23	−0.41	2.32**
	(0.45)	(0.37)	(0.45)	(0.52)
Left-right	0.63	−2.26**	−1.11	4.26**
	(0.54)	(0.48)	(0.61)	(0.67)
Moral liberalism	−0.68*	0.16	1.13**	−0.63
	(0.33)	(0.28)	(0.37)	(0.38)
Cynicism	−0.68*	−0.11	0.13	0.61
	(0.32)	(0.28)	(0.36)	(0.37)
Identity	1.67**	0.53	−0.85	−1.42**
	(0.49)	(0.39)	(0.46)	(0.50)
AttachSC	1.69*	0.24	0.15	−0.99
	(0.79)	(0.52)	(0.60)	(0.57)
AttachUK	−0.68	0.63	−0.65	0.46
	(0.40)	(0.39)	(0.48)	(0.60)
Values	0.19	−0.45	0.03	0.23
	(0.35)	(0.31)	(0.40)	(0.42)
Market	0.20	−0.47	−0.12	0.41
	(0.41)	(0.35)	(0.44)	(0.45)
Independence	1.41**	−1.17**	−0.60	−0.50
	(0.25)	(0.24)	(0.31)	(0.34)
More powers	0.85**	0.39	−0.03	−0.79**
	(0.31)	(0.22)	(0.27)	(0.27)
IMPCONST	0.94*	0.51	−0.54	−1.11*
	(0.42)	(0.35)	(0.41)	(0.45)
Constant	−5.31**	0.67	−1.23	−2.51**
	(1.01)	(0.74)	(0.92)	(0.96)
Nagelkerke pseudo-R^2	0.32	0.09	0.08	0.34
N	812	812	812	812

$**p \leq 0.01$; $*p \leq 0.05$ (two-tailed tests). Entries represent unstandardized logistic regression coefficients (with standard deviations in parentheses).

Table D13
Logistic regression models of support for Scotland independence

	(1)	(2)	(3)	(4)
Age	−0.78**	−0.49	−0.69	−0.86*
	(0.29)	(0.35)	(0.35)	(0.37)
Female	−0.46**	−0.46**	−0.44**	−0.50**
	(0.13)	(0.15)	(0.16)	(0.16)
Education	−0.28	−0.13	−0.28	−0.43
	(0.33)	(0.39)	(0.39)	(0.41)
Income	−1.20**	−1.13**	−1.20**	−0.95**
	(0.28)	(0.32)	(0.33)	(0.34)
Left-right	−2.16**	−1.06*	−1.00*	−1.33**
	(0.36)	(0.42)	(0.43)	(0.45)
Moral liberalism	−0.72**	−0.69**	−0.66**	−0.67*
	(0.21)	(0.25)	(0.26)	(0.27)
Cynicism	−2.21**	−1.67**	−1.56**	−1.43**
	(0.21)	(0.24)	(0.24)	(0.25)
Identity	–	1.28**	1.17**	1.06**
		(0.32)	(0.33)	(0.34)
AttachSC	–	1.70**	1.59**	1.53**
		(0.50)	(0.51)	(0.53)
AttachUK	–	−3.38**	−3.11**	−3.08**
		(0.33)	(0.34)	(0.34)
Values	–	–	0.77**	0.87**
			(0.28)	(0.29)
Market	–	–	1.32**	1.39**
			(0.33)	(0.34)
IMPCONST	–	–	–	1.14**
				(0.31)
Constant	3.38**	2.34**	1.39*	0.83
	(0.41)	(0.61)	(0.65)	(0.69)
Nagelkerke pseudo-R²	0.13	0.30	0.32	0.33
N	1,212	1,168	1,168	1,093

**$p \leq 0.01$; *$p \leq 0.05$ (two-tailed tests). Entries represent unstandardized logistic regression coefficients (with standard deviations in parentheses).

Table D14
Regression logistic models of support for more powers for Scotland

	(1)	(2)	(3)	(4)
Age	−0.38	−0.11	−0.31	−0.34
	(0.31)	(0.36)	(0.37)	(0.39)
Female	0.00	0.07	0.08	0.07
	(0.14)	(0.16)	(0.16)	(0.17)
Education	0.05	0.55	0.37	0.20
	(0.35)	(0.39)	(0.40)	(0.42)
Income	−1.23**	−1.25**	−1.33**	−1.34**
	(0.31)	(0.34)	(0.35)	(0.37)
Left-right	−1.40**	−0.43	−0.39	−0.59
	(0.38)	(0.43)	(0.44)	(0.47)
Moral liberalism	0.03	0.09	0.13	0.13
	(0.23)	(0.25)	(0.26)	(0.27)
Cynicism	−2.49**	−2.02**	−1.96**	−2.00**
	(0.22)	(0.25)	(0.25)	(0.26)
Identity	–	1.86**	1.75**	1.82**
		(0.32)	(0.33)	(0.34)
AttachSC	–	1.51**	1.42**	1.24**
		(0.45)	(0.45)	(0.47)
AttachUK	–	−1.73**	−1.34**	−1.39**
		(0.36)	(0.37)	(0.39)
Values	–	–	1.20**	1.25**
			(0.29)	(0.30)
Market	–	–	1.25**	1.37**
			(0.33)	(0.35)
IMPCONST	–	–	–	0.94**
				(0.32)
Constant	3.42**	1.02	−0.08	−0.39
	(0.43)	(0.58)	(0.62)	(0.69)
Nagelkerke pseudo-R²	0.14	0.26	0.28	0.30
N	1,136	1,101	1,101	1,025

**$p \leq 0.01$; *$p \leq 0.05$ (two-tailed tests). Entries represent unstandardized logistic regression coefficients (with standard deviations in parentheses).

Table D15
Change in probabilities for regression models of support for more powers for
Scotland, excluding supporters of independence

	(1)	(2)	(3)	(4)
Age	−0.05	0.02	−0.02	−0.02
Female	−0.02	−0.01	−0.01	−0.01
Education	0.01	0.06	0.02	0.03
Income	−0.21**	−0.23**	−0.24**	−0.24**
Left-right	−0.17	−0.00	−0.01	−0.02
Moral liberalism	0.26**	0.23**	0.22**	0.22**
Cynicism	0.15**	0.08	0.07	0.07
Identity	–	0.33**	0.30**	0.29**
AttachSC	–	0.19	0.17	0.16
AttachUK	–	−0.31**	−0.26*	−0.27**
Values	–	–	0.24**	0.25**
Market	–	–	0.11	0.12
IMPCONST	–	–	–	0.10
N	615	596	596	596

**$p \leq 0.01$; *$p \leq 0.05$ (two-tailed tests).

Notes

CHAPTER ONE

1   The Parti Libéral du Québec has been disaffiliated from the Liberal Party of Canada since the 1950s. While the Parti Québécois has some informal ties with the federal-level Bloc Québécois, the two parties are organizationally distinct.

2   In effect, the Parti Québécois came to replace the Union Nationale. Formerly the provincial Conservative Party, the Union Nationale was a right-leaning autonomist party that held power in Quebec for large periods between 1936 and 1970, mostly under Maurice Duplessis's leadership (see Quinn 1979). It progressively vanished during the 1980s once the PQ had broken through the party system.

3   Unanimity of the legislatures was necessary because the Accord proposed a modification to the 1982 Canadian Constitution's amending formula that would have granted Quebec a veto right on any future changes to the Constitution.

4   Technically there were two referendums, one in Quebec, regulated by the Directeur général des élections du Québec, and one in the rest of Canada, regulated by Elections Canada, but both asking the same question. The pan-Canadian result was 54.3 per cent against the Accord, similar to the level of opposition in Quebec (56.7 per cent).

5   In March 1979 the eleven SNP MPs voted with the Conservatives to bring down a Labour government in a vote of no confidence.

6   That conclusion seems to particularly apply to niche parties (Klüver and Spoon 2016).

7   Contrary to the Bloc Québécois, which was immediately successful in the first election it fought in 1993, the Scottish National Party received limited support for most of its history. Until 2015, its best ever performance was

eleven MPs in the October 1974 general election; in 2010 the party returned six, which represented neither a net gain nor a loss on the previous election. As just discussed in the previous section, this difference between the successes of the BQ and the SNP might be explained by the particular context that surrounded the creation of the Bloc in the early 1990s (see also chapter 2). Indeed, it is important to note that the BQ has had several unsuccessful predecessors at the federal level – like the Bloc Populaire and the Parti Nationaliste (see Bickerton, Gagnon, and Smith 1999, 164–92) – and that for a long time sovereignist Quebecers were encouraged to abstain in federal elections. Time will tell whether the SNP will be able to maintain a high level of support in UK general elections if the debate about the future of Scotland recedes from the political agenda in this region.

8 Although on some of its dimensions, the economy can also be construed as a positional issue (see Lewis-Beck and Nadeau 2011).

9 It must be acknowledged that some authors question the usefulness of distinguishing between valence and positional issues (e.g., Pardos-Prado 2012; Guinaudeau and Persico 2014; Green and Jennings 2017) while others dismiss outright the very notion of valence issues (e.g., van der Brug 2017).

10 One might even go as far as to say that *federal* elections are considered as second order in Quebecers' eyes.

11 Those interested in Scottish voting behaviour therefore had to determine which elements of voting behaviour were different because of the electoral scale – which in turn ties in with debates about first- and second-order voting – and which were related to the presence of two votes in the Additional Member electoral system. The simultaneous arrival of devolution and a proportional electoral system makes it more difficult to determine to what extent the decision-making calculus is more influenced by devolution tapping the national interest or by a new electoral system that encourages an expansion of the party system. Certainly we have evidence that voters were likely to experiment with their two votes, engaging in split ticket voting to varying degrees. Paterson et al. (2001) report 20 per cent ticket splitting in 1999, and Carman and Johns (2010) report 27 per cent by 2007.

CHAPTER TWO

1 Party manifestos from the September 2012 substate election in Quebec have also been coded and analyzed, but are not included here since the findings largely converged with those obtained for the April 2014 election.

2 To protect the confidentiality of our interviewees, we use the feminine throughout the book when we report their words even though we interviewed both male and female party representatives. Also of note is that we conducted all the interviews for this chapter in French and translated the quotations reported herein into English.

3 In Quebec parlance, an *adéquiste* is someone who belongs to the ADQ; a *péquiste* is someone who belongs to the PQ.

4 It must be kept in mind, however, that the BQ had by far the longest manifesto of all (190 pages).

5 It is worth noting that the two CAQ MNAs do not differ much in their assessment of the national question and the need for more constitutional autonomy and powers. The only slight but notable differences in their viewpoints are twofold: the former *adéquiste* always prefers to use the term "autonomist" while the former *péquiste* never uses it, preferring instead the label "nationalist"; and the former *péquiste* seems more willing than the former *adéquiste* to keep the door open to the idea that Quebecers should hold a new referendum on independence once the other, more pressing policy priorities have been effectively addressed (by a government formed by the CAQ).

6 See Pelletier (2001).

7 On the CPC's open federalism approach, see Banting et al. (2006).

8 See Policy Committee of the NDP (2005).

9 Government of Quebec, Bill 60: Charter affirming the values of state secularism and religious neutrality and of equality between women and men, and providing a framework for accommodation requests, National Assembly of Quebec, 40th Legislature, 1st Session, November 2013.

10 Government of Quebec, Bill 14: An Act to amend the Charter of the French language, the Charter of human rights and freedoms and other legislative provisions, National Assembly of Quebec, 40th Legislature, 1st Session, December 2012.

11 The Gérin-Lajoie doctrine basically states that any Canadian province has the right to negotiate treaties with foreign states when these treaties involve policy areas that fall under provincial jurisdiction; paradiplomacy therefore is viewed as the external extension of a province's domestic competencies (Bélanger 2002).

CHAPTER THREE

1 We were unsuccessful in being granted interviews with Conservative MPs for Scotland (of which there was only one at the time of our field-

work) and Liberal Democrat MPs for Scotland (of which there were eleven). As such, we have relied more heavily on the views of Conservative and LibDem MSPs for our interview analysis.

CHAPTER FOUR

1   Throughout the chapter, weighting procedures are used so as to make the sample more representative of the Quebec population. The weight variable used is based on official data on gender, age, region of residence, and language from the 2011 Statistics Canada census.

2   A more direct way to test these expectations would be to use a measure of the parties' reputational image related to the national question. We have done so in appendix table C7 using the survey question, "Which party best stands up for the interests of Quebec?" As can be seen in table 4.6 later in this chapter, the PQ ranks first on this item (33 per cent), followed by the PLQ (25 per cent), the CAQ (14 per cent), and QS (7 per cent). Direct measures of party reputations can be problematic because they are plagued by projection effects (van der Brug 2004; Wagner and Zeglovits 2014). To expunge this partisan bias, we used a two-step approach. We first regressed the four reputation variables on a measure of party identification and saved the residuals from this regression. We then entered these prediction errors in the final vote models as "purged" measures of each party's image on the national question (for more details, see appendix B). The results are displayed in table C7. Not surprisingly, the impact of the reputation variables is strong and significant for the four parties under study (the average change in probabilities for this variable is 0.15). This suggests that the parties' reputation at defending Quebec's interests adds to the explanation of voting behaviour in this province. Perhaps more interesting is the fact that all the results discussed in this chapter are left virtually unaltered by the inclusion of the party reputation variables even though these variables are still plagued by a significant projection effect.

3   Péladeau would go on to be leader of the Parti Québécois from May 2015 until his resignation a year later in May 2016.

4   Adding the attachment variables produces a greater increase in the level of explained variance as measured with Nagelkerke's pseudo-R^2 in all cases: +0.21 vs. +0.13; +0.23 vs. +0.21; +0.02 vs. +0.01; +0.02 vs. +0.00 for the PLQ, PQ, CAQ, and QS, respectively.

5   This result may explain, at least in part, why this party came to adopt a more explicit autonomist position in 2015 as already pointed out.

6 Despite this decrease in popular support, the BQ was able to increase its parliamentary representation from four in 2011 to ten MPs in 2015 thanks to the fragmentation of the vote and the first-past-the-post electoral system.

7 The question about recalled federal vote choice was not asked in our 2014 survey, and so that dataset could not be used for this section of the chapter.

8 In the 2011 election, the major federal political parties received the following support in Quebec: 23 per cent for the BQ, 14 per cent for the LPC, 17 per cent for the CPC, and 43 per cent for the NDP. The responses from our 2012 survey quite faithfully reproduce these results, since support for these parties is 26 per cent for the BQ, 15 per cent for the LPC, 13 per cent for the CPC, and 44 per cent for the NDP. The 2012 survey was also conducted online by Léger Marketing. It was administered to 1,505 adult Quebecers through web-based interviews between 12 September 2012 and 25 September 2012.

9 In fact, we carried out these two 2012 surveys (Quebec and Scotland) at the exact same time in both territories.

10 The NDP coefficient for the attachment to Quebec variable is significant at a 92 per cent level of confidence for the entire sample and becomes significant at 95 per cent when the analysis is limited to French speakers (but then the variable measuring attachment to Canada ceases to be significant).

11 The finding that a Quebec voter's left-right orientation is not significantly linked to support for the NDP in the 2011 federal election may seem surprising. But it should be noted that the marginal effect associated with the left-right variable for the NDP in table 4.17 is close to achieving statistical significance ($p < 0.06$ using a one-tailed test) and indicates that the NDP is the party that had the most left-leaning voters compared to the other three parties (-0.12, versus -0.06 for the BQ, 0.05 for the LPC, and 0.20 for the CPC; recall that a negative sign for this coefficient means support coming from the left while a positive sign indicates support coming from the right, on a -1 to + 1 scale). The fact that the relationship for the NDP is not statistically significant may be due to a number of factors including the strong impact of the national question itself on voter choice.

12 Since support for more powers is almost unanimous (94 per cent) among partisans of independence, we have re-estimated the model of table 4.19 by excluding these respondents so as to isolate the "moderate nationalists," a sizeable group (25 per cent) that is favourable to a transfer of powers for Quebec but opposed to its political sovereignty. This new

estimation, which is presented in appendix table C15, thus examines the differences between moderate nationalists and partisans of the status quo (i.e., voters opposed to both independence and more powers for Quebec). The results of table C15 can be compared to those of table 4.18 to assess the differences between the profile of these strict autonomists (or devolutionists) and that of independence supporters. These results indicate that moderate nationalists are older and more sensitive to the difference in values between Quebecers and other Canadians than partisans of independence are, and that the impact of identity, attachment to Quebec and to Canada, the preference for more political autonomy over belonging to a larger market, and the salience of the constitutional issue is lesser for moderate nationalists than it is for supporters of independence. That said, all of these conclusions were already clearly on display in table 4.19.

13 Recent events support this interpretation. The PLQ launched in May 2017 a new constitutional proposal asking for more powers and a formal recognition of Quebec's distinct status within Canada (Canadian Press 2017) without fuelling any debates on this question among its ranks. Meanwhile, the decision of the PQ's leader Jean-François Lisée to postpone a referendum on independence for the coming years has demobilized the radical supporters of independence in his party. The same uneasiness is sometimes palpable with the CAQ, a party opposed to independence but still reluctant to label itself as "federalist."

CHAPTER FIVE

1 To be sure, a strand of the academic literature has concluded that by their values Scots were not dissimilar to residents elsewhere in the UK with whom they share a similar sociodemographic profile (e.g., Curtice 1996; Miller, Timpson, and Lessnoff 1996). That said, Scots vary consistently from other Britons on three key issues: partisan preferences, national identity, and constitutional preferences. For example, when we compare Scottish voters with Welsh voters, the former show greater support for more powers and independence. When we compare Scots with English voters, we see lower levels of support in England not only for any form of English devolution but also for further devolution to Scotland (or Scottish independence) (Henderson, Delaney, and Liñeira 2014; Jeffery et al. 2014).

2 Throughout the chapter, weighting procedures are used so as to make the sample more representative of the Scotland population. The weight

variable used is based on official data about gender, age, and region of residence from Scotland's Census 2011.

3   As mentioned in chapter 4, a more direct way to perform the same test would be to rely on measures of the parties' reputational image. We have done so in appendix table D7, following the same two-step strategy presented in the previous chapter, in order to purge these perceptions from their partisan bias. Unsurprisingly, the impact of the reputation variables is strong (particularly for Labour) and significant for the four parties under study (the average change in probabilities for the four parties is 0.25). This suggests that the parties' reputation at defending Scotland's interests adds to the explanation of voting behaviour in this region. Given that party image variables are close to the dependent variable, it is not surprising that the coefficients for the other independent variables in the models decrease in magnitude following their inclusion. That said, most of these coefficients remain statistically significant, which is indicative of the robustness of these effects.

4   The results in table 5.6 should be interpreted keeping in mind that they partly reflect partisan projection effects. The percentages in this table are calculated taking into account the percentages of don't knows and refusals. The comparable figures for the vote intentions (i.e., with don't knows and refusals excluded as well) are 41 per cent for the SNP, 22 per cent for Labour, 12 per cent for the Conservatives, and 9 per cent for the LibDems. These percentages help to better appreciate the SNP's domination as the defender of Scotland's identity and culture (the 41 percentage point gap between SNP and Labour on this question is twice as large as the SNP's 19 percentage point lead over Labour in voting intentions) and Labour's stronger position on social issues (Labour and SNP are practically on par on the issue of fighting poverty despite the SNP's clear lead over Labour in vote intentions).

5   Responses to the recalled constituency vote question in our survey largely reproduce the 2011 election's actual results despite the sixteen months that separate the survey from the election. These responses indicate 46 per cent of the constituency vote for the SNP, 25 per cent for Labour, 13 per cent for the Conservative Party, and 10 per cent for the LibDems. These estimates all fall within ± 2 percentage points of the actual results, except for Labour support which is underestimated by 7 percentage points.

6   Interestingly, this pattern is not replicated for moral liberalism. In this case, Labour and LibDem voters express more liberal attitudes on moral issues whereas SNP and Tory supporters display more conservative moral

attitudes. For the SNP, this may reflect that its clientele is a large coalition of voters unified primarily by their views about the political future of Scotland.

7 The fact that the SNP was forming a majority government at the time of the survey may also explain the impact of "cynicism" on political choices. In that sense, the effect of this variable could also be interpreted as a short-term factor endogenous to party support. But the magnitude of this effect, particularly when compared with Quebec, suggests that this factor also reflects a more structural, long-term component of voting behaviour in Scotland.

8 About 61 per cent of SNP voters think that Scottish people have distinct values, a perception that is shared by only 30 per cent of Labour partisans. The difference is lesser for the market-sovereignty trade-off: 43 per cent of SNP voters against 26 per cent of Labour supporters express support for greater political sovereignty.

9 The quasi-unanimous opposition of Conservative voters to Scotland's independence produces a high level of collinearity among these variables, which makes the regression coefficients difficult to interpret.

10 As might be expected given the twenty-eight months that passed between the 2010 general election and the time of data collection, the survey tends to overestimate SNP support and to underestimate the Labour vote in that election, although it closely reflects Scots' support for the Conservatives and the LibDems.

11 As observed in Quebec, support for more powers is almost unanimous (94 per cent) among partisans of independence in Scotland. For this reason, and as we did for Quebec, we have re-estimated the model of table 5.19 by excluding these respondents so as to isolate the "true" devolutionists, who make up around 27 per cent of the sample. These new estimates are presented in appendix table D15. The results pertaining to the exclusive preference for the devolution option differ markedly from those obtained for independence (table 5.18), although they do so in ways that were already made apparent in table 5.19's estimates. Table D15 basically confirms, with greater clarity, that true devolutionists are older, more liberal, and more to the right than supporters of independence; that the variables of identity and distinct Scottish values have a greater impact on support for devolution than for independence; and that the variables of attachment to Scotland and the UK, preference for more political autonomy over belonging to a larger market, and salience of the constitutional issue have a lesser impact on support for devolution than for Scotland's independence.

CHAPTER SIX

1   Despite one of Québec Solidaire's ancestors, the Parti de la Démocratie Socialiste/Nouveau Parti Démocratique du Québec, previously having links to the federal NDP.

2   Another of Quebec's pro-independence parties – Québec Solidaire – also proposed the maintenance of various links between the "independent states" of Canada and Quebec, including currency, defence, and a newly created supranational institution (see chapter 2).

3   Although the SNP's tax policy in 2016 had a clear progressive orientation.

4   The wording of the questions used in our public opinion surveys is as follows: "When you cast your ballot in Quebec (Scottish) elections, how important are each of the following when you make your voting choice: How well the party understands Quebec's (Scotland's) history and culture? How well the party defends Quebec's (Scotland's) current and future interests? The party's constitutional preferences?"

5   Support for independence has fluctuated over time in both regions. As previously noted in chapter 1, it reached 40 and 49.4 per cent in the 1980 and 1995 Quebec referendums, respectively, and 45 per cent in Scotland in the 2014 referendum. That said, on all three occasions, independence has been rejected by a majority of Quebecers and Scots. Furthermore, support for independence has rarely gone above 50 per cent in any survey carried out in either region. During the 2016 Scottish election campaign, SNP leader Nicola Sturgeon claimed that there would not be a second referendum on Scottish independence, as public opinion did not seem favourable to it, although this situation may change in the aftermath of the June 2016 Brexit referendum's outcome (where Scotland rejected the winning option of the UK leaving the European Union).

6   The percentages corresponding to a strong attachment to Quebec and Canada are 85 per cent and 6 per cent for Parti Québécois, 48 per cent and 72 per cent for Parti Libéral du Québec, 59 per cent and 7 per cent for Québec Solidaire, and 48 per cent and 26 per cent for Coalition Avenir Québec. The percentages corresponding to a strong attachment to Scotland and the UK are 75 per cent and 16 per cent for the Scottish National Party, 43 per cent and 66 per cent for the Conservatives, 59 per cent and 39 per cent for Labour, and 64 per cent and 61 per cent for the LibDems. (For Quebec, see table 4.3 in chapter 4; for Scotland, see table 5.2 in chapter 5.)

7   Recall that the public opinion analyses presented in chapter 4 (see table 4.7) clearly indicate that PLQ voters locate themselves more to the right than CAQ voters.

8   Former PQ leader Bernard Landry used to say, "Sovereignty is neither left nor right, but forwards" (*la souveraineté n'est ni à gauche ni à droite, mais en avant*; Société Radio-Canada 2010).

9   The probability of supporting Labour decreases by 34 percentage points in the initial model when going from the extreme left to the extreme right. This effect slightly increases to 40 percentage points when all variables related to the national question are included in the model. In the case of the Conservative Party, the effect is 41 percentage points in the initial model and 35 percentage points in the final model.

10   Some interpretations of the 2016 Scottish election put forward the idea that the impact of the national question might become greater in coming years (this point is discussed further in the conclusion to this chapter).

11   Québec Solidaire is officially a sovereignist party. That said, as seen in chapters 2 and 4, its discourse focuses on social issues, and its voters, who are divided on the question of independence, are massively in favour of a transfer of powers from the federal government to Quebec.

12   Including identity and attachment variables into the vote choice model contributes to raising the pseudo-R^2 by 0.09 for the SNP and 0.07 for the Conservative Party. Their contribution to explaining vote choice is much smaller than that for the PQ (0.25) and PLQ (0.22). The contrast is even more striking in models explaining support for independence. In the Quebec case, these variables add 0.43 to the pseudo-R^2, whereas they only add 0.17 in Scotland.

13   Empirical studies have begun to look at the cyclicality of nationalist opinions; for Quebec see Pinard (2002), Yale and Durand (2011), Richez and Bodet (2012); for Scotland see Paterson et al. (2001), Henderson (2007), Curtice and Seyd (2009), Carman, Johns, and Mitchell (2014).

14   More anecdotally, the noted presence in Scotland of many Quebecers and Catalans during the 2014 independence referendum campaign suggests that Scottish strategies and arguments pertaining to the national question may soon cross borders. Similarly, significant exchanges between Quebec and Scottish strategists – nationalist and non-nationalist alike – during the three years preceding that same referendum have been reported and documented (Castonguay 2014; Brie 2016). Given the way in which the wording of the Scottish referendum question was adopted (after negotiation between Holyrood and Westminster governments, with echoes of the Canadian "Clarity Act") and the way the arguments – even the "No Thanks" slogan – used by the Better Together campaign closely mirrored those of the 1980 "No" campaign in Quebec (for instance, the 1980 "No" campaign's slogan in Quebec was *Non merci*), it seems fair to say that the evidence of learning (in

recent years at least) appears greater in the case of unionists/federalists than independentists (Brie 2016). In fact, former SNP leader Alex Salmond's alleged interest in the Quebec secessionist case may have been motivated by a will to avoid the PQ's strategic mistakes (Murray 2014). In any case, better documenting the existence of such diffusion effects might provide for a richer understanding of how substate elites manage to (re)mobilize their support base in the long term. While our party elite interviewees remained elusive when questioned on the issue of reciprocal links, the Parti Québécois representative we spoke to pointed out that "Scotland keeps alive the idea of independence. At a time when we sometimes feel that the project of Quebec independence is in a dead end, Scotland proves that that project is still alive. Scotland is thus a source of hope and, to some extent, an inspiration" (interview with PQ MNA, 15 August 2013).

15 While the labels change, the underlying meanings remain the same. The more nationalist political parties in Quebec have often adopted the label of "autonomist." For example, the now defunct Action Démocratique du Québec explicitly did so during the 2007 Quebec provincial election. Today, the Coalition Avenir Québec employs the label "nationalist" to present its position as a compromise between the PQ's sovereignty and the PLQ's federalism. It is possible that these positions may eventually come to be called "sovereignty," "devolution," and "unionism" in the Scottish context. Paradoxically, the "federalist" option of the Liberal Democrats corresponds to an autonomist position in Scotland, whereas in Quebec the same option refers to the constitutional status quo. Going beyond labels, the debates over the national question tend to revolve around three types of claims that can be made about powers for a substate region. The first is claiming all powers, called "sovereignty" in Quebec and "independence" in Scotland. The second is claiming no further powers, called "federalism" in Quebec and "unionism" in Scotland. The third category consists of claiming new powers while still remaining part of the larger state, called "autonomism" (or "nationalism") in Quebec and either "devolution" or "federalism" in Scotland.

16 A rival interpretation would be that Scottish Labour's poor performance in 2016 is explained less by the party's position on Scotland's constitutional future and more by its marked ideological turn to the left, a move that was made under the influence of the party's statewide organization.

17 Quebec's well-known humorist Yvon Deschamps has most famously encapsulated this state of mind by noting that Quebecers' favourite option is "an independent Quebec within a strong Canada" (in a 1977 skit called "La fierté d'être Québécois").

References

Adams, James, Michael Clark, Lawrence Ezrow, and Garrett Glasgow. 2006. "Are Niche Parties Fundamentally Different from Mainstream Parties? The Causes and the Electoral Consequences of Western European Parties' Policy Shifts, 1976–1998." *American Journal of Political Science* 50 (3): 513–29.

Adams, James, Lawrence Ezrow, and Zeynep Somer-Topcu. 2011. "Is Anybody Listening? Evidence That Voters Do Not Respond to European Parties' Policy Statements during Elections." *American Journal of Political Science* 55 (2): 370–82.

Aldecoa, Francisco, and Michael Keating, eds. 1999. *Paradiplomacy in Action: The Foreign Relations of Subnational Governments.* Abingdon: Routledge.

Alonso, Sonia. 2012. *Challenging the State: Devolution and the Battle for Partisan Credibility.* New York: Oxford University Press.

Alonso, Sonia, Laura Cabeza, and Braulio Gómez. 2015. "Parties' Electoral Strategies in a Two-Dimensional Political Space: Evidence from Spain and Great Britain." *Party Politics* 21 (6): 851–65.

Alonso, Sonia, Braulio Gómez, and Laura Cabeza. 2013. "Measuring Centre-Periphery Preferences: The Regional Manifestos Project." *Regional and Federal Studies* 23 (2): 189–211.

Atikcan, Ece Ozlem. 2015. *Framing the European Union: The Power of Arguments in Shaping European Union.* Cambridge: Cambridge University Press.

Aughey, Arthur. 2011. "The Con-Lib Coalition Agenda for Scotland, Wales and Northern Ireland." In *The Cameron-Clegg Government: Coalition Politics in an Age of Austerity,* edited by Simon Lee and Matt Beech, 168–84. Basingstoke: Palgrave Macmillan.

Bakvis, Herman, and Laura G. Macpherson. 1995. "Quebec Block Voting and the Canadian Electoral System." *Canadian Journal of Political Science* 28 (4): 619–35.

Balfour, Sebastian, and Alejandro Quiroga. 2007. *The Reinvention of Spain: Nation and Identity Since Democracy*. Oxford: Oxford University Press.

Banting, Keith G., Roger Gibbins, Peter M. Leslie, Alain Noël, Richard Simeon, and Robert Young. 2006. *Open Federalism: Interpretations, Significance*. Kingston: Institute of Intergovernmental Relations.

Barker, Fiona. 2015. *Nationalism, Identity and the Governance of Diversity*. Basingstoke: Palgrave Macmillan.

Basile, Linda. 2015. "A Dwarf among Giants? Party Competition between Ethno-Regionalist and State-wide Parties on the Territorial Dimension: The Case of Italy 1963–2013." *Party Politics* 21 (6): 887–99.

Bastien, Frédérick, Éric Bélanger, and François Gélineau, eds. 2013. *Les Québécois aux urnes: les partis, les médias et les citoyens en campagne*. Montreal: Presses de l'Université de Montréal.

BBC. 2014. "Scottish Independence: UK Leaders Pledge Parliament Powers," 5 August.

Bechhofer, Frank, and David McCrone. 2010. "Choosing National Identity." *Sociological Research Online*. http://www.socresonline.org.uk/15/3/3.html> 10.5153/sro.2191.

Béland, Daniel, and André Lecours. 2008. *Nationalism and Social Policy: The Politics of Territorial Solidarity*. Oxford: Oxford University Press.

Bélanger, Éric, and Chris Chhim. 2016. "National Identity and Support for Sovereignty in Quebec." In *Quebec Questions: Quebec Studies for the Twenty-First Century*, 2nd ed., edited by Stéphan Gervais, Christopher Kirkey, and Jarrett Rudy, 332–47. Don Mills, ON: Oxford University Press.

Bélanger, Éric, and Eva Falk Pedersen. 2015. "The 2014 Provincial Election in Quebec." *Canadian Political Science Review* 9: 112–20.

Bélanger, Éric, and François Gélineau. 2011. "Le vote économique en contexte de crise financière: l'élection provinciale de 2008 au Québec." *Canadian Journal of Political Science* 44 (3): 529–51.

Bélanger, Éric, and Bonnie M. Meguid. 2008. "Issue Salience, Issue Ownership and Issue-Based Vote Choice." *Electoral Studies* 27 (3): 477–91.

Bélanger, Éric, and Richard Nadeau. 2009. *Le comportement électoral des Québécois*. Montreal: Presses de l'Université de Montréal.

– 2014. "Economic Crisis, Party Competence and the Economic Vote." *Acta Politica* 49 (4): 462–85.

– 2016. "The Bloc Québécois in a Rainbow-Coloured Quebec." In *The Canadian Federal Election of 2015*, edited by Jon H. Pammett and Christopher Dornan, 117–39. Toronto: Dundurn Press.

Bélanger, Éric, and Andrea M.L. Perrella. 2008. "Facteurs d'appui à la souveraineté du Québec chez les jeunes: une comparaison entre francophones, anglophones et allophones." *Politique et sociétés* 27 (3): 13–40.

Bélanger, Louis. 2002. "The Domestic Politics of Quebec's Quest for External Distinctiveness." *American Review of Canadian Studies* 32 (2): 195–214.

Bernard, André, and Bernard Descôteaux. 1981. *Québec: élections 1981.* Montreal: Hurtubise HMH.

Better Together. 2014. *Scottish Referendum: Money and the Economy.* London: HM Government.

Bickerton, James, Alain-G. Gagnon, and Patrick J. Smith. 1999. *Ties That Bind: Parties and Voters in Canada.* Don Mills, ON: Oxford University Press.

Bilodeau, Antoine. 2016. "Usage du français et préférences politiques des néo-Québécois." *Canadian Journal of Political Science* 49 (1): 41–62.

Bilodeau, Antoine, and Luc Turgeon. 2014. "L'immigration: une menace pour la culture québécoise? Portrait et analyses des perceptions régionales." *Canadian Journal of Political Science* 47 (2): 281–305.

Bischof, Daniel. 2017. "Towards a Renewal of the Niche Party Concept: Parties, Market Shares and Condensed Offers." *Party Politics* 23 (3): 220–35.

Blair, Tony. 2006. "The Duty to Integrate: Shared British Values." Speech by UK Prime Minister Tony Blair, 8 December.

Blais, André, Elisabeth Gidengil, Richard Nadeau, and Neil Nevitte. 2002. *Anatomy of a Liberal Victory: Making Sense of the Vote in the 2000 Canadian Election.* Peterborough: Broadview Press.

Blais, André, Pierre Martin, and Richard Nadeau. 1995. "Attentes économiques et linguistiques et appui à la souveraineté du Québec." *Canadian Journal of Political Science* 28 (4): 637–57.

Blais, André, and Richard Nadeau. 1984a. "L'appui au Parti québécois: évolution de la clientèle de 1970 à 1981." In *Comportement électoral au Québec*, edited by Jean Crête, 279–318. Chicoutimi: Gaëtan Morin.

– 1984b. "La clientèle du OUI." In *Comportement électoral au Québec*, edited by Jean Crête, 321–34. Chicoutimi: Gaëtan Morin.

– 1992. "To Be or Not to Be Sovereignist: Quebeckers' Perennial Dilemma." *Canadian Public Policy* 18 (1): 89–103.

Blake, Donald E. 1985. *Two Political Worlds: Parties and Voting in British Columbia.* Vancouver: University of British Columbia Press.

Böhmelt, Tobias, Lawrence Ezrow, Roni Lehrer, and Hugh Ward. 2016. "Party Policy Diffusion." *American Political Science Review* 110 (2): 397–410.

Bond, Ross. 2000. "Squaring the Circles: Demonstrating and Explaining the Political 'Non-Alignment' of Scottish National Identity." *Scottish Affairs* 32 (1): 15–35.

Bouchard, Gérard. 2015. *Interculturalism: A View from Quebec*. Toronto: University of Toronto Press.

Bourque, Gilles L. 2000. *Le modèle québécois de développement: de l'émergence au renouvellement*. Sainte-Foy: Presses de l'Université du Québec.

Bradbury, Jonathan. 2006. "British Political Parties and Devolution: Adapting to Multi-Level Politics in Scotland and Wales." In *Devolution and Electoral Politics*, edited by Dan Hough and Charlie Jeffery, 21–3. Manchester: Manchester University Press.

Brancati, Dawn. 2008. "The Origins and Strengths of Regional Parties." *British Journal of Political Science* 38 (1): 135–59.

Brand, Jack, James Mitchell, and Paula Surridge. 1993. "Identity and the Vote: Class and Nationality in Scotland." In *British Elections and Parties Yearbook*, edited by David Denver, Pippa Norris, David Broughton, and Collin Rallings, 143–57. Hemel Hempstead: Harvester Wheatsheaf.

Brie, Evelyne. 2016. "Diplomatie référendaire: transmission et interprétation de l'exigence de clarté référendaire au Royaume-Uni (2011–2014)." MSc thesis, Université Laval.

Brown, Alice, David McCrone, and Lindsay Paterson. 1996. *Politics and Society in Scotland*. Basingstoke: Macmillan.

Brown, Alice, David McCrone, Lindsay Paterson, and Paula Surridge. 1999. *The Scottish Electorate: The 1997 General Election and Beyond*. Basingstoke: Macmillan Press.

Budge, Ian, and Dennis J. Farlie. 1983. *Explaining and Predicting Elections*. London: Allen and Unwin.

Budge, Ian, Hans-Dieter Klingemann, Andrea Volkens, Judith Bara, and Eric Tanenbaum. 2001. *Mapping Policy Preferences: Estimates for Parties, Electors, and Governments 1945–1998*. Oxford: Oxford University Press.

Budge, Ian, and Derek W. Urwin. 1966. *Scottish Political Behaviour: A Case Study in British Homogeneity*. London: Longmans.

Bulmer, Simon, Martin Burch, Patricia Hogwood, and Andrew Scott. 2006. "UK Devolution and the European Union: A Tale of Cooperative Asymmetry." *Publius: The Journal of Federalism* 36 (1): 75–93.

Calder, Angus. 1994. *Revolving Culture: Notes from the Scottish Republic*. London: I.B. Tauris.

Cameron, David. 2011. Prime Minister's Speech at the Munich Security Conference, 5 February. www.number10.gov.uk/news/pms-speech-at-munich-security-conference/.

Canadian Press. 2017. "Québec relance le débat constitutionnel," 31 May.

Carman, Christopher, and Robert Johns. 2010. "Linking Coalition Attitudes and Split Ticket Voting: The Scottish Parliament Elections of 2007." *Electoral Studies* 29 (3): 381–91.

Carman, Christopher, Robert Johns, and James Mitchell. 2014. *More Scottish than British: The 2011 Scottish Parliament Election*. Basingstoke: Palgrave Macmillan.

Caron, Jean-François. 2013. "The Exclusive Nature of Quebec's Contemporary Nationalism: The Pitfalls of Civic Nationalism." *International Journal of Canadian Studies* 47 (1): 221–38.

Carrell, Severin. 2014. "Scottish Labour Unveils Mini-Manifesto to Woo Disillusioned Voters." *The Guardian*, 21 March.

Castonguay, Alec. 2014. "Référendum écossais: petits complots entre amis." *L'Actualité*, 24 August.

– 2015. "Le pari nationaliste de François Legault." *L'Actualité*, 9 November.

Cento Bull, Anna, and Mark Gilbert. 2001. *The Lega Nord and the Northern Question in Italian Politics*. New York: Palgrave.

Chaney, Paul. 2013. "An Electoral Discourse Approach to State Decentralisation: State wide Parties' Manifesto Proposals on Scottish and Welsh Devolution, 1945–2010." *British Politics* 8 (3): 333–56.

Chhibber, Pradeep K., and Ken Kollman. 2004. *The Formation of National Party Systems: Federalism and Party Competition in Canada, Great Britain, India and the United States*. New Jersey: Princeton University Press.

Chhim, Chris. 2016. "The Nationalist Niche? Parties and Voters in Sub-state Nationalist Mobilisation." PhD thesis, McGill University.

Chhim, Chris, and Éric Bélanger. 2017. "Language as a Public Good and National Identity: Scotland's Competing Heritage Languages." *Nations and Nationalism* 23 (4): 929–51.

Clarke, Harold D., Allan Kornberg, and Thomas Scotto. 2009. *Making Political Choices: Canada and the United States*. Toronto: University of Toronto Press.

Clarke, Harold D., David Sanders, Marianne C. Stewart, and Paul F. Whiteley. 2004. *Political Choice in Britain*. Oxford: Oxford University Press.

– 2009. *Performance Politics and the British Voter*. Cambridge: Cambridge University Press.

– 2011. "Valence Politics and Electoral Choice in Britain, 2010." *Journal of Elections, Public Opinion and Parties* 21 (2): 237–53.

Commission on Scottish Devolution. 2009. *Serving Scotland Better: Scotland and the United Kingdom in the 21st Century*. Final Report. Edinburgh: Commission on Scottish Devolution.

Cook, James. 2013. "Alex Salmond Talks Up UK-Scottish Links." *BBC News*, 12 July.

Crête, Jean, ed. 1984. *Comportement électoral au Québec.* Chicoutimi: Gaëtan Morin.

Cross, William P., Jonathan Malloy, Tamara A. Small, and Laura B. Stephenson. 2015. *Fighting for Votes: Parties, the Media, and Voters in an Ontario Election.* Vancouver: University of British Columbia Press.

Curtice, John. 1996. "One Nation Again?" In *British Social Attitudes: The 13th Report,* edited by Roger Jowell, John Currie, Alison Park, Lindsay Brook, and Katarina Thomson. Aldershot: Dartmouth.

– 2013. *Who Supports and Opposes Independence – and Why?* Edinburgh: ScotCen.

Curtice, John, David McCrone, Nicola McEwen, Michael Marsh, and Rachel Ormston. 2009. *Revolution or Evolution? The 2007 Scottish Elections.* Edinburgh: Edinburgh University Press.

Curtice, John, and Ben Seyd. 2009. "The Citizens' Response: Devolution and the Union." In *Has Devolution Worked? The Verdict from Policy Makers and the Public,* edited by John Curtice and Ben Seyd, 116–37. Manchester: Manchester University Press.

Cutler, Fred. 2008. "One Voter, Two First-Order Elections?" *Electoral Studies* 27 (3): 492–504.

Dalton, Russell J. 1988. *Citizen Politics in Western Democracies: Public Opinion and Political Parties in the United States, Great Britain, Germany and France.* New Jersey: Chatham House Publishers.

Dandoy, Régis, Geoffroy Matagne, and Caroline Van Wynsberghe. 2013. "The Future of Belgian Federalism: An Analysis of Party Preferences." *Regional and Federal Studies* 23 (3): 331–51.

David, Michel. 2015. "Le dangereux pari du vide." *Le Devoir,* 23 May.

Demuro, Gianmario, Francesco Mola, and Ilenia Rúggiu, eds. 2013. *Identità e autonomia in Sardegna e Scozia.* Bologna: Maggioli Editore.

Denver, David, and Robert Johns. 2010. "Scottish Parliament Elections: 'British not Scottish' or 'More Scottish than British'?" *Scottish Affairs* 70 (1): 9–28.

Deschouwer, Kris. 2003. "Political Parties in Multi-Layered Systems." *European Urban and Regional Studies* 10 (3): 213–26.

– 2013. "Party Strategies, Voter Demands and Territorial Reform in Belgium." *West European Politics* 36 (2): 338–58.

Dinkel, Reiner. 1978. "The Relationship between Federal and State Elections in West Germany." In *Elections and Parties,* edited by Max Kaase and Klaus Von Beyme, 53–190. London: Sage.

Dion, Léon. 1975. *Nationalismes et politique au Québec.* Montreal: Hurtubise HMH.

Downs, Anthony. 1957. *An Economic Theory of Democracy*. New York: Harper.

Dupré, Jean-François. 2012. "Intercultural Citizenship, Civic Nationalism, and Nation Building in Quebec." *Studies in Ethnicity and Nationalism* 12 (2): 227–48.

Egan, Patrick J. 2013. *Partisan Priorities*. Cambridge: Cambridge University Press.

van der Eijk, Cees, Mark N. Franklin, and Michael Marsh. 1996. "What Voters Teach Us about Europe-wide Elections: What Europe-wide Elections Teach Us about Voters." *Electoral Studies* 15 (2): 149–66.

Elias, Anwen, Edina Szöcsik, and Christina Isabel Zuber. 2015. "Position, Selective Emphasis and Framing: How Parties Deal with a Second Dimension in Competition." *Party Politics* 21 (6): 839–50.

Enelow, James M., and Melvin J. Hinich. 1984. *The Spatial Theory of Voting: An Introduction*. New York: Cambridge University Press.

Esman, Milton J. 1977. *Ethnic Conflict in the Western World*. Ithaca, NY: Cornell University Press.

Fabre, Elodie, and Enric Martínez-Herrera. 2009. "Statewide Parties and Regional Party Competition. An Analysis of Party Manifestos in the United Kingdom." In *Territorial Party Politics in Western Europe*, edited by Wilfried Swenden and Bart Maddens, 229–48. Basingstoke and New York: Palgrave Macmillan.

Fontecilla, Andrés. 2016. "Partenariat transpacifique: moins de souveraineté." *Le Devoir*, 16 February.

Fournier, Patrick, André Blais, Richard Nadeau, Elisabeth Gidengil, and Neil Nevitte. 2003. "Issue Importance and Performance Voting." *Political Behavior* 25 (1): 51–67.

Fournier, Patrick, Fred Cutler, Stuart Soroka, Dietlind Stolle, and Éric Bélanger. 2013. "Riding the Orange Wave: Leadership, Values and Issues in the 2011 Canadian Election." *Canadian Journal of Political Science* 46 (4): 863–97.

Franklin, Mark N., Thomas T. Mackie, and Henry Valen, eds. 1992. *Electoral Change: Responses to Evolving Social and Attitudinal Structures in Western Countries*. Cambridge: Cambridge University Press.

Fuchs, Dieter, and Hans-Dieter Klingemann. 1989. "The Left-Right Schema." In *Continuities in Political Action*, edited by M. Kent Jennings and Jan van Deth, 203–34. Berlin: Walter de Gruyter.

Gabel, Matthew J., and John D. Huber. 2000. "Putting Parties in Their Place: Inferring Party Left-Right Ideological Positions from Party Manifestos Data." *American Journal of Political Science* 44 (1): 94–103.

Gagnon, Alain-G., and François Boucher. 2017. "Party Politics in a Distinct

Society: Two Eras of Block Voting in Quebec." In *Canadian Parties in Transition*, 4th ed., edited by Alain-G. Gagnon and A. Brian Tanguay, 277–95. Toronto: University of Toronto Press.

Geekie, Jack, and Roger Levy. 1989. "Devolution and the Tartanisation of the Labour Party." *Parliamentary Affairs* 42 (3): 399–411.

Gidengil, Elisabeth, Neil Nevitte, André Blais, Joanna Everitt, and Patrick Fournier. 2012. *Dominance and Decline: Making Sense of Recent Canadian Elections*. Toronto: University of Toronto Press.

Godbout, Jean-François. 2013. "Les élections au Québec de 1973 à 2012." In *Les Québécois aux urnes*, edited by Frédérick Bastien, Éric Bélanger, and François Gélineau, 23–43. Montreal: Les Presses de l'Université de Montréal.

Godbout, Jean-François, and Éric Bélanger. 2002. "La dimension régionale du vote économique canadien aux élections fédérales de 1988 à 2000." *Canadian Journal of Political Science* 35 (3): 567–88.

Golder, Sona N., Ignacio Lago, André Blais, Elisabeth Gidengil, and Thomas Gschwend. 2017. *Multi-Level Electoral Politics: Beyond the Second-Order Election Model*. Oxford: Oxford University Press.

Government of Quebec. 2013. "Bill 60: Charter Affirming the Values of State Secularism and Religious Neutrality and of Equality between Women and Men, and Providing a Framework for Accommodation Requests." National Assembly of Quebec, 40th Legislature, 1st Session, 7 November.

Green, Jane. 2007. "When Voters and Parties Agree: Valence Issues and Party Competition." *Political Studies* 55 (3): 629–55.

Green, Jane, and Will Jennings. 2017. *The Politics of Competence: Parties, Public Opinion and Voters*. Cambridge: Cambridge University Press.

Guinaudeau, Isabelle, and Simon Persico. 2014. "What Is Issue Competition? Conflict, Consensus and Issue Ownership in Party Competition." *Journal of Elections, Public Opinion and Parties* 24 (3): 312–33.

Guinjoan, Marc, and Toni Rodon. 2016. "A Scrutiny of the Linz-Moreno Question." *Publius: The Journal of Federalism* 46 (1): 128–42.

Gunther, Richard, and Larry Diamond. 2003. "Species of Political Parties: A New Typology." *Party Politics* 9 (2): 167–99.

Hamilton, Paul. 1999. "The Scottish National Paradox: The Scottish National Party's Lack of Ethnic Character." *Canadian Review of Studies in Nationalism* 26 (1–2): 17–36.

Hassan, Gerry, and Eric Shaw. 2012. *Strange Death of Labour in Scotland*. Edinburgh: Edinburgh University Press.

Henderson, Ailsa. 2007. *Hierarchies of Belonging: National Identity and Political Culture in Scotland and Quebec*. Montreal: McGill-Queen's University Press.

– 2014. "The Myth of Meritocratic Scotland: Political Culture(s) in the UK." In *Sex, Lies and the Ballot Box*, edited by Philip Cowley and Rob Ford, 103–7. London: Biteback Press.

Henderson, Ailsa, and Colin Coates. 2005. "Introduction: Scotland and Québec: An Evolving Comparison." *British Journal of Canadian Studies* 18 (2): 207–13.

Henderson, Ailsa, Liam Delaney, and Robert Liñeira. 2014. *Risk and Attitudes to Constitutional Change.* Edinburgh: Centre on Constitutional Change.

Henderson, Ailsa, Charlie Jeffery, and Robert Liñeira. 2015. "National Identity or National Interest? Scottish, English and Welsh Attitudes to the Constitutional Debate." *Political Quarterly* 86 (2): 265–74.

Henderson, Ailsa, Charlie Jeffery, and Daniel Wincott, eds. 2013. *Citizenship after the Nation State.* Basingstoke: Palgrave Macmillan.

Henderson, Ailsa, and Robert Liñeira. 2014. *Public Attitudes towards Additional Devolution to the Scottish Parliament.* Edinburgh: Centre on Constitutional Change.

Henderson, Ailsa, and Nicola McEwen. 2005. "Do Shared Values Underpin National Identity? Examining the Role of Values in National Identity in Canada and the United Kingdom." *National Identities* 7 (2): 173–91.

– 2010. "A Comparative Analysis of Voter Turnout in Regional Elections." *Electoral Studies* 29 (3): 405–16.

– 2015. "Regions as Primary Political Communities: A Multi-Level Comparative Analysis of Turnout in Regional Elections." *Publius: The Journal of Federalism* 45 (2): 189–215.

Hepburn, Eve. 2006. "Scottish Autonomy and European Integration: The Response of Scotland's Political Parties." In *European Integration and the Nationalities Question*, edited by John McGarry and Michael Keating, 225–38. London and New York: Routledge.

– 2008. "The Rise and Fall of a Europe of the Regions." *Regional and Federal Studies* 18 (5): 537–55.

– 2009a. "Introduction: Re-conceptualizing Sub-state Mobilization." *Regional and Federal Studies* 19 (4–5): 477–99.

– 2009b. "Degrees of Independence: SNP Thinking in an International Context." In *The Modern SNP: From Protest to Power*, edited by Gerry Hassan, 190–203. Edinburgh: Edinburgh University Press.

– 2010a. "Small Worlds in Canada and Europe: A Comparison of Regional Party Systems in Quebec, Bavaria and Scotland." *Regional and Federal Studies* 20 (4–5): 527–44.

– 2010b. "Can Scotland Unite against Cameronism?" *Holyrood Magazine*, 15 March.

- 2010c. *Using Europe: Territorial Party Strategies in a Multilevel System.* Manchester: Manchester University Press.
- 2011. "'Citizens of the Region': Party Conceptions of Regional Citizenship and Immigrant Integration." *European Journal of Political Research* 50 (4): 504–29.
- 2014a. "Spreading Demands for Self-Determination: The 'Contagion Effect' of Substate Nationalist and Regionalist Parties on the Territorial Stances of Other Parties." Paper presented at the international conference Self-Determination in Europe: Contemporary Challenges of Minorities in Multinational States, University of Bern, 9–11 October.
- 2014b. "Independence and the Immigration Debate in Scotland." *British Politics Review* 9 (2): 10–12.
- 2014c. "Scotland's 'Hidden' Policy Competence: Immigrant Integration and Policy Divergence in Scotland since Devolution." Paper presented at the Annual Policy and Politics Conference, University of Bristol, 15–16 September.
Hepburn, Eve, and Michael Rosie. 2014. "Immigration, Nationalism and Political Parties in Scotland." In *The Politics of Immigration in Multilevel States: Governance and Political Parties,* edited by Eve Hepburn and Ricard Zapata-Barrero, 241–60. Basingstoke: Palgrave Macmillan.
Hinich, Melvin J., Michael C. Munger, and Scott De Marchi. 1998. "Ideology and the Construction of Nationality: The Canadian Elections of 1993." *Public Choice* 97 (3): 401–28.
Hooghe, Lisbet. 1991. *A Leap in the Dark: Nationalist Conflict and Federal Reform in Belgium.* Ithaca, NY: Cornell University Press.
Hough, Dan, and Charlie Jeffery. 2006. *Devolution and Electoral Politics.* Manchester: Manchester University Press.
Hutchinson, John. 1999. "Re-interpreting Cultural Nationalism." *Australian Journal of Politics and History* 45 (3): 392–409.
Inglehart, Ronald. 1984. "The Changing Structure of Political Cleavages in Western Society." In *Electoral Change in Advanced Industrial Societies: Realignment or Dealignment?* Edited by Russell J. Dalton, Scott C. Flanagan, and Paul Allen Beck, 25–69. Princeton: Princeton University Press.
- 1990. *Culture Shift in Advanced Industrial Society.* Princeton: Princeton University Press.
Inglehart, Ronald, and Hans-Dieter Klingemann. 1976. "Party Identification, Ideological Preference and the Left-Right Dimension among Western Mass Publics." In *Party Identification and Beyond: Representations of Voting and Party Competition,* edited by Ian Budge, Ivor Crewe, and Dennis J. Farlie, 243–76. London: Wiley.

Irvine, J.A. Sandy, and Kim Richard Nossal. 2005. "Constitutional Constraints on the International Activities of Non-Central Governments: Scotland and Québec Compared." *British Journal of Canadian Studies* 18 (2): 340–57.

Jeffery, Charlie. 2005. "Devolution and the European Union: Trajectories and Futures." In *The Dynamics of Devolution: The State of the Nations 2005*, edited by Allan Trench, 179–200. Thorverton: Imprint Academic.

– 2009a. "New Research Agendas on Regional Party Competition." *Regional and Federal Studies* 19 (4–5): 639–50.

– 2009b. "Multi-Level Party Competition in Federal and Regional States." In *Handbook on Multi-Level Governance*, edited by Henrik Enderlein, Sonja Walti, and Michael Zurn, 136–52. Cheltenham: Edward Elgar Publishing.

Jeffery, Charlie, and Dan Hough. 2003. "Regional Elections in Multi-Level Systems." *European Urban and Regional Studies* 10 (3): 199–212.

Jeffery, Charlie, and James Mitchell, eds. 2010. *The Scottish Parliament: The First Decade*. Edinburgh: Luath Press.

Jeffery, Charlie, Richard Wyn Jones, Ailsa Henderson, Roger Scully, and Guy Lodge. 2014. *Taking England Seriously: The New English Politics*. Edinburgh: Future of the UK and Scotland.

Jensen, Christian B., and Jae-Jae Spoon. 2010. "Thinking Locally, Acting Supranationally: Niche Party Behaviour in the European Parliament." *European Journal of Political Research* 49 (2): 174–201.

Johns, Robert. 2011. "Credit Where It's Due? Valence Politics, Attributions of Responsibility and Multi-Level Elections." *Political Behavior* 33 (1): 53–77.

Johns, Robert, Christopher J. Carman, and James Mitchell. 2013. "Constitution or Competence? The SNP's Re-election in 2011." *Political Studies* 61 (S1): 158–78.

Johns, Robert, David Denver, James Mitchell, and Charles Pattie. 2009. "Valence Politics in Scotland: Towards an Explanation of the 2007 Election." *Political Studies* 57 (1): 207–33.

Johns, Robert, and James Mitchell. 2016. *Takeover: Explaining the Extraordinary Rise of the SNP*. London: Biteback Publishing.

Johnston, Richard. 2000. "Canadian Elections at the Millennium." *IRPP Choices* 6 (6): 4–36.

– 2008. "Polarized Pluralism in the Canadian Party System." *Canadian Journal of Political Science* 41 (4): 815–34.

Johnston, Richard, André Blais, Henry E. Brady, and Jean Crête. 1992. *Letting the People Decide: Dynamics of a Canadian Election*. Montreal: McGill-Queen's University Press.

Journet, Paul. 2014. "Pour la souveraineté et la prospérité." *La Presse*, 10 March.

Keating, Michael. 1996. *Nations against the State: The New Politics of Nationalism in Quebec, Catalonia, and Scotland*. London: Macmillan.

– 2005. "Semantics and Sovereignty, or Is There a Coherent Post-sovereignty Stance? Evidence from Quebec and Scotland." *British Journal of Canadian Studies* 18 (2): 246–68.

– ed. 2007. *Scottish Social Democracy: Progressive Ideas for Public Policy*. Brussels: Peter Lang.

– 2009. *The Independence of Scotland: Self-Government and the Shifting Politics of Union*. Oxford: Oxford University Press.

– 2010. *The Government of Scotland*. 2nd ed. Edinburgh: Edinburgh University Press.

Keating, Michael, and David Bleiman. 1979. *Labour and Scottish Nationalism*. London: Macmillan.

Kennedy, James. 2013. *Liberal Nationalisms: Empire, State, and Civil Society in Scotland and Quebec*. Montreal: McGill-Queen's University Press.

Keren, Michael. 2000. "Political Perfectionism and the 'Anti-System' Party." *Party Politics* 6 (1): 107–16.

Klingemann, Hans-Dieter, Andrea Volkens, Judith Bara, Ian Budge, and Michael McDonald. 2006. *Mapping Policy Preferences II: Estimates for Parties, Electors, and Governments in Eastern Europe, European Union, and OECD 1990–2003*. Oxford and New York: Oxford University Press.

Klüver, Heike, and Iñaki Sagarzazu. 2016. "Setting the Agenda or Responding to Voters? Political Parties, Voters and Issue Attention." *West European Politics* 39 (2): 380–98.

Klüver, Heike, and Jae-Jae Spoon. 2016. "Who Responds? Voters, Parties and Issue Attention." *British Journal of Political Science* 46 (3): 633–54.

Kuznetsov, Alexander. 2015. *Theory and Practice of Paradiplomacy: Subnational Governments in International Affairs*. Abingdon: Routledge.

Kymlicka, Will. 2001. "Immigrant Integration and Minority Nationalism." In *Minority Nationalism and the Changing International Order*, edited by Michael Keating and John McGarry, 61–83. Oxford: Oxford University Press.

– 2011. "Multicultural Citizenship within Multination States." *Ethnicities* 11 (3): 281–302.

Lachapelle, Guy, and Stéphane Paquin, eds. 2004. *Mondialisation, gouvernance et nouvelles stratégies subétatiques*. Quebec City: Presses de l'Université Laval.

Laponce, Jean A. 1970. "Note on the Use of the Left-Right Dimension." *Comparative Political Studies* 2 (4): 191–225.

Latouche, Daniel, Guy Lord, and Jean-Guy Vaillancourt, eds. 1976. *Le

processus électoral au Québec: les élections provinciales de 1970 et 1973.
Montreal: Hurtubise HMH.

Lecours, André. 2007. *Basque Nationalism and the Spanish State.* Reno: University of Nevada Press.

Leith, Murray Stewart, and Daniel P.J. Soule. 2011. *Political Discourse and National Identity in Scotland.* Edinburgh: Edinburgh University Press.

Lemieux, Vincent, ed. 1969. *Quatre élections provinciales au Québec.* Quebec City: Presses de l'Université Laval.

Lemieux, Vincent. 2006. "Le gouvernement Charest et les valeurs libérales." In *Le Parti libéral: enquête sur les réalisations du gouvernement Charest,* edited by François Pétry, Éric Bélanger, and Louis M. Imbeau, 41–50. Quebec City: Presses de l'Université Laval.

– 2008. *Le Parti libéral du Québec: alliances, rivalités et neutralités.* Quebec City: Presses de l'Université Laval.

– 2011. *Les partis générationnels au Québec: passé, présent, avenir.* Quebec City: Presses de l'Université Laval.

Lemieux, Vincent, Marcel Gilbert, and André Blais. 1970. *Une élection de réalignement: l'élection générale du 29 avril 1970 au Québec.* Montreal: Éditions du Jour.

Létourneau, Jocelyn. 2006. *Que veulent vraiment les Québécois?* Montreal: Boréal.

Levy, Naomi. 2014. "Measuring Multiple Identities: What Is Lost with a Zero-Sum Approach." *Politics, Groups, and Identities* 2 (4): 624–42.

Lewis, Hannah, and Gary Craig. 2014. "'Multiculturalism Is Never Talked About': From Multiculturalism to Community Cohesion at the Local Level in England." *Policy and Politics* 42 (1): 21–38.

Lewis-Beck, Michael S., William Jacoby, Helmut Norpoth, and Herbert Weisberg. 2008. *The American Voter Revisited.* Ann Arbor: University of Michigan Press.

Lewis-Beck, Michael S., and Richard Nadeau. 2011. "Economic Voting Theory: Testing New Dimensions." *Electoral Studies* 30 (2): 288–94.

Libbrecht, Liselotte, Bart Maddens, and Wilfried Swenden. 2013. "Party Competition in Regional Elections: The Strategies of State-wide Parties in Spain and the United Kingdom." *Party Politics* 19 (4): 624–40.

Libbrecht, Liselotte, Bart Maddens, Wilfried Swenden, and Elodie Fabre. 2009. "Issue Salience in Regional Party Manifestos in Spain." *European Journal of Political Research* 48 (1): 58–79.

Linz, Juan J., Manuel Gómez-Reino, Francisco Andrés Orizo, and Darío Vila, eds. 1981. *Informe sociológico sobre el cambio político en España, 1975–1981.* Madrid: Euramerica.

Lipset, Seymour Martin, and Stein Rokkan. 1967. *Party Systems and Voter Alignments: Cross National Perspectives*. New York: Free Press.

Lublin, David. 2014. *Minority Rules: Electoral Systems, Decentralization, and Ethnoregional Party Success*. Oxford: Oxford University Press.

Lynch, Peter. 2005. "Scottish Independence, the Quebec Model of Secession and the Political Future of the Scottish National Party." *Nationalism and Ethnic Politics* 11 (4): 503–31.

Macdonell, Hamish. 2012. "Scottish Labour Plans to End Free Universal Benefits." *The Independent*, 26 September.

Mahéo, Valérie-Anne, and Éric Bélanger. Forthcoming. "Is the Parti Québécois Bound to Disappear? A Study of the Current Generational Dynamics of Electoral Behaviour in Quebec." *Canadian Journal of Political Science*.

Maioni, Antonia. 2014. "The Québec Election of 2014 and the Unresolved Challenges of the Parti Québécois." *Québec Studies* 58 (1): 139–52.

Marsh, Michael. 1998. "Testing the Second-Order Election Model after Four European Elections." *British Journal of Political Science* 28 (4): 591–607.

Martin, Pierre. 1997. "When Nationalism Meets Continentalism: The Politics of Free Trade in Quebec." In *The Political Economy of Regionalism*, edited by Michael Keating and John Loughlin, 236–61. London: Frank Cass.

Martin, Pierre, and Richard Nadeau. 2002. "Understanding Opinion Formation on Quebec Sovereignty." In *Citizen Politics: Research and Theory in Canadian Political Behaviour*, edited by Joanna Everitt and Brenda O'Neill, 142–58. Don Mills, ON: Oxford University Press.

McCrone, David. 1992. *Understanding Scotland: The Sociology of a Stateless Nation*. London and New York: Routledge.

McEwen, Nicola. 2006. *Nationalism and the State: Welfare and Identity in Scotland and Quebec*. Brussels: Presses Interuniversitaires Européennes/Peter Lang.

McLeod, Wilson. 2001. "Gaelic in the New Scotland: Politics, Rhetoric and Public Discourse." *Journal of Ethnopolitics and Minority Issues in Europe*. www.ecmi.de/jemie/download/JEMIE02MacLeod28-11-01.pdf.

Meadwell, Hudson. 1991. "A Rational Choice Approach to Political Regionalism." *Comparative Politics* 23 (4): 401–21.

Meguid, Bonnie M. 2008. *Party Competition between Unequals: Strategies and Electoral Fortunes in Western Europe*. Cambridge: Cambridge University Press.

Mendelsohn, Matthew. 2002. "Measuring National Identity and Patterns of Attachment: Quebec and Nationalist Mobilization." *Nationalism and Ethnic Politics* 8 (3): 72–94.

Meyer, Thomas M., and Bernhard Miller. 2015. "The Niche Party Concept and Its Measurement." *Party Politics* 21 (2): 259–71.

Miller, Warren E., and J. Merrill Shanks. 1996. *The New American Voter*. Cambridge: Harvard University Press.

Miller, William L., Annis May Timpson, and Michael Lessnoff. 1996. *Political Culture in Contemporary Britain*. Oxford: Clarendon Press.

Mitchell, James. 1998. "The Evolution of Devolution: Labour's Home Rule Strategy in Opposition." *Government and Opposition* 33 (4): 479–96.

– 2009. *Devolution in the United Kingdom*. Manchester: Manchester University Press.

– 2014. *The Scottish Question*. Oxford: Oxford University Press.

Mitchell, James, Lynn Bennie, and Rob Johns. 2011. *The Scottish National Party: Transition to Power*. Oxford University Press.

Monière, Denis, and Jean-Herman Guay, eds. 1995. *La bataille du Québec. Deuxième épisode: les élections québécoises de 1994*. Montreal: Fides.

Mooney, Gerry, Gill Scott, and Charlotte Williams. 2006. "Rethinking Social Policy through Devolution." *Critical Social Policy* 26 (3): 483–97.

Moreno, Luis. 1988. "Scotland and Catalonia: The Path to Home Rule." In *The Scottish Government Yearbook*, edited by David McCrone and Alice Brown, 166–82. Edinburgh: The Unit for the Study of Government in Scotland.

Müller-Rommel, Ferdinand. 1998. "Ethnoregionalist Parties in Western Europe." In *Regionalist Parties in Western Europe*, edited by Lieven De Winter and Huri Türsan, 17–27. London and New York: Routledge.

Murray, Don. 2014. "What Scotland Independence Crusader Alex Salmond Learned from Quebec." *CBC News*, 17 September. http://www.cbc.ca/news/world/what-scotland-independence-crusader-alex-salmond-learned-from-quebec-1.2766564.

Nadeau, Richard, and Éric Bélanger. 2012. "Quebec versus the Rest of Canada, 1965–2006." In *The Canadian Election Studies: Assessing Four Decades of Influence*, edited by Mebs Kanji, Antoine Bilodeau, and Thomas J. Scotto, 136–53. Vancouver: University of British Columbia Press.

– 2013. "Un modèle général d'explication du vote des Québécois." In *Les Québécois aux urnes: les partis, les médias et les citoyens en campagne*, edited by Frédérick Bastien, Éric Bélanger, and François Gélineau, 191–208. Montreal: Presses de l'Université de Montréal.

Nadeau, Richard, Éric Bélanger, Michael S. Lewis-Beck, Bruno Cautrès, and Martial Foucault. 2012. *Le vote des Français de Mitterrand à Sarkozy*. Paris: Presses de Sciences Po.

Nadeau, Richard, and André Blais. 1990. "Do Canadians Distinguish Between Parties? Perceptions of Party Competence." *Canadian Journal of Political Science* 23 (2): 317–33.

Nadeau, Richard, André Blais, Elisabeth Gidengil, and Neil Nevitte. 2001. "Perceptions of Party Competence in the 1997 Election." In *Party Politics in Canada*, 8th ed., edited by Hugh Thorburn and Alan Whitehorn, 413–30. Toronto: Prentice-Hall.

Nadeau, Richard, and Christopher Fleury. 1995. "Gains linguistiques anticipés et appui à la souveraineté du Québec." *Canadian Journal of Political Science* 28 (1): 35–50.

Nadeau, Richard, Daniel Guérin, and Pierre Martin. 1995. "L'effondrement du Parti progressiste-conservateur à l'élection fédérale de 1993." *Revue québécoise de science politique* 27 (printemps): 123–48.

Nevitte, Neil, André Blais, Elisabeth Gidengil, and Richard Nadeau. 2000. *Unsteady State: The 1997 Canadian Federal Election*. Don Mills, ON: Oxford University Press.

Newell, James L. 1998. "The Scottish National Party: Development and Change." In *Regionalist Parties in Western Europe*, edited by Lieven De Winter and Huri Türsan, 105–24. London and New York: Routledge.

Noël, Alain. 1994. "Distinct in the House of Commons: The Bloc Québécois as Official Opposition." In *Canada: The State of the Federation 1994*, edited by Douglas M. Brown and Janet Hiebert, 19–35. Kingston: Institute of Intergovernmental Relations.

Norris, Pippa, and Karlheinz Reif. 1997. "Second-Order Elections." *European Journal of Political Research* 31 (1): 109–14.

Pallarés, Francesc, and Michael Keating. 2003. "Multi-Level Electoral Competition: Regional Elections and Party Systems in Spain." *European Urban and Regional Studies* 10 (3): 239–55.

Paquin, Stéphane. 2001. *La revanche des petites nations: le Québec, l'Écosse et la Catalogne face à la mondialisation*. Montreal: VLB Éditeur.

Pardos-Prado, Sergi. 2012. "Valence beyond Consensus: Party Competence and Policy Dispersion from a Comparative Perspective." *Electoral Studies* 31 (2): 342–52.

Paterson, Lindsay, Alice Brown, John Curtice, and Kerstin Hinds. 2001. *New Scotland, New Politics*. Edinburgh: Polygon.

Paterson, Lindsay, Fiona O'Hanlon, Rachel Ormston, and Susan Reid. 2014. "Public Attitudes to Gaelic and the Debate about Scottish Autonomy." *Regional and Federal Studies* 24(4): 429–50.

Pelletier, Benoît. 2001. *A Project for Quebec: Affirmation, Autonomy and Leadership*. Parti Libéral du Québec orientation document, October.

Pelletier, Réjean. 2012. "L'évolution du système de partis au Québec." In *Les partis politiques québécois dans la tourmente: mieux comprendre et évaluer leur rôle*, edited by Réjean Pelletier, 19–40. Quebec City: Presses de l'Université Laval.

Petrocik, John R. 1996. "Issue Ownership in Presidential Elections, with a 1980 Case Study." *American Journal of Political Science* 40 (3): 825–50.

Pinard, Maurice. 2002. "The Quebec Independence Movement: From Its Emergence to the 1995 Referendum." In *Political Sociology: Canadian Perspectives*, edited by Douglas Baer, 238–68. Don Mills, ON: Oxford University Press.

– 2005. "Political Ambivalence towards the Parti Québécois and Its Electoral Consequences, 1970–2003." *Canadian Journal of Sociology* 30 (3): 281–314.

Pinard, Maurice, Robert Bernier, and Vincent Lemieux. 1997. *Un combat inachevé*. Sainte-Foy: Presses de l'Université du Québec.

Pinard, Maurice, and Richard Hamilton. 1977. "The Independence Issue and the Polarization of the Electorate: The 1973 Quebec Election." *Canadian Journal of Political Science* 10 (2): 215–59.

– 1978. "The Parti Québécois Comes to Power: An Analysis of the 1976 Quebec Election." *Canadian Journal of Political Science* 11 (4): 739–75.

Piroth, Scott. 2004. "Generational Replacement, Value Shifts, and Support for a Sovereign Quebec." *Québec Studies* 37 (4): 23–43.

Pogorelis, Robertas, Bart Maddens, Wilfried Swenden, and Elodie Fabre. 2005. "Issue Salience in Regional and National Party Manifestos in the UK." *West European Politics* 28 (5): 992–1014.

Policy Committee of the NDP. Quebec Section. 2005. *Quebec's Voice and a Choice for a Different Canada: Federalism, Social-Democracy and the Quebec Question*. New Democratic Party orientation document, October.

Quinn, Herbert F. 1979. *The Union Nationale: Quebec Nationalism from Duplessis to Lévesque*. Toronto: University of Toronto Press.

Rayside, David M. 1978. "Federalism and the Party System: Provincial and Federal Liberals in the Province of Quebec." *Canadian Journal of Political Science* 11 (3): 499–528.

Reid Foundation. 2013. *The Common Weal: A Model for Economic and Social Development in Scotland*. Edinburgh: The Jimmy Reid Foundation.

Reif, Karlheinz, and Hermann Schmitt. 1980. "Nine Second-Order Elections: A Conceptual Framework for the Analysis of European Elections." *European Journal of Political Research* 8 (1): 3–44.

Richez, Emmanuelle, and Marc André Bodet. 2012. "Fear and Disappointment: Explaining the Persistence of Support for Quebec Secession." *Journal of Elections, Public Opinion and Parties* 22 (1): 77–93.

Robertson, David. 1976. *A Theory of Party Competition*. New York: Wiley.

Sartori, Giovanni. 1971. "Opposition and Control: Problems and Prospects." In *Studies in Opposition*, edited by Rodney Barker, 31–7. London: Macmillan Press.

Schakel, Arjan H., and Charlie Jeffery. 2013. "Are Regional Elections Really 'Second-Order' Elections?" *Regional Studies* 47 (3): 323–41.

Schedler, Andreas. 1996. "Anti-political Establishment Parties." *Party Politics* 2 (3): 291–312.

Schlesinger, Philip. 2009. "The SNP, Cultural Policy and the Idea of the 'Creative Economy.'" In *The Modern SNP: From Protest to Power*, edited by Gerry Hassan, 135–46. Edinburgh: Edinburgh University Press.

Scottish Executive. 2002. *Working Together for Race Equality: The Scottish Executive's Race Equality Scheme*. Edinburgh: Scottish Executive.

– 2004. *New Scots: Attracting Fresh Talent to Meet the Challenge of Growth*. Edinburgh: Scottish Executive.

Scottish Government. 2008. *Scottish Government Race Equality Statement*. Edinburgh: Scottish Government.

– 2013a. *Scotland's Future: Your Guide to an Independent Scotland*. Edinburgh: Scottish Government.

– 2013b. *Building Security and Creating Opportunity: Economic Policy Choices in an Independent Scotland*. Edinburgh: Scottish Government.

Scottish Labour. 2014a. *Powers for a Purpose: Strengthening Accountability and Empowering People. Scottish Labour Devolution Commission Report*. Edinburgh: Scottish Labour.

– 2014b. *Together We Can*. Edinburgh: Scottish Labour.

Scottish Liberal Democrats. 2012. *Federalism: The Best Future for Scotland. The Report of the Home Rule and Community Rule Commission of the Scottish Liberal Democrats*. Edinburgh: Scottish Liberal Democrats.

Scottish National Party. 2015. *Stronger for Scotland: Manifesto 2015*. Glasgow: SNP.

Seawright, David. 1996. "The Scottish Unionist Party: What's in a Name?" *Scottish Affairs* 14 (1): 90–102.

– 2004. "The Scottish Conservative and Unionist Party: The Lesser Spotted Tory?" POLIS Working Paper No. 13, University of Leeds.

Sinnott, Richard. 2006. "An Evaluation of the Measurement of National, Subnational and Supranational Identity in Crossnational Surveys." *International Journal of Public Opinion Research* 18 (2): 211–23.

Smith Report. 2014. *Report of the Smith Commission for Further Devolution of Powers to the Scottish Parliament*. Edinburgh: The Smith Commission.

Société Radio-Canada. 2010. "Bernard Landry dénonce la 'troisième voie,'" 22 October.

Spectator. 2013. "Alex Salmond's Economic Policies Would Drive an Independent Scotland into the Ground," 23 November.

Steenbergen, Marco, Erica Edwards, and Catherine de Vries. 2007. "Who's Cueing Whom? Mass-Elite Linkages and the Future of European Integration." *European Union Politics* 8 (1): 13–35.

Stokes, Donald E. 1963. "Spatial Models of Party Competition." *American Political Science Review* 57 (2): 368–77.

Stokes, Donald E., and John J. Dilulio. 1993. "The Setting: Valence Politics in Modern Elections." In *The Elections of 1992*, edited by Michael Nelson, 1–20. Washington, DC: Congressional Quarterly Press.

Swyngedouw, Marc, and Gilles Ivaldi. 2001. "The Extreme Right Utopia in Belgium and France: The Ideology of the Flemish Vlaams Blok and the French Front National." *West European Politics* 24 (3): 1–22.

Tanguay, Brian. 2013. "Epitaph for a Conservative Insurgency in Quebec. The Rise and Fall – and Rise and Fall – of the Action Démocratique du Québec, 1994–2008." In *Conservatism in Canada*, edited by James Farney and David Rayside, 317–38. Toronto: University of Toronto Press.

Tannahill, Kerry, and Mebs Kanji. 2016. "Quebec." In *Big Worlds: Politics and Elections in the Canadian Provinces and Territories*, edited by Jared J. Wesley, 82–102. Toronto: University of Toronto Press.

Tessier, Charles, and Éric Montigny. 2016. "Untangling Myths and Facts: Who Supported the Québec Charter of Values?" *French Politics* 14 (2): 272–85.

Thorlakson, Lori, and Michael Keating. 2017. "Party Systems and Party Competition." In *Constitutional Politics and the Territorial Question in Canada and the United Kingdom*, edited by Michael Keating and Guy Laforest, 135–58. Basingstoke: Palgrave Macmillan.

Tierney, Stephen. 2004. *Constitutional Law and National Pluralism*. Oxford: Oxford University Press.

Tremblay, Rodrigue. 1970. *Indépendance et marché commun Québec – États-Unis*. Montreal: Éditions du Jour.

Trench, Alan, ed. 2007. *Devolution and Power in the United Kingdom*. Manchester: Manchester University Press.

van der Brug, Wouter. 2004. "Issue Ownership and Party Choice." *Electoral Studies* 23 (2): 209–33.

– 2017. "Issue Ownership: An Ambiguous Concept." In *The SAGE Handbook of Electoral Behaviour*, edited by Kai Arzheimer, Jocelyn Evans, and Michael S. Lewis-Beck, 521–37. London: Sage.

Wagner, Markus. 2012. "Defining and Measuring Niche Parties." *Party Politics* 18 (6): 845–64.

Wagner, Markus, and Eva Zeglovits. 2014. "Survey Questions about Party

Competence: Insights from Cognitive Interviews." *Electoral Studies* 34 (2): 280–90.

Wyn Jones, Richard, Guy Lodge, Ailsa Henderson, and Daniel Wincott. 2012. *The Dog That Finally Barked: England as an Emerging Political Community*. London: Institute for Public Policy Research.

Wyn Jones, Richard, Guy Lodge, Charlie Jeffery, Glenn Gottfried, Roger Scully, Ailsa Henderson, and Daniel Wincott. 2013. *England and Its Two Unions: The Anatomy of a Nation and Its Discontents*. London: Institute for Public Policy Research.

Yale, François, and Claire Durand. 2011. "What Did Quebeckers Want? Impact of Question Wording, Constitutional Proposal and Context on Support for Sovereignty, 1976–2008." *American Review of Canadian Studies* 41 (3): 242–58.

Young, Lori, and Éric Bélanger. 2008. "BQ in the House: The Nature of Sovereigntist Representation in the Canadian Parliament." *Nationalism and Ethnic Politics* 14 (4): 487–522.

Index

Page references in italics indicate a figure; page references in bold indicate a table.

Action Démocratique du Québec
 (ADQ): "autonomist" label of, 41,
 263n15; constitutional position of,
 41; creation of, 8; merger with
 CAQ, 8; position on multiculturalism, 48; in reform movement, 53
Aussant, Jean-Martin, 8

Basque Country, 3, 194
Beaulieu, Mario, 37
Bloc Québécois (BQ): constitutional
 issue and, 37, 38–9, 172; creation
 of, 64, 121, 254n7; electoral performance of, 7, 9–10, 33, 121–2,
 196; issue of cosmopolitanism
 and, 46–7, 65; language issue and,
 49–50; model of immigrant integration, 45; national question and,
 65, 184; parliamentary representation, 257n6; popular support of,
 185, 195–6, 257n6; position on
 federalism, 63; Quebec economic
 interests and, 56–7, 56–8, 61; Quebec social interests and, 52, 53, 55;
 support of Quebec independence,

15–16, 42–4; supranational inter-
 ests in Quebec and, 59 60, 60; ties
 with Parti Québécois, 253n1; voter
 profile, 123–4, 127–8
Bourassa, Robert, 7–8
Brexit, 94, 98, 166, 198, 261n5
Brown, Gordon, 73
Budge, Ian, 24

Calman Commission on Scottish
 Devolution, 73–4
Catalonia, 3, 194, 198, 262n14
Charlottetown Accord, 7
Charter of Quebec Values, 21, 45, 48,
 103
Clegg, Nick, 145
Coalition Avenir Québec (CAQ):
 2014 electoral campaign, 108; constitutional issue and, 19, 37–8, 38–
 9, 40–1, 104, 171–2, 182, 187, 195;
 cosmopolitanism issue and, 45,
 46–7; criticism of Quebec government, 55–6; electoral strategy,
 196–7; language issue and, 49–50,
 192; merger with ADQ, 8; national